P9-CJQ-251

N AMER

THE DEVELOPMENT
OF BLACK THEATER
IN AMERICA

THE DEVELOPMENT OF BLACK THEATER IN AMERICA

FROM SHADOWS TO SELVES

LESLIE CATHERINE SANDERS

LOUISIANA STATE UNIVERSITY PRESS
BATON ROUGE AND LONDON

Designer: Sylvia Loftin
Typeface: Novarese Book
Typesetter: G&S Typesetters, Inc.
Printer: Thomson-Shore, Inc.
Binder: John H. Dekker & Sons, Inc.

10 9 8 7 6 5 4 3 2 1

The author gratefully acknowledges the Hatch-Billops Archives, New York, for permission to publish passages from plays by Willis Richardson. "Note on Commercial Theatre" is Copyright 1948 by Langston Hughes. Reprinted from *Selected Poems of Langston Hughes*, by permission of Alfred A. Knopf, Inc.

Library of Congress Cataloging-in-Publication Data

Sanders, Leslie Catherine, 1944–
    The development of black theater in America.

    Bibliography: p.
    Includes index.
    1. American drama—Afro-American authors—
History and criticism.   2. Afro-American theater—
History.   3. Afro-Americans in literature.   I. Title.
PS338.N4S26   1987   812'.009'896073   87-13542
ISBN 0-8071-1328-X

For my dear friend Thadious,
who is responsible only for
what herein is true,
and
to Harold

CONTENTS ⁊

ACKNOWLEDGMENTS ❧

Many people helped me with this book. I would like to thank especially Thadious Davis, Frederick Flahiff, and Brian Parker. So much of my thinking about Afro-American literature is a product of my long discussions with Thadious Davis, her endless suggestions, and her loving encouragement. I can never thank her enough. Frederick Flahiff is an old and dear friend who on reading every version kept telling me I could do it better. Also, he is the most remarkable thinker on literature I have ever encountered. As teacher and as friend, he opened my mind to the relevance of everything and thus handed me my intellectual freedom. Among other things, he pushed me into Marshall McLuhan's undergraduate and graduate courses. Working with McLuhan as a student of literature, particularly with Fred as interpreter and guide, was perhaps the most important intellectual experience I have had. I hope that McLuhan would see his influence here and be pleased. Brian Parker was the most patient, best humored, most encouraging, most insightful, and warmest supervisor a body could wish for, and in spite of his ordeal remains my friend.

Several other people whose help I value and appreciate are Jim Hatch, who opened his arms and his files to the stranger who came knocking on his loft door; Sheldon Zitner, whose wisdom, humor, and precise vocabulary pulled me out of some intellectual boxes; Arnold Rampersad, who generously allowed access to the theatrical papers in the Beinecke Hughes collection, and who shared his ideas and his own work; Donald Gallup at the Beinecke Library, without whom the Hughes chapter could never have been written; and my lifelong friend Virginia Smith, who can spot and untangle any troubled sentence.

THE DEVELOPMENT
OF BLACK THEATER
IN AMERICA

INTRODUCTION ⚜

This play . . . is intended for a white audience, but if . . . it is ever performed before a black audience, then a white person . . . should be invited every evening.

But what if no white person accepted? Then let white masks be distributed to the black spectators as they enter the theatre. And if the blacks refuse the masks, then let a dummy be used.

—Jean Genet
The Blacks: A Clown Show

Widely acclaimed, the 1961 off-Broadway production of Jean Genet's *The Blacks* seemed prophetic of the black theater of the sixties and a radical exposé of black rage. However, Eugene O'Neill's *The Emperor Jones* rather than LeRoi Jones's *Dutchman* is the prototype of the play, for the prescription with which Genet prefaces his work signals the traditional relation of black character to a white audience, a problem that has long hampered the development of black theater. Genet insists on the presence of whites in the audience not only as objects of the black characters' hatred but also as components of the play's formulation of color. *The Blacks* defines color as existentially relative: black exists only in relation to white. If there were no whites in the audience, there would be no blacks on stage: "One evening an actor asked me to write a play for an all-black cast. But what exactly is a black? First of all, what's his color?" [1]

Although the play's exposition of the relation between colonized and colonizer speaks eloquently to the racial situation in the United States, *The Blacks* is not primarily concerned with black people. Rather, it uses them and their experience both as metaphor of more general aspects of the human predicament and as mask for Genet's personal experience and philosophy. This use of the black as projection and mask has particularly affected the development of black theater, for on the stage the many problems confronting black American artists and their black audience, problems that arise not only from the concrete effects of racism but also from the complex role the Negro plays in the American imagination, become disconcertingly literal. [2]

1. Jean Genet, *The Blacks: A Clown Show* (New York, 1960), 3.
2. Generally, I will refer to black people as black or Afro-American. However, I will use the older term *Negro* when the texts discussed or alluded to use the term or when, for reasons of historical accuracy, the term *Negro* seems more appropriate than *black*.

Genet's injunction itself makes literal the underlying source of black artists' dilemma: in a predominantly white society, the cultural ground is white, for it consists of the thoughts, history, and artistic creations of white people. In the theater, then, the stage reality, the conscious and unconscious assumptions mutually accepted by the theater and its audience, is white, unless white assumptions have been replaced by black assumptions, giving a black stage reality.[3] Until those assumptions are replaced, black figures on stage exist in a white ground, and their color is charged with significance. Black artists thus employ an essentially alien—even alienating—medium, and their audience reacts uncomfortably to the disruptive influence of the vehicle for their expression.

This study approaches the history of black theater as the process of creating a black stage reality, of freeing black figures of their metaphoric burden and making the ground on which they stand their own, and at the same time, of transforming conventions borrowed from white European culture into forms appropriate to black artists and audiences. Only when these things were accomplished could the aim of black playwrights, often articulated as "realistic portrayal of the Negro," be fully realized.

Black artists and critics have defined and understood the question of stage reality in various ways and proposed various solutions. In 1928, James Weldon Johnson used the metaphor of theater and audience in a manner much like Genet's to define the Negro dramatist's problem: "[The Negro's audience] is more than a double audience; it is a divided audience, an audience made up of two elements with differing and often opposite and antagonistic points of view. His audience is always both white America and black America. . . . The Negro author can try the experiment of putting black America in the orchestra chairs, so to speak, and keeping white America in the gallery, but he is likely at any moment to find his audience shifting places on him, and sometimes without notice."[4]

Generally, white audiences find credible only those portraits of the Negro they are prepared to believe, and perceive each black character

3. By *theater* in this context I mean "the entire occasion of acted drama—that is, the performance of parts by actors according to some kind of shaping intent." This definition of *theater* is taken from Michael Goldman, *The Actor's Freedom: Toward a Theory of Drama* (New York, 1975), ix. My concept of "stage reality" is influenced by Goldman's entire discussion; see especially 82–86.

4. James Weldon Johnson, "The Dilemma of the Negro Author," *American Mercury*, XV (December, 1928), 477, 481.

as symbol of the entire race. Accordingly, black artists and audiences fear any negative portraits and thus shy away from the richness and variety of depiction that realistic portrayal of the Negro requires. Johnson resolves the dilemma by demanding that the writer, "standing on his racial foundation . . . |rise| above race and |reach| out to the universal"—a solution that rests precariously on an assumption that is both a critical truth and a truism: good art has a universal level of meaning, and the artist should aspire to work that is most vivid at this highest level of significance.[5] Johnson's injunction suggests that one can separate the imaginative world through which meaning is articulated from the meaning itself. It fails to take into account that the vehicle shapes meaning and modulates the experience of apprehending it. No matter how good the play, *Othello* is not the same experience for a black audience as for a white.

Another frequent solution derives from the assumption that when the American cultural ground becomes color-free, race will cease to be of importance in shaping perception. This assumption is consistent with those of American pluralist democracy. The illusiveness of this solution has become increasingly apparent with the repeated failure of that democracy for the black American.

A third solution, not new to contemporary playwrights, but made a reality by them, is to reverse the black-figure / white-ground configuration, to demetaphorize the figure of the black and make that of the white metaphorical.[6] Some recent black theater, principally during the sixties and early seventies, deliberately employed this approach. Initially, the reversal appeared as a tactic, a self-conscious and obvious statement. The reversal thus made reference to the conventional relation it was overturning. Gradually, however, the stage reality absorbed the shift and became a black stage reality, without unwanted implied reference to a white cultural ground. Thus the black and white figures began to assume rightful and appropriate significance.

5. *Ibid.*, 481.

6. The term "figure / ground" is taken from Gestalt psychology and defines a gestalt, that is, an "integrated structure or pattern . . . that has particular properties which can neither be derived from the elements of the whole nor considered simply as the sum of those elements" (*Webster New World Dictionary*, Second College Edition, 1974). According to the Gestalt theory, all experience consists of responses to these patterns, or gestalten. Like the gestalten, the responses are unanalyzable wholes rather than responses to constituent parts. See, for example, F. S. Perls, *Ego, Hunger and Aggression: The Beginning of Gestalt Therapy* (New York, 1969), esp. chapters I-IV.

These "solutions" reflect and embody the social and political contexts in which the artists create and through which their works are
perceived and understood. While many artists, black and white, have
not overtly defined the effect of context on their depiction of black life
or the reception of their work as a political issue most have, of necessity, been aware of the special problems these contexts raised for
them. During the period from the Harlem Renaissance to the Black
Arts Movement, three symposia, all in black publications, and two
consisting exclusively of the work of black critics and artists, specifically addressed these issues.

In 1926, as the Harlem Renaissance was beginning and "the Negro
was in vogue," the *Crisis* sent out a seven-part questionnaire to the
"artists of the world" concerning how the Negro should be portrayed
in art, publishing the replies as a symposium.[7] In answer to the first
question, black and white contributors all agreed the artist ought to
have absolute freedom in portraying the Negro. But responses to the
other six questions indicated the complexity of the "agreement." Julia
Peterkin ended her response: "I write about Negroes because they
represent human nature obscured by so little veneer; human nature
groping among its instinctive impulses and in an environment which
is tragically primitive and often unutterably pathetic. But I am no
propagandist for or against any race. I devoutly hope I shall never be
one. I am interested in humanity *per se* without regard to color or
conditions."[8]

Her comments validated Countee Cullen's concern: "It is a question
of whether the work is the *thing*, or its moral, social and educational
effect." Although all insisted on artistic freedom, they disagreed
about whether portraits of low-life suggest racial characteristics.
Some whites denied that the stereotypical image of the Negro in art
affected their perceptions; others suggested that the Negro was overly
sensitive. H. L. Mencken challenged black artists to make the white
appear as ridiculous as he had made the black appear: "He looks ridiculous even to me. . . . To a Negro, he must be an hilarious spectacle, indeed. . . . Let the Negro sculptors spit on their hands! What a

7. "The Negro in Art: How Shall He Be Portrayed: A Symposium" first ap-
pered in *Crisis*, XXXI (March, 1926), 219–20, and subsequently in XXXI (April,
1926), 278–80; XXXII (May, 1926), 35–36, (June, 1926), 71–73, (August, 1926),
193–94, (September, 1926), 238–39; and XXXIII (November, 1926), 28–29.

8. "The Negro in Art: How Shall He Be Portrayed: A Symposium," *Crisis*,
XXXII (September, 1926), 239.

chance!" In short, both black and white writers expressed intense self-consciousness concerning the Negro as subject for art. Langston Hughes's statement is most succinct: "I think like this: What's the use of saying anything—the true literary artist is going to write about what he chooses anyway regardless of outside opinions. . . . It's the way people look at things, not what they look at, that needs to be changed."[9]

Almost twenty-five years later, in 1950, *Phylon* published a similar symposium, celebrating the "coming-of-age" of the Negro writer.[10] Partly a retrospective on the Harlem Renaissance, the symposium shifted in emphasis from the image of the Negro to the writers themselves—a revealing change. Ten years after the publication of Richard Wright's *Native Son* and a year after Gwendolyn Brooks won the Pulitzer Prize, the first black so honored, the symposium celebrated the fact that black American poets and novelists had achieved international reputations with regularity. Assured of a formal literature, several contributors turned their attention to a criticism for it, concurring with Blyden Jackson's comment in his "Essay in Criticism" that the next task was to provide their literature with the "sort of scholarly and critical framework which adds the needed marginal dimension to the established European literatures."[11]

However, the *Phylon* contributors disagreed on the nature of the Negro writers' task. Most defended the writers' right to avoid the topic of race, seeing the career of Frank Yerby as a sign of progress. While some suggested Negroes' place in society afforded them special insight into its shortcomings, only L. D. Reddick, Nick Aaron Ford, and Alain Locke insisted that racial perspective and heritage are black writers' greatest assets.[12] In 1926, race was considered the subject for and source of creativity; in 1950, race was minimized, even perceived as hampering Negro artists' vision.

Like their *Crisis* counterparts, the *Phylon* writers assumed that whites are the primary audience of Negro literature and thus that the artist

9. *Ibid.*, XXXII (August, 1926), 193, XXXI (March, 1926), 220, and XXXI (April, 1926), 278.
10. *Phylon*, XI (November, 1950). The entire 4th-quarter issue is devoted to the symposium.
11. Blyden Jackson, "An Essay in Criticism," *Phylon*, XI (1950), 338.
12. Nick Aaron Ford, "A Blueprint for Negro Authors," *Phylon*, XI (1950), 374–77; Alain Locke, "Self-Criticism: The Third Dimension in Culture," *ibid.*, 391–94; L. D. Reddick, "No Kafka in the South," *Phylon*, XI (1950), 380–83.

determines the place the Negro will take in the larger American imaginative world. When some contributors describe Negro writers as American in their orientation, however, the image suggests a kind of intellectual "passing," as though the absence of the racial perspective allows a writer to become part of the mainstream. Except for the first part of Sterling Brown's well-known article "Folk Expression," the symposium is remarkably barren of any discussion of the black heritage. It is as though the imaginative ground of the American artist had become truly color-free.

Just fifteen years later, in 1965, *Negro Digest* solicited a similar discussion but radically altered the terms of the discussion: "What is the task of the Negro writer concerned with creating a work of art in a segregated society and how does his task differ from that of the white writer—if it differs at all?"[13] The question acknowledges segregation as fact, and thus the very premise of the discussion differs from that of the two earlier symposia. The thirty-six writers concurred with the debate's assumptions.

Almost all remarked that the Negro writers' task, or at least their point of view, must differ from that of white writers. Lerone Bennett, Jr., used the term *engagement* to describe the Negro writer's role, and most of the others described it similarly. When Dudley Randall suggested that Negro writers model themselves after writers of other "oppressed minorities," his choice of language marked the distance from the view implied by the term *ethnic writers* in the *Crisis* symposium.[14]

While the *Negro Digest* contributors varied in the degree of their militancy, almost all suggested that the Negro artists' vision derives from their special position in American society and that this vision must dictate their themes. Clearly the acknowledgment of figure / ground relationship had returned; in 1965 it was seen as the measure of the artist's performance. Moreover, the contributors' attitude toward the audience differed from that of their *Phylon* counterparts. While that aspect of an artist's vision expressed as social critique may still be directed primarily to a white audience, the artist's search for identity, a theme of which many of the writers spoke, is on behalf of the black audience. Most respondents subscribed to the sentiments and criticisms thus summarized by William M. Kelley: "The task of the

13. "The Task of the Negro Writer as Artist," *Negro Digest*, XIV (April, 1965), 54–83.
    14. *Ibid.*, 78,77.

Negro writer should differ from that of the white writer in that, among other things, he should be addressing himself to the Negro. . . . The Negro writer believes that he must tell the white man where it's at, as if the white man oppressed the Negro for the last 346 years without really being aware of it. . . . Thomas Paine did not address himself to the British. If he had done otherwise, America today might still be a colony." [15]

The shift in emphasis in the three symposia allows us to chart changing perspectives on black artists and the nature of their art. During the 1920s, elevating the figure of the Negro beyond that of a buffoon constituted a victory; by exploiting racial characteristics when creating Negro characters, both black and white writers deliberately opposed black and white in the American imaginative world. By 1950, the fight for integration was reflected in thinking about the role of the black artist. Integration underplays difference in favor of homogeneity, and correspondingly, black artists insisted on their right to be and to write like anyone else. By 1965, America was an openly divided society. Having tested integration, black Americans began to question its desirability. Accordingly, the black figure assumed a new position in the white ground and became critic, judge, possibly saviour.

If viewed as revealing development toward a black stage reality, the symposia suggest that the question of identity can be asked only after the ground for the figure is determined. The question "Who am I?" only occurs after the questions "Where am I?" and "Who am I to them?" In concluding thus, we are only stating as an artistic problem what, in 1903, W. E. B. Du Bois described as an existential situation.

After the Egyptian and Indian, the Greek and Roman, the Teuton and Mongolian, the Negro is a sort of seventh son, born with a veil, and gifted with second-sight in this American world—a world which yields him no true self-consciousness, but only lets him see himself through the revelation of the other world. It is a peculiar sensation, this double-consciousness, this sense of always looking at one's self through the eyes of others, of measuring one's soul by the tape of a world that looks on in amused contempt and pity. One ever feels his two-ness,—an American, a Negro.[16]

Anthologies of Negro plays published over the same periods reveal how the playwrights wrestled with the artistic implications of this

15. *Ibid.*, 64, 78.
16. W. E. B. Du Bois, *The Souls of Black Folk* (1903; rpr. Greenwich, Conn., 1961), 16–17.

"two-ness" and with the burden of taking "America's metaphor" as subject for their art. The earliest anthology, *Plays of Negro Life: A Source-Book of Native American Drama*, published in 1927, which includes works by both black and white writers, through its subtitle links itself to the nascent folk drama movement in American theater. Alain Locke's introduction, "The Drama of Negro Life," reveals the multiple purposes and contradictory effects of art concerning the Negro. Locke refers to the Negro experience "as inherently dramatic. . . . No group experience in America has plumbed greater emotional depths, or passed so dramatically through more levels of life or caught up into itself more of those elements of social conflict and complication in which the modern dramatist must find the only tragedy that our realistic, scientific philosophy of life allows us." [17]

The "inherent drama of Negro life," a commonplace in discussions of the Negro theater during the twenties, constitutes the Negro's offer of self as American image. Elsewhere, Du Bois suggested that white writers take up the offer as a mode of indirection: "[White artists] cry for freedom in dealing with Negroes because they have so little freedom in dealing with whites. DuBose Heywood writes 'Porgy' and writes beautifully of the black Charleston underworld. But why does he do it? Because he cannot do a similar thing for the white people of Charleston, or they would drum him out of town. The only chance he had to tell the truth of pitiful human degradation was to tell it of colored people." [18]

Locke's introductory essay seeks to resolve what he sees as the two approaches to Negro material. The first is that of the Negro writer attempting to provide the Negro actor with appropriate scripts; the second is that of the white writer "quest[ing] . . . for new material and a deeper, firmer grip on the actualities of American life." Locke diplomatically opposes the strength of each, crediting the white writer with "objectivity" and greater theatrical experience, and the Negro with access to "the heart and spirit of Negro life." [19] While he insists it is the Negro playwright, theater, and audience that will bring to fruition the Negro theater's potential, Locke is forced to admit the primitive

17. Alain Locke, Introduction to Alain Locke and Montgomery Gregory (eds.), *Plays of Negro Life: A Source-Book of Native American Drama* (New York, 1927).
18. W. E. B. Du Bois, "Criteria of Negro Art," *Crisis*, XXXII (October, 1926), 297.
19. Locke, Introduction to Locke and Gregory (eds.), *Plays of Negro Life*.

quality of its beginnings. He suggests that the Negro theater is hampered both by the convention of the problem play and by the Negro
writer's tendency to sentimentality.

More important, Locke suggests, "The Negro's situation . . . has
forced him to a counter-attitude in life and a spectator's attitude toward himself [which has] cut at the roots of fine drama in him." [20] His
comments clearly reveal the debilitating effects of seeing oneself as a
figure in another's ground, and his insight is inconsistent with his ap-
plauding of the use of the Negro by white writers. He supports their
use of black material because he hopes their greater license will
broaden the possibilities of a genuine Negro theater.

The anthology's plays exhibit all the problems Locke delineates in
his essay. They vary in quality and in their handling of the Negro, but
in most, two apparently contradictory qualities predominate: the
characters are black, but there is little to distinguish them from white
characters other than dialect or specific situations, for example, miscegenation. Only Jean Toomer's *Balo*, a portrait of the black religious
experience, attempts to explore black material. *Plumes*, by Georgia
Douglas Johnson, centers both action and image on the traditional
black taste for a big funeral but unfolds the meaning of neither image
nor custom. Essentially, the volume's plays are important only because they depict black characters and because most use the folk play
to do so.

The folk play did seem to offer a ready vehicle for serious depiction
of Negro life, but white use of the form for this purpose created many
problems for the black writer. The two Eugene O'Neill plays in the collection, *The Dreamy Kid* and *The Emperor Jones*, epitomize several of
them. In *The Dreamy Kid*, the characters are black, one suspects, because only stereotypical assumptions about Negro superstition make
plausible Dreamy's fear of his dying grandmother's curse. Superstition
motivates *The Emperor Jones* as well. As surrogate for the white audience, Brutus Jones endures the dark night of the soul, the jungle of
the unconscious. Commonly regarded as a play about Negro life, *The
Emperor Jones* established a pattern for white use of Negro material.
The dramatic attraction of Negro figures lies in their primitiveness,
which is imagined either as exotic or as innocent. The exotic fre-

20. *Ibid.*

quently surfaced as a jungle or a sexual motif; the innocent reached its almost literal apogee in the 1930 production of Marc Connelly's *The Green Pastures*.

Many of the folk plays placed their characters in the rural South, and this too raised problems for black playwrights. White audiences for "plays of Negro life" were neither rural nor southern. In part because the rural Negro was remote from such audiences, and in part because the twenties' search for the folk expressed a desire, not only to solidify the roots of American culture, but also to flee industrialism and the vacuity of the jazz age, the figure of the rural Negro became idealized. As image, it constituted the flip side of Harlem high life, the innocent from a purer historical past.

To a black audience, of course, the rural South even now constitutes an imaginative landscape and a reality of very different significance. It suggests roots in an immediate sense and recalls not only a history of slavery and oppression but a locus of community and value. Moreover, it exists within the experience of much of its audience. No sooner was the image presented on stage, however, than it was burdened with white projections, and when black writers turned to the material in their quest for realism, they found it tainted.

Frustrated by the portrayals of the Negro on the American stage, all black commentators during the twenties called for a national Negro theater to provide drama meaningful to black audiences.[21] The Irish and Jewish theaters were frequently cited as models for the Negro theater, but as analogues they suggest two very different paths. Integral to the Irish theater is the desire to subsume the voice of the folk into mainstream culture: the work of Frederick Koch and the Carolina Playmakers, for example, aimed at this synthesis.[22] The Jewish theater in

21. For example, Montgomery Gregory, "For a Negro Theatre," *New Republic*, November 16, 1921, p. 350. Most consistent was the commenting of Theophilus Lewis, drama critic for *Opportunity* magazine from 1923 to 1927. For a good summary of his work during those years see Theodore Kornweibel, Jr., "Theophilus Lewis and the Theatre of the Harlem Renaissance," in Arna Bontemps (ed.), *The Harlem Renaissance Remembered* (New York, 1972), 171–89.

22. Sterling Brown specifically connects the work of Ridgely Torrence to that of William Butler Yeats, John Millington Synge, and Lady Gregory in the chapter "Folk Drama of the Negro," in his influential work *Negro Poetry and Drama* (1937; rpr. New York, 1969), 115. See also Carl Van Vechten's enthusiastic review of the 1914 blackface production of Torrence's *Granny Maumee*, which he compares to the work of Synge in *Literary Digest*, May 9, 1914, p. 1114.

New York, however, remained insistently discrete from mainstream American theater for ethnic and linguistic reasons.

While Locke's anthology indicates a theater more closely modeled on the Irish, two other anthologies, compiled and published at the instigation of the black historian and popularizer Carter G. Woodson, and addressing themselves solely to a black audience, suggest a theater more like that developed by the Jewish community. Both were edited by Willis Richardson. *Plays and Pageants from the Life of the Negro*, published in 1930, he compiled alone, and *Negro History in Thirteen Plays*, published in 1935, he edited with May Miller.[23]

Plays and Pageants includes plays about historical figures and contemporary problems, and pageants on the history of the Negro. It contains no folk plays because, Richardson wrote in his introduction, the volume is intended for schools, where dialect is deemed "inappropriate." However, several plays in his second anthology, those depicting slavery, use dialect as realistic detail. The plays in both volumes further Woodson's concentrated efforts during the 1930s to promulgate Negro history and thus to encourage racial pride. In his introduction to the second anthology, Woodson wrote: "The stage in America, moreover, is often an agency for racial propaganda which fair-minded people are not anxious to promote. . . . Why does not the Negro dramatize his own life and bring the world unto him? Paul Green, Eugene O'Neill and Marc Connelly cannot do it. They see that the thing is possible, and they are trying to do it; but at best they misunderstand the Negro because *they cannot think black.*"[24]

Woodson's own historical works during the 1930s were aimed at popularizing black history. For example, he defined the purpose of his high-school text *African Heroes and Heroines* as the demonstration that these "leaders of a despised people measure up to the full stature of the heroic in the histories of other nations."[25] The same sense of comparative standards informs the plays in Richardson's anthologies. With few exceptions, the plays' characters are black in skin only, and the

23. Willis Richardson (ed.), *Plays and Pageants from the Life of the Negro* (Washington, D.C., 1930); Willis Richardson and May Miller (eds.), *Negro History in Thirteen Plays* (Washington, D.C., 1935).

24. Carter G. Woodson, Introduction to Richardson and Miller (eds.), *Negro History in Thirteen Plays*, iii, emphasis added.

25. Quoted in James O. Young, *Black Writers of the Thirties* (Baton Rouge, 1973), 116.

situations in which they find themselves are designed to provide them opportunities to act heroically rather than to illuminate black history. Not only the limited experience or ability of the playwrights, but also the very conception of many of the plays limits their effectiveness. The plays seek to establish the conventional figure / ground relationship. The stage reality is that of Western history, in which Negroes assert their rightful place.

The intention of the Richardson anthologies, to provide a black audience with plays that address its concerns, is more confidently and even defiantly the province of the next anthology published, the *Drama Review* "Black Theatre Issue," Summer, 1968. Although thirty years and integration have intervened, the *Drama Review* issue, which became a manifesto for the new black theater, is quite close to its predecessor in its theory, and the *Drama Review* playwrights are similarly concerned with creating theater relevant to the lives of black people. However, their idea of what is relevant to a black audience differs radically from their predecessors'. The issue's editor, Ed Bullins, separated the plays of the collection into two categories: "Black Revolutionary Theatre" and the "Theatre of Black Experience." Plays in the first category are characterized by images of victorious struggle, which is either literal or implicit in the clear choices the play defines for its black audience. Theatre of Black Experience delineates situations familiar to the imaginative world of a black audience and inquires into their meanings.

The plays also reveal a profound, deliberate shift in stage reality. Some, for example, those about violent revolution, directly address the issue of whether the ground for the characters is white or black. These "revolutionary" plays differ radically from plays about the "angry black," who has a long tradition in the American imagination as an image of social injustice or of the nightmarish aspects of the American Dream. Rather, Black Revolutionary Theatre is about the revolution that, unless or until it becomes actual, is an overturning of imaginative rather than physical reality. The plays often depict the taking over of a ghetto, proudly and defiantly declared black territory—an apparently redundant activity that is the crucial imaginative act with which Black Revolutionary Theatre is concerned.

Theatre of Black Experience is a kind of transvalued folk drama. In these plays, the setting is usually urban, delineated not only by concrete detail but also by the characters' speech and behavior. The plays clearly and unselfconsciously address themselves to a black audience and inquire into the meaning of the black experience, not so that a white audience can understand it, but so that a black audience's insight may be enriched. If the white world enters these plays, it enters as image; it is only important as it impinges on the black reality depicted.

The articles in the *Drama Review* anthology define the changes reflected in the plays. The issue's manifesto is Larry Neal's "The Black Arts Movement," an analysis of the career of LeRoi Jones, who had already become the movement's principal spokesman. In his essay, Neal argues that the material produced by the Black Arts Movement signals a break, not only with American theater, but with Western aesthetics. He declares that art is important for its social significance, for its contribution to the mythology that validates the consciousness and values of a people. As he defines it, however, the aesthetic question is still comparative: "The motive behind the Black aesthetic is the destruction of the White thing, the destruction of ideas, and white ways of looking at the world. The new aesthetic is mostly predicated on an Ethics which asks the question: whose vision of the world is finally more meaningful, ours or the white oppressor's? What is the truth? Or, more precisely, whose truth shall we express, that of the oppressed or of the oppressors?" [26]

Neal's concept of aesthetics assumes that aesthetic judgments arise from particular perceptual fields and cultural milieux. His either-or question proposes that to discuss aesthetics at all is to address a critical establishment that insists aesthetic values are culture-free, even absolute. Neal's dialogue is also internal. The language of aesthetics is a white European language. Thus, for example, when Alain Locke, in the 1920s, spoke of the "drama" and the "tragedy" of Negro life, his use of language arising from European dramatic tradition made of Negro life an artifact in that tradition. Developing a black aesthetic at first requires working with the tools available. The break with Western aesthetics of which Neal speaks involves not only a rejection of its claim to universality but also a reversing of a figure/ground relationship.

While the theory articulated in the *Drama Review* issue still operates in terms of dichotomies, the black theater it represents solidifies the black stage reality. In many of these plays, the fact that black charac-

26. Larry Neal, "The Black Arts Movement," *Drama Review*, XII (Summer, 1968), 30.

ters command the stage is no longer in itself a meaning, nor do those characters function as easily generalized racial representatives. Moreover, the works do not assume a double audience or direct explanations to any whites present. In those plays in which violence is done to whites, the function of the violence usually is to indulge the imagination of the black audience rather than to threaten any whites who might be present, much as war movies serve the imaginative needs of the home front. The plays of the Black Arts Movement indeed declared the black theater's autonomy.

Developmental arguments, however, must always be made with caution. Loften Mitchell's lively history of the American Negro in the theater, *Black Drama*, which chronicles the activities of black playwrights, actors, and actresses both on the mainstream American stage and in various Harlem community theaters, reminds us that, especially in theater, practical matters shape the progression of art.[27] Playwrights need productions, theaters need financial backers, and backing for plays by black playwrights has always been scarce. Moreover, not until the creation of the Negro Unit of the Federal Theater Project did large numbers of black actors and actresses, stagehands, technicians, and designers receive training and experience in professional theater. Mitchell concludes that financial difficulties and the lure of the "Great White Way," which often co-opted successful community productions, were the chief obstacles to the development of black community theater. Mitchell also reminds us that some black playwrights have always unselfconsciously asserted a black reality in their works, but their plays were rarely produced, at least on the professional stage. Their work was ignored because it clashed with the dominant image of the Negro, the subject to which we must now briefly turn.

In 1933, two plays were running concurrently in New York, *The Green Pastures* and Hall Johnson's *Run, Little Chillun'*. After seeing the latter, Kenneth Burke reflected:

> The appeal of *The Green Pastures* may have arisen in part from the fact that, for all the honest pleasantness in its dialogue, it did contrive to exploit the old minstrel show conception of the Negro (naive, good-natured, easily put upon) which would naturally provide an endearing symbol for the eliciting of White warmth. Nothing is so expansive as comfort—and such childlike fancies were highly comforting. . . . Americans, driven by some deep competitive fear, seem to open their hearts most easily to such symbols of

27. Loften Mitchell, *Black Drama* (New York, 1967).

"contented indigence" . . . the child symbol is the symbol par excellence of innocence (*innocentia*: "harmlessness"; thence derivatively, "blameless-ness"; thence, lo! "integrity"). . . . *Run, Little Children* [*sic*], written "from within," by a Negro, Hall Johnson, brings out an aspect of the Negro-symbol with which our theatre-going public is not theatrically at home: the power side of the Negro.[28]

Burke's comments about *The Green Pastures* illuminate not only the popular image of the Negro as the "folk" but the entire history of the Negro, or rather the "Negro-symbol," on the American stage. During the nineteenth century, when Negro roles, particularly on stage, ranged from entertainer to buffoon, with the occasional exception of an Uncle Tom or a tragic mulatto, the meaning of the Negro-symbol was elo-quently suggested by the use of blackface. Nathan Huggins describes it thus: "The black mask that white men put on was the antithesis of proper character and proper manners. These white faces in black masks were, one might say, their own alter-egos. . . . The Negro stereo-type and the blackface minstrel provided performer and audience with a way of being themselves—part of themselves, at least."[29]

In the twenties, the licentious primitive shared the stage with the innocent folk; both objectified for the white audience aspects of their own experience that they could not directly acknowledge. While the Puritan perspective denied sensuality, American innocence and opti-mism denied the tragic experience, and both were attributed to the Negro folk. Their supposed ability to suffer gracefully became a sym-bol of human endurance; ironically, this suffering was caused by the white audience that derived inspiration from theatrical depictions of it.

During the thirties, the Negro-symbol entered another arena. De-pression writers concerned with social and political issues often treated the plight of the black in America. Negroes became a potent symbol of American injustice; their suffering rendered America vul-nerable, particularly to its critics from the left. Moreover, their help-lessness aptly reflected the feeling of helplessness experienced by most Americans in the grips of the Great Depression. The Negro's situation *was* realistically depicted, but the depiction still functioned symbolically, as evidence of the failure of American ideals. At best, the truthful portraits served to prod the conscience of white America,

28. Kenneth Burke, "The Negro's Pattern of Life," in *The Philosophy of Literary Form* (Berkeley, 1973), 361–62.
29. Nathan Huggins, *Harlem Renaissance* (New York, 1971), 256.

not to investigate the meaning of the black experience for people living it.

Also during the thirties, the Federal Theater Project encouraged the development of black theater. However, the program actually produced few plays by black writers. A "Living Newspaper," Liberty Deferred, by John Silvera and Abram Hill, was never performed, and the Negro Arts Committee of the Festival Arts Council felt impelled to criticize the Federal Theater Project for neglecting this and other plays by black playwrights.[30]

If the thirties elevated the oppressed-Negro symbol, the forties and fifties popularized two that still persist. The first is that of the angry black and the second may be called, from the title of Ralph Ellison's 1952 novel, the invisible man. As popular stereotype, the angry black originated with Richard Wright's novel Native Son, published in 1940, in which Bigger Thomas' fate made vivid to the American reading public not only the fact of American injustice but the experience of that injustice eloquently understood. The name "Bigger Thomas" came to represent the image of the angry black in the American imagination.

The more various origins of the invisible-man symbol can be traced to the politics of integration rather than just to Ellison's work. The unnamed protagonist of Invisible Man is invisible because he is not perceived by others. While the epilogue suggests that he will be ready to be seen only when he fully perceives himself, there is a tension in the novel between the protagonist's desire to fit into American society at large and his growing sense of an identity that threatens the society he proposes to become visible in. The concept of invisibility, in a novel two years after the Phylon symposium, reflects ironically on integration as image of black Americans' relatedness to American society in general. The Negro-symbol of the integrated Negro or invisible man is ultimately an ambivalent one. For example, Lorraine Hansberry's Raisin in the Sun presents characters with whom a white audience can readily identify; the play reveals essential similarities between black people and white.[31] If a white audience can accept the similarity, then possibly the aims of the characters can be achieved: movement into a white neighborhood. The integrated Negro is the Other who is not

30. Doris Abramson, Negro Playwrights in the American Theatre, 1925–1959 (New York, 1969), 65.

31. H. Keyassar-Franke, "Strategies in Black Drama" (Ph.D. dissertation, University of Iowa, 1974), 241.

really Other—the one who seems strange and therefore disquieting is made similar and thus familiar. However, the insistence on familiarity is, more accurately, a refusal to allow those perceived as Other their uniqueness.

The Negro-symbols, then, are numerous, and overcoming them— or making them productive—is a crucial aspect of establishing the black stage reality. We will observe the process of establishing the black stage reality by examining the work of five black American playwrights: Willis Richardson, Randolph Edmonds, Langston Hughes, LeRoi Jones / Imamu Amiri Baraka, and Ed Bullins. The most prolific of the black American playwrights, all have contributed significantly to the creation of American black theater. All are aware that the stage is dominated by the assumptions and expectations of white culture. All but Bullins assume that the first task of the black dramatist is to counter that cultural domination. However, each writer understands the problem differently and thus responds in a different fashion.

Willis Richardson and Randolph Edmonds take up the primary task of countering the stereotypical images of the Negro in order to redeem the theater for black audiences and to create new images for inclusion in the American stage tradition. While both men write to serve the needs of black audiences, they also feel compelled to respond to the dominant culture by correcting the images of the Negro it promulgates and by creating drama "worthy" of inclusion in the larger canon of what Edmonds calls "world drama." Langston Hughes is less self-conscious in his approach to the stage. In his early plays, he addresses the problem of the figure / ground relationship directly, through his use of setting, or dramatic landscape. While several of his early works depict the landscape as contested, others carefully establish that the landscape is indisputably black. Sometimes his setting is literally black—Harlem or Haiti, for example—not only because blacks normally inhabit it but also because these locations are part of the imaginative landscape of black Americans. However, landscape alone does not create a black stage reality. In other plays, folk forms, particularly the black sermon, shape the dramatic events, and thus the stage reality is black by virtue of being subsumed into another and, for a black audience, prior tradition. These dramatic experiments constitute a limited but important solution to the problem of stage reality.

LeRoi Jones continues the process of transforming the stage as part of his vehement, comprehensive attack on white culture and society. Many of Jones's plays depict direct, violent confrontation between blacks and whites, and between their differing perspectives on the world. In these contests much more than territory is at stake, for Jones challenges as well the very language and forms that the dominant culture uses to describe the world, and thereby challenges what that culture sees as reality. Particularly in *Dutchman*, Jones takes issue with the various meanings the image of the Negro has had in America. In his work, the metaphoric relation between whites and blacks is played out; as a result, the black figure is finally divested of its metaphoric quality and the white made metaphor of aspects of the black experience.

In dissimilar but equally complex ways, Hughes and Jones address the problem of claiming and transforming the stage. In Ed Bullins' work the transformation is complete. Bullins' characters are no longer black figures in a white ground, nor are they haunted by degrading stereotypes or by fears of judgment by an ultimately hostile white audience. Rather, they are fully themselves and fully a part of their dramatic landscape. Bullins' imaginative and artistic assurance and the resulting black stage reality allow him to explore the black experience with a freedom denied his predecessors; his plays mark the maturity of black theater.

ONE ❧
"HOW SHALL THE NEGRO BE PORTRAYED?"
Willis Richardson and Randolph Edmonds, the Pioneers

Willis Richardson and Randolph Edmonds had few models for their ambition to create viable black theater. The American theater had so often ridiculed its Negro characters that blacks understandably had come to view the stage itself with suspicion. Moreover, when the stage was not used to humiliate them, it seemed to portray a level of culture toward which they were urged to aspire but assured they could never attain. Thus Richardson, Edmonds, and their contemporaries inherited the complex task of redeeming both black stage characters and the boards on which they walked.

Richardson's and Edmonds' work was not only shaped by their reactions to the traditional stage Negro. More generally, their perceptions of what Edmonds called "world drama," essentially drama in the West, influenced their artistic choices. This latter preoccupation was an inevitable, essential element of their work. By formulating a reaction to the tradition of Western drama, both made many of its cultural biases evident. This groundwork enabled later writers to operate more freely, even within conventional dramatic modes.

Although they were concerned with all aspects of the tradition, Richardson and Edmonds devoted special attention to the American folk play, for it was the form favored by white dramatists who took the Negro as their subject. The American folk drama movement, influenced by the work of John Millington Synge and the 1911 tour of the Abbey Players, was centered at the University of North Carolina at Chapel Hill. It grew from the playwriting seminars of Frederick Koch, who encouraged his students to draw on local landscape, people, and language for their materials. Eventually, a journal and a theater troupe were established; the journal, *Carolina Magazine*, even published works by black dramatists, although blacks could not attend the university. Beginning in 1920, the theater troupe, the Carolina Playmakers, toured plays written for them as far south as Georgia. Koch's most famous student, Paul Green, won the 1927 Pulitzer Prize for a Negro folk play, *In Abraham's Bosom*.

White writers of Negro folk plays met with great success, but the work of Paul Green, Ridgely Torrence, DuBose Heywood, and Marc Connelly provided black dramatists with an irritant as well as a model. By virtue of its subject, the folk play seemed an appropriate form for black writers to adopt. The simple, rural, and often illiterate folk these plays depicted did in fact resemble much of the black population, particularly before 1920. However, the form contained certain intolerable restrictions, as Frederick Koch's definition of the folk play makes clear. He called it "the work of a single author dealing consciously with his materials, the folkways of our less sophisticated people living simple lives. . . . The chief concern of the folk dramatist is man's conflict with the forces of nature and his simple pleasure in being alive. . . . The ultimate cause of all dramatic action we classify as 'folk,' whether it be physical or spiritual, may be found in man's desperate struggle for existence and in his enjoyment of the world of nature." [1]

Even when their characters fit into the world of folk drama, black dramatists have concerns that extend beyond depicting their subjects as "naked, unaccommodated man." They desire to treat the entire range of social, moral, and political problems that face black people, both as a group and as individuals trying to make sense of their lives and heritage. Thus the black dramatists' plays appear to fall under the rubric of the folk play, but the similarity is limited. Indeed, the perception of their plays as folk plays itself constituted a problem for black playwrights and the black theater.

However, the popularity of the Negro folk play provided powerful precedents. As so few scripts depicting Negro life were available, early black drama groups often turned to Negro folk plays by white writers, even while expressing discomfort with aspects of the works.[2] Langston Hughes characterized the problems they raised thus: "Ninety percent of the plays about Negroes drop their final curtain on defeat—usually death. A serious drama about Negroes simply cannot

1. Frederick Koch, Introduction to Koch (ed.), *American Folk Plays* (New York, 1939), xv–xvi.
2. In the twenties, black critics were torn because, although they were pleased that there were plays depicting serious black characters and that therefore black actors had expanded opportunities for work, the tenor of the plays did not escape them. For example, Theophilus Lewis entitled his review of the publication of *The Field God and In Abraham's Bosom* "The Paul Green Menace Increases," in *Messenger*, X (January, 1928), 18.

end happily. From *Uncle Tom's Cabin* to *Blues for Mr. Charlie* if every Negro who had died impotent and defeated on stage were to be buried end to end, their assembled corpses would reach around the world. . . . The stereotype of the Negro drama is the unhappy ending—spiritually and physically defeated, lynched, dead—gotten rid of to the relief of the dramatist and audience, in time for a late supper."[3]

Although black playwrights, Hughes included, were often as guilty of creating these endings as were whites, from the very beginning many deliberately countered the unrelieved grimness of the typical Negro folk play. The way Richardson and Edmonds did so reveals a complex understanding of the genre as applied to black people. Neither Richardson nor Edmonds confined himself to folk plays, however. In order to provide black theater groups with a range of materials, both wrote history plays, drama about the middle class, plays for children, and historical pageants. They desired not only to challenge artistic stereotypes but also to educate black people about their history and, usually but not always, to counteract "race literature"— literature whose chief aim was to uphold, even to idealize, black people and to protest racial prejudice and persecution. Finally, Edmonds, in particular, hoped his work in the theater would help provide black Americans with a formal literature.

When W. E. B. Du Bois established his Krigwa Little Theatre Movement in 1926, he postulated four fundamental principles: "The plays of a real Negro theatre must be: 1. *About us.* That is, they must have plots which reveal Negro life as it is. 2. *By us.* That is, they must be written by Negro authors who understand from birth and continual association just what it means to be a Negro today. 3. *For us.* That is, the theatre must cater primarily to Negro audiences and be supported and sustained by their entertainment and approval. 4. *Near us.* The theatre must be in a Negro neighborhood near the mass of ordinary Negro people." In 1926 there were few plays that satisfied the Krigwa criteria, but for its first production, the New York Krigwa group discovered two, *Compromise* and *The Broken Banjo*. Both were by Willis Richardson, a Washington, D.C., resident and United States government worker, who began writing plays because after seeing a 1916 production of Angelina Weld Grimke's *Rachel*, he felt he "could do

3. Langston Hughes, "The Negro and American Entertainment," in John T. Davis (ed.), *The American Negro Reference Book* (Englewood Cliffs, N.J., 1966), 847.

better than that." His first efforts, three one-act plays completed shortly thereafter, were judged by a mentor at Howard University "the best plays he'd seen by a person of our race."[4]

Richardson's impulse coincided quite precisely with the first stirrings of serious Negro theater. When, in April, 1917, Ridgely Torrence's *Three Plays for a Negro Theatre* was performed at the Old Garden Theatre in New York, critics hailed the event as "mark[ing] an epoch for the Negro on stage . . . by giving the American Negro his first opportunity in serious legitimate drama."[5] This production of the Torrence plays did signal the beginnings of serious drama about the Negro, but it is not the appropriate event to mark the beginnings of black theater. Theater that satisfies the Krigwa criteria, particularly the last two, "for us" and "near us," had long existed in black colleges, black churches, and other black community organizations all over the country. However, these manifestations of black drama as yet remain unchronicled because the productions were collegiate or amateur, and the theater groups ephemeral. Histories of black theater, like histories of American theater in general, have largely been confined to professional productions, especially those on the New York stage. Because black access to the professional stage has been so restricted, productions there are an unreliable gauge of black theatrical activity. Consideration only of professional drama gives an incomplete view of the contexts that shaped the writing of black dramatists, especially the early ones.[6]

Several aspects of Richardson's career make it more appropriate to take up a history of black theater with his work than with the Torrence production. Richardson lived in what was, prior to the 1920s, the intellectual capital of black America, Washington, D.C., and the first production, as well as several subsequent productions, of his plays

4. W. E. B. Du Bois, "Krigwa Little Theatre Movement," *Crisis*, XXXII (July, 1926), 134; recorded interview with Willis Richardson, March 5, 1972 (Hatch-Billops Oral Black History Collection, City College of New York, hereafter called the Hatch-Billops Collection). Richardson does not name these three plays.

5. James Weldon Johnson's review of the Torrence plays in New York *Age*, quoted in Edith Isaacs, *The Negro in the American Theatre* (New York, 1947), 59. This production was actually the second of the Torrence plays, but the first with black actors. The original production of one of the plays, *Granny Maumee*, in 1914 was so enthusiastically received that Torrence wrote two more one-act plays about Negro life. See Mitchell, *Black Drama* (New York, 1967), 69.

6. Thus a comprehensive understanding of the origins of black theater must derive from a study of the theater of black colleges and black communities.

were at one of the country's foremost black universities, Howard. Two Richardson plays, *The Broken Banjo* and *The House of Sham*, were among the most successful plays in both community and college theaters.[7] Richardson has claimed, apparently with justification, that his plays have been more frequently produced by black colleges and community groups than those of any other black playwright.[8]

That the 1916 production of Grimke's *Rachel* served as his catalyst is symbolically appropriate. A "race" play, *Rachel* is a melodramatic exposition of the traumatic effects of racial persecution, especially lynching, on a respectable middle-class Washington, D.C., family. The debate resulting from the 1916 production by the Drama Group of the National Association for the Advancement of Colored People (NAACP) caused a split in the community that sponsored it.[9] The rift presaged by ten years the rebellion of the Harlem Renaissance against the limited conception and purpose of "race art" and the demand of the movement for freedom to explore artistically the realities of black life. Those who disapproved of the play, Alain Locke and Montgomery Gregory among them, were later instrumental in founding the Howard Players, which "promot[ed] the purely artistic approach and the folk drama idea."[10]

Willis Richardson sided with the dissidents. While he recognized the importance of the propaganda play, a genre in which he included the work of John Galsworthy, George Bernard Shaw, and Eugène Brieux, as well as Grimke, he believed the hope for Negro drama lay in "the play that shows the soul of a people." He cited Torrence's *Three Plays for a Negro Theatre* and Mary Burrill's *Aftermath* as evidence of the fruitful possibilities in Negro material, and as model for Negro

7. Randolph Edmonds, "The Negro Playwright in the American Theatre," SADSA *Encore* (Spring, 1950), 12.

8. Richardson makes this claim during the March 5, 1972, interview in the Hatch-Billops Collection. It seems valid, for almost any report by a black community or college drama group from about 1920 until the late 1930s records the production of several of Richardson's plays. The other dramatists most frequently cited for plays about black people are Paul Green and Eugene O'Neill.

9. For accounts of the 1916 production of *Rachel* and the ensuing events, see Montgomery Gregory, "A Chronology of the Negro Theatre," in Locke and Gregory (eds.), *Plays of Negro Life*, 413–15, and Introduction to *Rachel* in James V. Hatch (ed.), *Black Theatre, U.S.A.: Forty-five Plays by Black Americans, 1847–1974* (New York, 1974), 137–38.

10. Montgomery Gregory, "A Chronology of the Negro Theatre," in Locke and Gregory (eds.), *Plays of Negro Life*, 414.

drama and dramatists he proposed the Irish national theater and its playwrights.[11]

The Chip Woman's Fortune, Richardson's best-known play, was the first serious play by a black playwright to be produced on Broadway. The way it reached Broadway reveals an important network in the early development of black theater. The Ethiopian Art Players, a Chicago group sponsored by Mrs. Sherwood Anderson and Raymond O'Neill, had written W. E. B. Du Bois at the *Crisis* for plays by Negro authors. Du Bois put the group in touch with Richardson, whose work he had twice published: first, in 1920, some children's plays in the *Brownies' Book* (the children's magazine briefly published by the *Crisis*), and second, *The Deacon's Awakening*, in the November issue of the *Crisis* for the same year. Richardson sent the Ethiopian Art Players his most recent work, *The Chip Woman's Fortune*, and it became the curtain raiser in a program they brought to New York in 1923. The play was well reviewed. In "Willis Richardson: Pioneer Playwright," Bernard Peterson quotes the New York *Times* review: "*The Chip Woman's Fortune* . . . is an unaffected and wholly convincing transcript of everyday character. No one is glorified or otherwise tricked out to please; no one is blackened to serve as a 'dramatic' contrast. I am referring, of course, to points of essential character, not to that matter of walnut stain."[12]

Richardson wrote more than forty other plays, all but seven in one act.[13] They fall into four categories: children's plays, history plays, plays depicting the black bourgeoisie, and folk plays. Only a handful are important to the history and development of black theater, since relatively few were disseminated or produced. Yet from these few and from his two anthologies, *Plays and Pageants from the Life of the Negro* and *Negro History in Thirteen Plays*, emerge a sense both of Richardson's conception of black theater and of the realities of that theater.

11. Willis Richardson, "The Hope of a Negro Drama," *Crisis*, XIX (November, 1919), 338–39. Burrill was Richardson's English teacher in high school, according to Bernard Peterson, Jr., "Willis Richardson: Pioneer Playwright," *Black World*, XXIV (April, 1975), 43.

12. Peterson, "Willis Richardson," 45. Richardson's account of how *The Chip Woman's Fortune* reached Broadway is quoted in Hatch (ed.), *Black Theatre*, U.S.A., 233. The other two plays on the program were Oscar Wilde's *Salome* and a jazz version of Shakespeare's *Comedy of Errors*.

13. The three-act plays are "The Amateur Prostitute," "The Visiting Lady," "Joy Rider," and "The Bootblack Lover." Three-act versions of *The Chip Woman's Fortune*, "The Flight of the Natives," and *The Broken Banjo* also exist. Mr. James V. Hatch has all but "Joy Rider," "The Bootblack Lover," and the expanded version of *The Chip Woman's Fortune*.

The least interesting of Richardson's plays are those he wrote for children. Moral tales set in an imaginary landscape, the plays always include, as central or peripheral to their story, a lesson on racial equality and brotherhood. They must have filled a need, for in 1956, Richardson collected and published the plays as *The King's Dilemma and Other Plays for Children*.[14] It is likely that they were used by teachers seeking appropriate material for children affected by school integration.

More important are Richardson's history plays, for they typify the kind of race literature against which such writers as Randolph Edmonds and Langston Hughes reacted in their plays depicting historical characters. Describing himself, as well as others, in his preface to *Negro History in Thirteen Plays*, Richardson remarked: "The writers have not attempted to reproduce definitive history, but have sought to create the atmosphere of a time past or the portrait of a memorable figure . . . in many instances, imagination has supplied the necessary details."[15] In most of his history plays, Richardson seeks only to depict black persons of stature in situations that allow them to display admirable traits. Like Carter Woodson, whose press published both his anthologies, Richardson thus sought to instill in black people pride in a "glorious past." As was Woodson's, however, his measure of glory is comparative. The plays evoke not African history but rather black history in the West or historical contact between Africa and Europe. Their aim, finally, is to place black heroes in the Western historical landscape.

The Black Horseman concerns white Carthage's treachery toward black Numidia and the subsequent alliance between Massinassa and Scipio. Set in 204 B.C. and written in iambic pentameter, the play clearly alludes not only to historical events but to Shakespeare's Roman plays as well. *In Menelik's Court*, set in Abyssinia in 1896, depicts a successfully repulsed attack by Italian spies on the court of Menelik. Published in 1935, the play reminded black Americans that Ethiopia, which had just fallen to Benito Mussolini, had been more powerful in the past. *Antonio Maceo* and *Attucks the Martyr* concern North American heroes. The former depicts the Cuban hero's assassination by Spanish soldiers. The latter portrays Attucks as loyal to the American cause in the American Revolution and as vehemently hating King George III,

14. Willis Richardson, *The King's Dilemma and Other Plays for Children: Episodes of Hope and Dream* (New York, 1956).
15. Richardson, Preface to Richardson and Miller (eds.), *Negro History in Thirteen Plays*, vi.

but not his master, even though he has just been declared a fugitive slave and is in danger of capture.

Most of Richardson's history plays are slight, but one deserves some extended discussion. *The Flight of the Natives* is set in the more familiar historical and imaginative landscape of American slavery and treats issues that also arise in Richardson's plays about the middle class and the folk. *The Flight of the Natives* was first performed by the Krigwa Players of Washington, D.C., in 1927 and was selected by Locke and Gregory for their anthology *Plays of Negro Life*, published the same year.

The play's title links black slaves to the indigenous American population, an intriguing suggestion that Richardson does not pursue. Rather, he uses flight, a traditional theme in literature about slavery, to correct the images of slavery in plantation literature, such works as Harriet Beecher Stowe's *Uncle Tom's Cabin*, and history books as well. In striking contrast to the individual heroes depicted in Richardson's later history plays is the group protagonist, which, James Hatch suggests, gives the play historical credibility.[16] The group protagonist also allows Richardson to raise the question of racial solidarity, one of his continual concerns, without overtly moralizing about its modern application.

The Flight of the Natives opens with a discussion about Slim, who has just been captured because Jude, a favorite slave of the master, disclosed Slim's escape route. The conversation reveals a range of personalities; it also provides insight into and counters some common beliefs about slave behavior. For example, through the central figure, Mose, Richardson insists on the integrity of the slave family. Mose has sworn he will never be whipped, but he has never attempted flight to escape punishment because he believes his wife could not endure its rigors. He also endures compromising behavior because he fears being sold away from her.

Mose's resolve is soon tested by a confrontation with his master, so he decides to escape and take his friends with him. Through the co-operatively determined escape plan, Richardson raises issues of racial solidarity. Mose mistrusts light-skinned Luke, who is clearly the master's offspring, but it is Luke's skin color that finally makes their escape possible. Dressed as his master, Luke will play a planter trav-

16. James Hatch, Introduction to *The Flight of the Natives,* in Hatch (ed.), *Black Theatre, U.S.A.,* 382.

eling with a group of his slaves. The ruse is preferable to the plan presented by Mose, for it enables them to take along Slim, crippled by the beating he received upon capture. Mose's plan, which requires physical agility and endurance, would necessitate abandoning him. In the play's resolution, skin color and group loyalty are divorced, for traitorous Jude is dark, while light-skinned Luke's ability to pass as a white is the group's key to freedom. Moreover, Mose, who protests that he will flee if any difficulty arises, prefers to trust selfishly in physical strength rather than in what the play implies is Luke's superior intellect. These strains on group loyalty in *The Flight of the Natives* reflect debates in the black community.[17]

Richardson's plays about the middle class are relentlessly critical. His central charge is that members of the middle class deny and disrupt the kind of racial solidarity depicted in *The Flight of the Natives* through their social pretension and avarice. The titles of two of his plays succinctly summarize his view of middle-class people: *Mortgaged* and *The House of Sham*. In three other plays from the twenties, *The Deacon's Awakening*, "A Pillar of the Church," and "The Peacock's Feather," he depicts them as narrow-minded, reactionary, hypocritical, and shallow.

The earliest published play in this category, *The Deacon's Awakening*, which appeared in 1920, concerns women's rights. It depicts the conflict between a narrow-minded deacon and his wife and daughter over their involvement in the suffrage movement and concludes with the deacon acknowledging the irrationality of his position. Published in the *Crisis*, the most influential magazine among the black middle class, *The Deacon's Awakening* may have been the first play portraying middle-class blacks involved in contemporary issues not directly related to race and critical of the reactionary attitudes of the black church. "A Pillar of the Church," which is undated, but clearly from the same period, similarly attacks religious conservatism.[18] In this play, a tyrannical, religious father's attitude toward modern education for his daughters triumphs over their young teacher's attempts to intercede for them.

17. The expanded "Flight of the Natives" (undated typescript, Hatch-Billops Collection) has the band of slaves meet Sojourner Truth, who helps them reach freedom. The portrait of Mose and the emphasis on the solidarity of the black family are even more pronounced in this version.
18. Willis Richardson, *The Deacon's Awakening*, *Crisis*, XXI (November, 1920), 10–15, and "A Pillar of the Church" (typescript in Hatch-Billops Collection).

Social pretension, wealth based on ill-gotten gains, and racial divisiveness are the themes of *Mortgaged*, "The Peacock's Feather," and *The House of Sham*. *Mortgaged*, written in 1923, is typical of Richardson's portraits of the wealthy bourgeoisie. His critique of the Fields is unremitting: they care for nothing but money and social position, and have spoiled their children. Thomas Fields has acquired at least some of his wealth by exploiting his own people as a slum landlord. Moreover, Fields scorns his poorer, intellectual brother and nephew.

An encounter between the brothers not only serves as vehicle for Richardson's attack but also replays the debate in which Booker T. Washington's trust in financial independence as a prerequisite to racial equality was challenged by W. E. B. Du Bois's insistence that the future of the race lay in nurturing its "Talented Tenth." When Uncle John, a brilliant but as yet unsuccessful chemist, comes to borrow money to send his equally talented son to school, Fields assents only on the condition that John give up his laboratory. John capitulates bitterly.

> Yes, but first let me tell you something about yourself and your kind. You have your money and I have my science. Perhaps you think you're helping to advance the race by piling up dollars, but you're not! It's not money that's going to make this race of ours respected, but what its men and women accomplish in science and the arts. . . . You may think you're doing a fine thing by getting richer and richer; but if nothing is ever done to make the race respected, you'll soon find out that your dollar that you love so well is not worth as much as the other fellow's dollar.[19]

The play clearly vindicates John's position, for at the end he becomes successful and wealthy. What is important about *Mortgaged* is not its intrinsic merit but the fact that Alain Locke and Montgomery Gregory chose it when, in 1924, they gave Richardson his first Howard University production. Clearly they believed *Mortgaged* spoke to the concerns of a Howard audience.

In "The Peacock's Feather," written in 1928, and *The House of Sham*, written in 1929, those who claim superiority based on wealth or culture are unmasked.[20] The earlier play directly pits character against class. Mrs. Adams, a social climber, prefers her daughter Dorothy's wealthy suitor, Clarence, to her poor but honest suitor, Joe. When

19. Willis Richardson, *Mortgaged*, in Othelia Cromwell, Lorenzo Dow Turner, and Eva B. Dykes (eds.), *Readings from Negro Authors* (New York, 1931), 157–58.
20. Willis Richardson, "The Peacock's Feather" (typescript in Hatch-Billops Collection), and *The House of Sham*, in *Plays and Pageants from the Life of the Negro*.

Clarence is exposed as vicious and petty, and Mrs. Adams as a hypo-
crite, Dorothy and Joe are free to wed. Underlying Richardson's criticism of social pretension in "The Peacock's Feather" is his concern
with racial solidarity. Mr. Adams sounds the theme when in defense of
Dorothy's preference for Joe, he comments that there are "too many
kinds of people among us [to put up] social barriers that are too hard
to pass." [21] In *The House of Sham*, pretensions of a more serious nature
are unmasked. In this play, the Cooper family's wealthy life-style rests
on exploitative business practices and borrowed money. When the
truth of their financial situation is revealed, the daughter's suitor
flees, but her cousin's remains faithful. The truly loving couple are
unaffected by the family's catastrophe because they had lived "without sham."

While Richardson's wholesale condemnation of the black bourgeoisie may in part have been a reaction to what he felt and observed
in his contact with Washington, D.C., society, his focus on social pretension and the blindness of the clergy also derives from the obses-
sions of his favorite author, George Bernard Shaw. [22] Yet, unlike Shaw,
neither the clery nor even the bourgeoisie are his real concern; he
pursues them only in the interest of his underlying preoccupation
with racial solidarity and right action, and this emerges most clearly
in his folk plays.

Richer and more lyrical than his other plays, Richardson's folk plays
are his most fully realized. In them, as elsewhere, he insists that
though singled out for oppression, black people must, nonetheless,
resolve their life problems morally and with integrity. His refusal to
idealize his characters challenged the proponents of race literature;
his focus on the black experience as context rather than as that which
must be explicated makes these plays the first models of what Ed
Bullins later called "Theatre of Black Experience." His focus also enabled Richardson to create at least a credible stage reality.

However, Richardson's talent as a playwright is limited; even his folk
plays suffer from his inability to make vivid his ideas and intentions.

21. Richardson, "The Peacock's Feather," 23.
22. From comments made by Richardson during the taped interview,
March 5, 1972, in the Hatch-Billops Collection, one gathers that he had frequent contact with at least the intellectual circle in Washington, D.C., particularly people at Howard University. He belonged to both the Krigwa Players in
Washington, D.C., and a Saturday-night group that met periodically to read
their work and to hold discussion.

He fails to fully utilize the elements of black language and tradition that he incorporates in his work, and he remains so conscious of working against dramatic stereotypes that his characters verge on the nondescript. Yet, in spite of his failings, his work set an important precedent in the development of black theater.

Richardson's folk plays were his most popular in part because they corrected the image of the Negro in folk plays by white writers. His characters are not the folk Koch meant when defining the genre: people living such basic lives that nature provides their most immediate source of joy and adversity. Rather, they are ordinary black men and women, hard-working, impoverished, but not necessarily without complexity, who try their best to make moral choices or to rectify mistakes of the past. All four extant folk plays from the 1920s, The Chip Woman's Fortune, The Broken Banjo, Compromise, and The Idle Head, published in 1923, 1925, 1925, and 1929, respectively, concern the complex decisions black people must make in painful circumstances. As in Negro plays by white authors, poverty and racism cause many of the characters' difficulties, but these in themselves are not the plays' concern. The black audiences to whom the plays were addressed were adequately familiar with the black experience and its hardships; while acknowledging them, they still had to resolve problems arising from the givens of their world.

Richardson's folk plays thus consider the impact of various resolutions to problems black people encounter in their daily living. He never evokes pity for his characters; indeed, one of the recurrent criticisms of his work has been that he fails to make his characters adequately sympathetic. The effect of his dispassionate attitude is to allow his audience likewise to evaluate dispassionately the rightness of a character's choice or action. Richardson's impulse is always didactic. He values honesty, loyalty, courage, personal integrity, and industry. All four plays depict what occurs when misfortune tempts his characters to abandon these virtues.

Although Richardson's characters possess human frailties, they also possess a stature and dignity lacking in black characters depicted by white playwrights. For example, in Ridgely Torrence's 1917 play The Rider of Dreams, which is heavily indebted to Synge's Playboy of the Western World, the man devoted to his music and his illicitly acquired guitar is a fool and a thief. His reformation involves submission to his virtuous wife and the turning of his music to profit. Felix Sper suggests

that The Broken Banjo is indebted to Torrence's play, and some connection is likely, for Richardson expressed his admiration for Torrence in
his essay "The Hope of the Negro Drama." [23] Yet Richardson's hero, Matt
Turner, who, like Torrence's Madison Sparrow, lives for his music, possesses his own banjo. The names of the characters themselves suggest
the differences between the two plays. While Torrence's Sparrow suggests those little ones whom God does not overlook (Luke 12:6–7,
24–25), Richardson's hero recalls Nat Turner, a man who took fate violently into his own hands. The principal characters' relation to music
is also significantly different. Matt Turner "is not by any means a good
player but his desire to play well is his religion," reads the character
description.[24] His banjo is an instrument emblematic of slavery and
the minstrel show, and he is so fiercely protective of it and so hot-
tempered that he kills once for it and almost twice. In The Rider of
Dreams, Sparrow's music is emblematic of a quite different attitude.
Early in the play, Sparrow says, "I boun' to play [the guitar] cause I'm
goin' to be er rich man soon an' I got to have a plenty music in me." At
the play's end, forced to combine music and work, he plaintively concludes: "Yes, but not all of my dreams is bad ones. All, [sic] I wants is
room to dream my good dreams an' make my own music." [25]

In the Torrence play, music becomes the signature of the simple,
happy-go-lucky, but now sobered, stereotypical man-child of the
Negro folk play. In The Broken Banjo, while the meaning of music to
Matt is not adequately articulated, clearly it is something fiercely private, sacred, and central to his self-conception. In short, the centrality
of music in The Broken Banjo reflects the place music actually holds in
black American culture. Although music in The Rider of Dreams is better
integrated into the symbolism and meaning of the play, the significance implied is the product of an outsider's imagination.

Richardson also differed markedly from white playwrights in his attitude toward the use of dialect. White dramatists sought in Negro
dialect the lyrical rhythms Synge had found in the speech of the Irish
folk. In 1924 Richardson wrote: "Every phase of life may be depicted

23. Felix Sper, From Native Roots: A Panorama of Our Regional Drama (Caldwell,
Idaho, 1948), 86. Sper makes a significant error in recounting the plot of The
Broken Banjo, but his comment is still valid.
24. Willis Richardson, The Broken Banjo, in Locke and Gregory (eds.), Plays of
Negro Life, 303. In 1925, Crisis awarded Richardson a prize for this play.
25. Ridgely Torrence, Granny Maumee, The Rider of Dreams, Simon the Cyrenian:
Plays for a Negro Theatre (New York, 1917), 45, 76.

in Negro drama. . . . The lives of the educated with their perfect language and manners may be shown as well as the lives and problems
of *the less fortunate who still use the dialect . . . we have learned the English language, but the dialect of the slave days is still the mother tongue of the American
Negro."* The image "mother tongue" related to dialect is a bold, significant connection. Dialect on stage is not merely realistic detail for
Richardson, nor is it "quaint." Rather, he insists on the link between
his dialect-speaking characters and the middle-class audience "sit-
[ting] in [their] stall[s] at the theatre and witness[ing] the interesting
things in the lives of [their] kinsmen, no matter what may be their
condition of life, speech or manners." [26]

Black audiences were uncomfortable with dialect on stage because,
traditionally, it provided much of the humor in the minstrel show and
marked the black stage comic. Perhaps one of the most novel aspects of the serious Negro theater was its use of dialect for sentiments other than comic—its demonstration that dialect could be
eloquent.[27] In rejecting dialect, an educated black audience rejected
not only stereotypical images of the Negro but also its own history in
America. Richardson insisted on the shared heritage of his characters
and the audience, as symbolized by dialect.

Richardson uses dialect and depicts other elements of black culture in his plays—for example, the banjo in *The Broken Banjo*, or folk
medicine in *The Chip Woman's Fortune*—because if he is to explore the
soul of his people, he must accept as part of the fabric of their world
all that it contains. It is ironic but also, in a sense, a measure of his
attitude and purpose that he is much poorer at exploiting these elements than other writers of folk plays, both black and white. For example, his dialect lacks the vivid imagery and rhythms characteristic
of black speech, more accurately reproduced by black writers Jean

26. Willis Richardson, "Propaganda in the Theatre," *Messenger*, VI (November, 1924), 354. Emphasis added to first quotation.
27. Debate about the use of dialect raged throughout the twenties. The
classic and highly influential statement about the use of dialect appears in
James Weldon Johnson's introduction to his volume of poetry, *God's Trombones:
Seven Negro Sermons in Verse* (1927; rpr. New York, 1969). Johnson cites the dream
speech from Torrence's *Rider of Dreams*, as delivered by Opal Cooper in the New
York production of the play, as the finest and only demonstration of the language and rhythms of a good black preacher. Five years later, in his preface to
Sterling Brown's volume of dialect poetry, *Southern Road*, Johnson changed his
evaluation of the range of literary dialect. See Sterling Brown, *Southern Road*
(1932; rpr. Boston, 1974).

Toomer, Georgia Douglas Johnson, and John Matheus, and white writers Paul Green and Ridgely Torrence.

Richardson does not explore and elaborate the elements of black culture included in his plays; however, neither does he, as did many white writers, turn the plays into set pieces, in which folk characters display talents or customs for which they are "noted"—generally, singing, dancing, or working themselves into a frenzy during a church service. As Richardson does not see his characters primarily as "folk," he is not particularly observant of "folkways," nor interested in them for themselves. All four of his folk plays concern rather the integrity of the black family and by extension the black people of America. In all of the plays, problems arise when the family is, in some way, compromised or denied, and the resolutions of the plays, as in *The Flight of the Natives*, comment as well on the strengths and weaknesses of the black community.

The first of the folk dramas, *The Chip Woman's Fortune*, in part addresses the relation between the modern generation and its folk past. The figure of the chip woman, Aunt Nancy, is described as a conventional folk figure: "Every one of us has seen her kind—those old women who go about the street picking up chips and lumps of coal. . . . She is old and her back is bent. . . . She is wearing a bonnet which partly hides her black, wrinkled face, and is wearing a shawl over her shoulders."[28] The Green family—Silas; his wife, Liza; and their daughter, Emma—have taken in Aunt Nancy; she, in return, has used her folk wisdom to nurse Liza through a long illness.

The Greens are poor and heavily in debt for a Victrola, the only modern convenience in their austere dwelling and their one luxury. The Victrola is an emblem of their progress into modern life, as well as a sign of some improvidence on their part. It precipitates the play's first crisis, in which Silas is sent home from his job "on account o' that old Victrola. Seems like it's bringin' us more trouble than it's worth."[29] His employer has given him furlough without pay for falling behind on his payments, and the Victrola is to be repossessed. The absurdity of this double bind is not commented on: the matter-of-factness with which Silas accepts it indicates the frequency of such absurd white behavior toward blacks. Rather, the play focuses on how

28. Willis Richardson, *The Chip Woman's Fortune*, in Darwin T. Turner (ed.), *Black Drama in America: An Anthology* (Greenwich, Conn., 1971), 20.
29. Ibid., 31.

the Green family can retain the Victrola and solve other money matters made more urgent because Silas will forfeit a few days' pay.

The play's central conflict erupts when Silas discovers buried in the backyard Aunt Nancy's store of money, which she has been saving for her son Jim, who is about to be released from jail. Silas demands that she contribute to the family finances; she refuses, saying the money belongs to her son. Fortunately, Jim arrives just as the men come to repossess the Victrola, and he readily gives half the savings to the Green family. The play ends with an awakening attraction between Emma and Jim and the entire family's affirmation of their love for Aunt Nancy.

In *The Chip Woman's Fortune*, the folk figure's wisdom and providence provide a solution to all difficulties. Aunt Nancy's knowledge of herbs, which she is gradually teaching Emma, has healed Liza; her carefully hoarded pennies finally provide, not only for her own needs and those of her son, but for the Greens' as well. Aunt Nancy points out that the old must be so provident not because it is their role but because the times have gone awry and the children astray: "When Ah was coming up . . . children used to get grown . . . [and] take care o' the old folks, but now it's different. The old folks has to take care o' the children." [30]

Even so, her nurturing of her son has not been perfect. Jim was jailed because he assaulted a man for harming his woman. The man, "one o' those big fellows that went to church every Sunday . . . [but] in the night trailed in the gutter," had Jim framed. Aunt Nancy answers Silas' criticisms of a man with a jail record: "Goin' to the pen ain' nothin'. Some o' the best men in the world's been to the pen. It ain't the goin' to the pen that counts, it's what you go there for . . . the people forgot that the Lord was locked up." [31]

However, having discovered his woman was "crooked," Jim had beaten her as well, and this act is not condoned—it causes his mother much pain. By separating the real wrong (doing violence to a woman) from the prison sentence, the play comments on the relationship between morality and the way the law is used against black people. Aunt Nancy's defense of Jim does not explore this social discrepancy; rather, it is directed against a bourgeois audience that might equate a prison record with lack of character. Yet, at the same

30. *Ibid.*, 40.
31. *Ibid.*, 41, 40–41.

time, Jim is not idealized; Aunt Nancy forgives his real crime, the beating of his woman, only because she is his mother.

As usual in Richardson's plays, several disruptive forces threaten the characters in *The Chip Woman's Fortune*: the white world; treacherous blacks, particularly the hypocritical among the middle class; and the characters' individual weaknesses. Correspondingly, Aunt Nancy's fortune can resolve their difficulties only because of a combination of forces: the Greens' hospitality, her own patience, and her son's goodness and generosity. Thus the play insists that only when all elements of the family, which represents the community, accept and cooperate with one another, can the world be set aright.

In contrast to *The Chip Woman's Fortune*, *The Broken Banjo*, as its title suggests, depicts family disruption. The play's setting is a "dull and dark" dining room with only two chairs. It opens on a quarrel between Emma and Matt about his banjo, their poverty, and Emma's parasitic relatives, Sam and Adam. Nonetheless, a real love exists between the couple. Matt admits, "If Ah didn't care nothin' about you Ah'd been gone long ago," and later, "Ain't nobody likes me but you, and you ain't crazy about me." Similarly, Emma protests: "Ah'm thinkin' for you every minute o' ma life, but you don't know it. You never will know it till you get in a big pinch." [32]

Matt has only recently begun working; until then, only Emma's labors had provided them with food. Matt resents Sam and Adam for devouring their meager resources, and he leaves to buy Emma a needed pair of shoes in return for her promise to tell her relatives they are no longer welcome. When Sam and Adam arrive, Emma does as she promised, much to their displeasure. However, they refuse to leave and, while playing around, break Matt's banjo. Both are terrified, for Matt has beaten them before. To counter Matt's anger, Sam reveals that he knows Matt once killed a white man who had attacked him and broken his banjo. When confronted, Matt readily confesses and compels Sam and Adam to swear secrecy. Nevertheless, Emma forces Matt to take some money she has saved and tells him to flee. Her instincts are accurate: Sam and Adam prove false, and the police arrive before Matt can escape.

If *The Chip Woman's Fortune* represents the binding together of a family through shared generosity, *The Broken Banjo* explores the destruction of a family in which guilt is similarly dispersed among its members.

32. Richardson, *The Broken Banjo*, in *Plays of Negro Life*, 303, 304, 305, 306.

Matt, in spite of his pugnacity, is likable for the genuine tenderness he shows toward Emma. However, like Jim's beating of his woman in *The Chip Woman's Fortune*, his conduct is sometimes criminal, unpremeditated but serious nonetheless. The same violence has earlier made enemies of Sam and Adam, though we side with Matt as soon as it becomes clear that they visit Emma not as friends but as parasites and that Sam, in contrast to the comical Adam, has a distinctly mean streak of which his final treachery is the logical outcome. Emma, the hub of the family, is helpless to hold it together. Her tears at the end of the play have the quality of incoherent pain rather than of focused mourning for a specific tragedy. Her love and providence were inadequate to the task of saving her family; she has lost both husband and kin. In spite of the unlikelihood of some elements of the plot, particularly that Matt could keep the murder hidden for so long and that he would trust the word of Sam and Adam, the theme and mood of brokenness in the play is effectively sustained. The final atmosphere of general lamentation suggests the mournful aspect of black music, particularly of the spirituals and the blues, to which the title also alludes.

Compromise depicts the destructive effect of relationships between blacks and whites on the black family. The title in its various meanings defines the tenor of the relationships. The play suggests that, finally, it is the blacks who must do all the compromising and that, as a result, they are the ones compromised.

Previous to the play's events, a white neighbor, Ben Carter, had accidentally killed Jane Lee's oldest son. Jim Lee drank himself to death with the hundred dollars Carter gave the Lee family in compensation. Thus, although Ben Carter frequently drops in to enjoy Jane's coffee, the black family bitterly resents its white neighbor. From the opening moments of the play, Carter's presence in the Lee house evokes the destructive impact of the white man on the black family, particularly suggesting the sexual meanings of the word *compromise*.

The first actual compromise was Jim Lee's decision to accept payment for his son's death. The second, Jane's, occurs seven years later. Jane discovers that young Jack Carter has impregnated her daughter Annie, and demands that Ben educate her two remaining children, Alec and Ruth, in compensation. Alarmed by hints of Alec's continued bitterness over the death of his brother, Ben agrees, but when Alec assaults Jack anyway, Ben revokes his promise and sets the sheriff on Alec. The second compromise has also proved disastrous, and as the play ends, Jane prepares her son's escape.

Like *The Chip Woman's Fortune*, *Compromise* reveals the different ways in which the generations cope with issues confronting them, but unlike *The Chip Woman's Fortune*, *Compromise* portrays the ways of the old as unacceptable and destructive of themselves and their progeny. When Alec admonishes his mother for having compromised over Joe and then again over Annie, she says: "Your fool daddy done that! Ah'll get somethin' out o' this." [33] But Alec refuses the fruits of her bargain and seeks to satisfy a revenge he can no longer suppress. As in *The Broken Banjo*, tragedy is the inevitable outcome of the decisions and actions of the characters. Yet, unlike in conventional tragedy, the characters do not choose wrongly due to blindness or hubris; rather, they have no realistic alternatives to the course of action they pursue. Moreover, *Compromise* depicts the impact of the humiliation inherent in the ways blacks have been forced to conduct their relationships with whites; as well, it illuminates the historical conflict of the black mother who understands and shares her son's rage but must force him to contain it for his own survival. Thus Jane defends her conduct to Alec although earlier she had used her son's rage as a veiled threat to obtain the very benefits to which he objects and which precipitate the final catastrophe.

The entire situation raises many basic issues; most powerfully depicted is the loss of personal integrity for which the characters are not blamed and which is the central cause of their suffering, rather than the events that precipitate the loss. This locating of the drama in how characters feel about events rather than in the events themselves marks another important difference between Richardson's work and plays by white writers with similar themes. The events were commonplace to a black audience. What needed dramatization was the crucial issue of how black people have coped with their tragic circumstances.

The fourth folk play, *The Idle Head*, examines the fate of a man who refuses to compromise. [34] At first view, George Broadus appears to be a loafer, and visiting clergy, demanding dues from his mother, imply as much. In fact, George has been branded a troublemaker and barred

33. Willis Richardson, *Compromise*, in Alain Locke (ed.), *The New Negro* (1925; rpr. New York, 1969), 192.
34. Willis Richardson, *The Idle Head*, in Hatch (ed.), *Black Theatre, U.S.A.*

from his employment as a waiter for a simple act of self-assertion before an insulting white patron. His mother supports her son's conduct in spite of its destructive effect: by asserting his manhood, George has forfeited the ability to support his family.

This conflict is subordinated to the central conflict in *The Idle Head*. While sorting a load of washing his mother has taken in, George discovers, left in the clothing, a pin of some value. Because his mother and sister are distraught by the minister's threat to expel them from the church unless they pay their dues, George pawns the pin and gives them the money. The owner misses the jewelry, and George is apprehended.

As in *Compromise*, the difficulty in which the characters find themselves is not perceived as extraordinary. The play focuses instead on the characters' experiences and the choices they make to resolve the situation. Both in his assertiveness and in his scornful attitude to the church, George clearly portrays the "New Negro." He refers to the clergymen deprecatingly as his mother's "class leaders" and pawns the pin only because the church is of such importance to her. Possibly, the play suggests that George's downfall is not merely his theft but also his resulting indirect support of the church, a frequent target of Richardson's anger.

In all four of his folk plays, then, Richardson depicts ordinary poor black people confronted with crises that require moral choice, and he queries what constitutes right action in their situations. Richardson's characters are also consciously and carefully portrayed as "not-stage-Negroes." Although they speak in dialect, little else identifies them as black because all suggestions of stereotype are studiously avoided. Each play points out what it is "not doing" in other ways as well. For example, we know Matt has been a profligate, but by the opening of *The Broken Banjo* he has reformed; Silas may have been improvident in buying the Victrola, but by the time *The Chip Woman's Fortune* opens, he is diligently attempting to provide for his family; and, similarly, George is only prevented from supporting his family by white injustice. Thus each play is "not upholding," and in fact is deliberately undermining, the stereotypical portrait of the irresponsible black male. Not until the comedies of Langston Hughes will the work of a serious black writer risk portraying the kind of behavior often labeled as "stereotype" without playing into the limits and degradation of racist cliches.

Randolph Edmonds declared a much broader intention than his predecessor's when, in 1930, then a young English instructor at Morgan College in Baltimore, Maryland, he wrote:

> There has been no riddle of the world given a solution in black terms; and after all this is the only thing that we can expect. For strictly speaking there is no such thing as Negro drama, Irish drama, French drama, and the like. Drama is a representation of universal life built around the feelings, thoughts, and clash of wills of particular people. When we speak of the drama of a nationality, we mean these universal truths colored by the temperament of a group. And certainly the reaction of Negroes to life should give us something that is distinctly different.

Impatient with what he viewed as the lack of originality and insight in the sparse offerings of his contemporaries, Richardson included, Edmonds proposed turning to black colleges and universities to increase the quantity and to improve the quality of Negro drama. For, he noted, "most of the great playwrights have been closely connected with the stage," and if black playwrights were to have stages on which to develop their art, they would have to provide their own.[35]

The idea was not new. In 1921, under the guidance of Alain Locke and Montgomery Gregory, Howard University had established an educational theater program; however, when Locke withdrew to his critical work and Gregory to employment elsewhere, the program disintegrated, and subsequent dramatic activity at Howard was extracurricular and sporadic. Edmonds certainly had this early attempt in mind when, in 1930, he proposed to Howard and three neighboring black colleges, Hampton Institute, Virginia State College, and Virginia Union, the organization of the Negro Intercollegiate Dramatic Association. Founded to promote the study of drama and performance at black colleges, this early organization provided a model for several others. In 1936, at Edmonds' instigation, the largest of these, the Southern Association of Dramatic and Speech Arts, became the National Association of Dramatic and Speech Arts, and he served as president for its first seven years. This organization currently includes drama departments in most of the black colleges.

Edmonds became a practitioner in the theater as a result of his research and teaching interests. Although his parents were born into slavery, his father was one of the first literate black men in Lawrence-

---

35. Randolph Edmonds, "Some Reflections on the Negro in American Drama," *Opportunity*, VIII (October, 1930), 305.

ville, Virginia, and Edmonds himself earned a bachelor of arts from
Oberlin College in 1926 and a master of arts from Columbia University in 1934, with a major in English and a minor in drama.[36] A Rockefeller grant in 1933 and a Rosenwald Fellowship in 1937 permitted
him two more years of study. The first he spent at the Yale Drama
School and the second in London and Dublin, where he worked with
the Abbey Players. Edmonds' university teaching career spanned
forty years at three institutions (Morgan College, 1929–1934; Dillard
University, 1935–1947; Florida A & M University, 1947–1969), where
he labored tirelessly to establish a little theater movement at black
colleges and universities. In addition to his organizational work, he
published numerous articles chronicling and publicizing black educational and community drama. To provide material for the theater he
sought to build, he wrote forty-eight plays.

Edmonds' academic interests shaped both his concept of the theater and his artistic work. Published in various journals and one anthology, his discussions of black theater, which span his academic career, changed little over the years. The preface to his first anthology of
black plays, *Six Plays for a Negro Theatre*, published in 1934, typifies his
position. The works in the volume are intended, he states, to provide
material written by a Negro for the Negro little theater, although he
hopes others will use the plays as well, for "if plays are really worthwhile, they ought to contain some universal elements." Edmonds observes that many Negroes will object to the use of dialect in the plays,
but believes their real objection is not to "the crude expressions of
the peasant characters . . . but rather [to] the repelling atmosphere
and the 'psychology of the inferior' that somehow creep into the peasant plays of even the most unbiased authors of other racial groups."
He expects to meet the "usual" objections to dialect plays by including in his plays four elements: "worthwhile themes, sharply drawn
conflict, positive characters, and a melodramatic plot." These elements prevent tragedies from being "too revolting in theme" and "too
subtle and psychological in their action and exposition" for the "average" theater-goer. His central characters are "positive" because they
have "courage and conviction and fight heroically in their losing
struggles." He includes melodramatic plot to satisfy "the average au-

36. His M.A. thesis at Columbia was "The Tragic Atmosphere in John
Webster." Listed on a bibliography submitted by the author, Hatch-Billops
Collection.

dience rather than the sophisticated theatre-goer." With only a slight change, a rewording of the fourth constituent to "theatrical rather than literary drama," Edmonds reiterated these elements in 1970 as a guideline for contemporary black playwrights.[37]

Ultimately, Edmonds' idea of black theater is more complex than his simple criteria suggest. However, he is torn between his literary and other artistic values on the one hand and his understanding both of the tradition he must combat and of what constitutes exciting performance, particularly for an "average" audience, on the other. His criteria "worthwhile themes" and "positive characters" counter the depressing situations and stereotypical characters commonly found in plays of Negro life. The criteria "sharply drawn conflict" and "melodramatic plots" cater to the unsophisticated audience he hoped to attract and then educate to an appreciation of serious drama.

By serious drama, Edmonds means both the tradition inherited from the West and drama as yet unwritten in which the lives of black people provide the imaginative landscape through which the human predicament is explored. For Edmonds, this drama requires a welding of the black experience to traditional dramatic forms, a union that could not occur until "'Uncle Tom' . . . [was] banished forever from the American stage," as Edmonds and his students at Dillard University expressed it in a pageant first performed in 1945.[38]

For Edmonds, not only the presence of Uncle Tom but that of any stereotype hindered the black theater's development. In "Black Drama in the American Theatre, 1700–1970," he defines thirteen Negro stereotypes created by white playwrights—and several more that he credits to contemporary black playwrights. As well in this article, Edmonds acknowledges white writers for their contribution to serious drama about the Negro, but he objects to their handling of both theme and character, and he claims black audiences have rejected their plays. Like Langston Hughes, Edmonds protests the inevitability of misfortune in plays about black people: "I do not contend that the tragic side of life should not be depicted . . . [but] it should be grounded in the natural laws of life, and the tragedy should come as a result of the fitness or unfitness of a character to perform a task."[39]

37. Randolph Edmonds, *Six Plays for a Negro Theatre* (Boston, 1934), 7–8, and "Black Drama in the American Theatre: 1700–1970," in *American Theatre: A Sum of Its Parts* (New York, 1971), 414.

38. Edmonds, "Black Drama," in *American Theatre*, 421.

39. *Ibid.*, 397–99; Edmonds, "Some Reflections," 304.

Underlying all Edmonds' discussions of black drama is his clear understanding of the fundamental dishonesty of the typical Negro folk play. Because of the degrading images of folk life that inform it, no characters can be accorded the stature of the tragic protagonist. Moreover, the nature of the typical conflict in which they are engaged also denies them such stature. "The chief concern of the folk dramatist is man's conflict with the forces of nature and his simple pleasure in being alive," wrote Frederick Koch.[40] Prototypically, Maurya's grief as the sea claims the last of her sons in Synge's *Riders to the Sea* celebrates human endurance within a larger pattern of meaning. However, the Negro folk play presents a special case because generally the black characters endure not "gods who kill for their sport," but other human beings who do so. Fate is the product of oppression rather than of natural forces—and need not simply be endured. The hostile reaction of black audiences to such plays is understandable.

In his preface to Edmonds' *Six Plays for a Negro Theatre*, Frederick Koch cites Paul Green's *Lonesome Road* as Edmonds' inspiration for turning to "Negro peasant plays." However, although Edmonds has described Paul Green as "coming nearer to depicting the black character than any other white playwright," he praises only five of his plays—*The No 'Count Boy*, *The Man Who Died at Twelve O'Clock*, *In Aunt Mahaly's Cabin*, *White Dresses*, and *Hymn to the Rising Sun*. Moreover, while he has observed that in Green's Negro plays, "realism and drama fused," and that "[his] folk speech and folk incidents ring true," he has added: "[Green's] realism is hopeless and depressing . . . and there is very little sympathy for his trouble-ridden characters."[41]

Even a cursory glance at a few of Green's plays makes clear what so disquiets Edmonds.[42] Abe McCranie, the mulatto of *In Abraham's Bosom*, is unaccountably both defiant and compliant before his white father. His noble ambition to save his people, which Green credits to his white blood, fades as he takes sexual comfort from his woman. In *Your Fiery Furnace*, the same Abe behaves contemptuously toward his black mother, who is portrayed as an aged slut, and he hates his no-

40. Koch, Introduction to Koch (ed.), *American Folk Plays*, xv–xvi.

41. Frederick Koch, Preface to Edmonds, *Six Plays*, 6; Interview with the author, August 21, 1973, in Hatch-Billops Collection; Edmonds, "Black Drama," in *American Theatre*, 388–89.

42. All the following plays are in Paul Green, *Lonesome Road: Six Plays for the Negro Theatre* (New York, 1926). The one-act version of *In Abraham's Bosom* and *Your Fiery Furnace* are both part of Green's 1927 Pulitzer Prize–winning play.

good son Doug. Doug informs on his father and thus precipitates the events leading to Abe's murder of his white brother and his own death at the hands of a mob.

In *White Dresses*, a young mulatto girl is attracted to Hugh, the son of her white employer, but is compelled to marry Jim, the black suitor the employer has provided for her. The marriage is urged because, the denouement reveals, Hugh is her half brother. In this play, the women are permitted some dignity, but the black male, Jim, appears incredibly dim-witted. Surely Edmonds felt more inspired to counter these plays than to model his own work after them.

Edmonds knew his audiences and their typical fare from his research into the Negro theater from emancipation on, and from the tours of his Morgan College Players in the early 1930s. In his article "The Negro Little Theatre Movement," Edmonds records that church groups and community centers often provided theatrical entertainment, primarily to raise funds. Religious plays, amateur minstrel shows, mock trials, womanless weddings, and dramatic readings and other types of recitation were popular and often the occasion for bazaars or fairs. Senior-high-school classes customarily offered a fund-raising graduation play, usually a rustic farce or an old-fashioned melodrama. Occasionally, a school might attempt Shakespeare, and universities generally mounted an annual Shakespeare production, but the most popular play among educational and community groups was Oscar Wilde's sophisticated, escapist *Lady Windermere's Fan.* Edmonds summarizes his evaluation of the Negro theatrical entertainment during the first fifty years of freedom as "akin to the crude phallic situations of pre-classical Greek comedy, the Italian farces before the Greek influence, the early interludes before Shakespeare. . . . Theatrical history shows that beginning audiences everywhere in the theatre like the crude, popular, ridiculous type of situations in their dramatic presentation. The Negro, as has been shown in this first period [1865–1920], was no exception." [43]

The plays Edmonds wrote attempt a compromise between the simplified characterization and unambiguous moral distinctions demanded by melodrama; the invincible, idealized heroes in works like Richardson's history plays; and his own desire for dramatic complexity. His various views of the hero reflect this tension. On the one hand,

43. Edmonds, "The Negro Little Theatre Movement," 83.

he held that the hero was simply "a man who does heroic things." [44] On the other, he hoped ultimately for black characters with the complexity of the classical tragic protagonists. His inclusion of Paul Robeson's 1943 Othello under the category "White Playwrights and Negro Characters: 1900 to the Present," for example, suggests this second view. Thus Edmonds creates characters who reveal weakness (for example, Thea, in Bad Man, is a bully; Nat, in Nat Turner, a fanatic), and deliberately alludes to Shakespearean characters and plays (notably in Old Man Pete and Nat Turner) to link the concerns of his characters to those in literary and other imaginative landscapes to which his black theater aspired.

Of Edmonds' forty-eight plays, nineteen have been published in three anthologies of his work and one in a recent collection of black drama by various playwrights. The first anthology, Shades and Shadows, published in 1930, was intended for reading only. Its subject matter is what Edmonds calls in the preface "imaginative literature" in the style of Maurice Maeterlinck and William Sharp. [45] His two later anthologies, Six Plays for a Negro Theatre and The Land of Cotton and Other Plays, published in 1942, provided material for educational theater and community drama groups for more than twenty years. Earth and Stars, according to Darwin Turner, has been staged more often than any other play by a black American. [46] Almost all of the plays in the last two anthologies were written during the 1930s to provide material for Edmonds' own university theater groups.

The Land of Cotton and Other Plays gathers together plays Edmonds wrote from 1927 (the date of Silas Brown) to 1941, when The Land of Cotton was finally completed and produced. The title play is the most important, for it fulfills all Edmonds' criteria for black theater. Its central theme, the battle against economic and racial oppression, waged with courage and interracial cooperation, is certainly worthwhile. The battle is made vivid through positive characters, men and women

44. Interview with the author, August 21, 1973, in Hatch-Billops Collection.
45. Randolph Edmonds, Shades and Shadows (Boston, 1930), 5. Edmonds did produce the title play in this collection at Florida A & M University in 1948 (Floyd Sandle, "A History of the Development of the Educational Theatre in the Negro Colleges and Universities, 1911–1959" [Ph.D. dissertation, Louisiana State University, 1959], 208).
46. Only the revised version of Earth and Stars has been published, in Darwin Turner (ed.), Black Drama in America: An Anthology (Greenwich, Conn., 1971). See the introduction to the play, 378.

who, although they are defeated in this particular incident, possess courage and dignity. Its central conflict is clear and the moral landscape unambiguous, yet various characters and situations create a complexity that may extend the audience's understanding of its own situation and conflicts. Moreover, although the play is highly theatrical, ending in carnage, its conclusion is neither defeatist or simply melodramatic. In the course of the play, the black community moves from laughing at its cowardice to declaring war on its oppressors. All the other plays in the collection are one act, and also provide insight into Edmonds' dramatic intention, although none have the reach and clarity of *The Land of Cotton*, the longest work. *The High Court of Historia*, written in 1939, and *The Yellow Death*, written in 1935, were composed for Negro History Week. The former, a pageant, promotes the teaching of black history. The latter celebrates the heroic service performed by the Twenty-fourth Infantry, which volunteered to nurse yellow-fever victims during the Spanish-American War.

The Yellow Death illuminates Edmonds' developing concept of the hero. When two privates, unable to withstand the agony of nursing the dying victims, plan to desert, Tom, the hero, persuades them to remain with their regiment by arguing that what they do will influence how the black race is regarded and provide a model for black children. Unlike in Richardson's plays, in *The Yellow Death*, the role of the individual is not subsumed into the collectivity of family or race. Rather, a tension remains between the individual and the group; collective heroism is the result of individual action. The nature of the connection between personal action and communal solidarity, between the heroism of an individual and the strength of the community, becomes a fruitful topic of exploration for later black drama, as well as for Edmonds' own *Land of Cotton* and *Earth and Stars*.

The relation of individual to community, as a dramatic problem, has a special significance for the black playwright still conscious of a white audience, and a white stage reality. As long as the individual symbolizes the race, the tragedy of the individual as defined by Western tradition cannot be written. For in that tradition social identity and individual identity rarely coincide. While *The Yellow Death* directly addresses the problem posed when the individual represents the race, Edmonds' later work addresses the matter less directly and thus provides a richer formulation of the relation between the hero and the community.

Another play in the anthology, *Gangsters over Harlem*, written in 1939, brings the gangster and his moll to Harlem. In his preface to the collection, Edmonds notes this play's popularity among little theater groups. Highly theatrical, and almost a parody, the play's white gangster stereotypes add an exhilarating element of impersonation to a cliche situation. Thus Edmonds deliberately makes productive the black-actor / white-stage configuration; *Gangsters* is a comic assertion of the black actor's rightful presence on the conventional stage.

Finally, among the plays in this anthology is *Silas Brown*, Edmonds' first folk play. Ironically, given Edmonds' sensitivity to the nuances of the genre, it is a grim piece about a tyrannical father who terrorizes and despises his wife and son, although he is generous to outsiders. When a situation reminiscent of the failure of Marcus Garvey's Black Star Lines leaves the family destitute, mother and son flee north. *Silas Brown* alludes to several problems within the black community, notably mistrust of black business and the failure to value intellect and education (in the person of Silas' son, who prefers reading to chores). As Silas' brutality is neither motivated nor made comprehensible, the play's grimness serves no purpose.

The title work of the volume, *The Land of Cotton*, is a full-length play based in part on Edmonds' father's experiences as a sharecropper.[47] Although it is melodramatic and derivative—particularly in its ideological conclusion—of Paul Peters and George Sklar's *Stevedore*, produced in 1934, the play presents an accurate portrait of attempts to unionize black and white sharecroppers in the South. Langston Hughes was also attracted to this subject because the unionizing of the sharecroppers, although brief and limited, involved interracial cooperation unprecedented in the South.[48]

In the first act, Clay Sherman, the union organizer, persuades a racially mixed group of sharecroppers and tenants to join the union. The exposition shows their economic plight, made more precarious

47. Interview with author, August 21, 1973, in Hatch-Billops Collection.

48. Hughes has two plays on this topic, both in MSS. in the Langston Hughes Papers, James Weldon Johnson Collection, Beinecke Library, Yale University, New Haven, hereinafter referred to as Langston Hughes Papers. "Blood on the Fields," written with Ella Winter about 1933 to 1934, is incomplete. It depicts the cotton strike in the San Joaquin Valley in 1933; the union organizers and the pickers themselves were an interracial group. "De Organizer," a blues opera in one act, dated 1939–1941, depicts organizing sharecroppers in the South.

when the landowner, Ben Jackson, announces that economic pressure is forcing him to switch to day labor. It also defines racial and class tensions through Jackson's challenge to Sherman, his use of a white sharecropper as a spy, and his threat to lynch Gurry, a black sharecropper who sides with Sherman.

The act comments not only on the details of oppression but on attitudes to it as well. When two black sharecroppers laugh over an account of one of their fellows fleeing from the Ku Klux Klan, Gurry admonishes them for making a joke of cowardice. They, in turn, suggest reading and union activity have destroyed his sense of humor. The tone of the play supports Gurry, and so disputes an important aspect of black tradition: the use of humor to mask aggression and defiance. The play portrays that tradition as reactionary, or at best irrelevant. The play also depicts as reactionary the older generation's attitudes and traditions. Gurry's mother mistrusts his alliance with whites and fears his union's activity will lead to the kind of trouble that will prevent her from having the big funeral she has planned for herself. The younger women, both black and white, also resist the union, primarily because they fear for their husbands' lives.

While certain attitudes and aspects of the black community are criticized, the play affirms that community as providing the ground for political progress. Acts 2 and 4 take place at Gurry's home, where a black "feast"—"a kind of bazaar where food and refreshments are sold for charitable purposes"—provides both the cover and the base for the county's organizing meeting.[49] The stage set for these acts emphasizes the shape of the house, which takes on added symbolic import in the last act, when the Klan attacks it from all sides, including that of the audience.

The feast in the second act provides opportunity for a display of other aspects of folk culture, as the black sharecroppers party before the arrival of their white companions. Dialect thickens while the characters sing, dance, play "dozens," and encourage each other as they dance. The merriment comes to an abrupt halt when the first white approaches. "Lawd hit's de white folks!" cries a woman ignorant of the real purpose of the festivities. Just as the men agree to strike if their leaders are arrested, the meeting is betrayed. Clay, Clint, Coggins, and Caleb are taken into custody, and in a finale undeniably reminiscent

49. Edmonds, *Land of Cotton*, 41.

of Clifford Odet's *Waiting for Lefty*, the remaining characters shout: "STRIKE! STRIKE! STRIKE!"

While the first two acts concentrate on groups, the third act focuses on individuals. Taking place in the sheriff's office, it portrays the deliberations that lead to the formation of another kind of community, equally a part of southern life, the lynch mob. The focus on individuals is ironic, for the mob, manipulated by the planters, who do not participate, is faceless, while the community of sharecroppers consists of vivid, distinct characters, whose strengths and weaknesses shape its destiny. The act ends as the sheriff forms the lynch party.

The opening of Act 4 parallels that of Act 2. This gathering, however, is for Gurry's mother's funeral and displays another aspect of black folk tradition: black religion. With a directness not typical of that tradition, the preacher joins the secular with the sacred: "I ain't scared to stick wid my people when I know dey's on de right track. And dey's on de right track when dey stick together to make things better on des here farms in de south. We's been thinking so much about de hell over de other side dat we ain't been looking at de hell right here. From now on we's got to pay mo' 'tention to dis hell right here on earth." [50]

From this declaration, he moves into his sermon, chanting in the rhythms and images of the traditional folk preacher. His sermon, taken from Rev. 22:14, envisions the drama of a soul brought home, but its image of God looking troubled at his earth suggests more vividly the new tragedy bearing down on the house even as he preaches.

> I see that awful sadness
> Hanging 'round the throne of mercy
> Like black clouds of smoke
> At hog killing time.
> And now as I look,
> Yes I see in my fancy.
> I see God leaning over whispering something
> to Michael.
> He's telling Old Michael
> That he needs a new saint in heaven.

Mother Lambert is never laid to rest, for the mob interrupts the sermon. In the ensuing battle all the principal characters are killed and the house destroyed by fire. "Oh Lord, ain't it awful to be colored!" weeps Gurry's widow, to which a white widow replies, "Colored and white mean the same thing in this place—if they be sharecroppers." [51]

---

50. *Ibid.*, 117.
51. *Ibid.*, 119, 144.

Although the play focuses on economic rather than racial injustice, its specific reference is to traditional black behavior in the South that accommodates an oppressive social order. Gurry repeatedly points out to Jackson that he is not the compliant Negro his father was, and he must break faith with his mother to pursue his rights. By depicting a time when a measure of interracial cooperation among the powerless occurred, the play suggests the possibility of alliance, but its focus is the black community within the alliance—and that community is portrayed with affection.

Even in 1941, when *The Land of Cotton* was first produced at the Longshoreman's Hall, by the People's Community Theater of New Orleans, black militancy was extremely dangerous. The play gives dramatic form to a sentiment most eloquently expressed in Claude McKay's poem often cited as proclaiming the position of the New Negro, "If We Must Die":

> If we must die, let it not be like hogs
> Hunted and penned in an inglorious spot . . .
> Like men we'll face the murderous, cowardly pack
> Pressed to the wall, dying, but fighting back! [52]

The militancy that ends *The Land of Cotton* is muted in Edmonds' earlier anthology, *Six Plays for a Negro Theatre*, a collection of folk plays acceptable to a black audience. But the collection is insistent in another way. Much more than Richardson's folk plays, Edmonds' counter almost every aspect of similar plays by white authors, particularly those in Paul Green's *Lonesome Road*.

For example, in *The New Window*, Edmonds seriously addresses the role of superstition in black culture, an aspect of the culture frequently used in white depictions of black folk life. In this play, omens prove accurate, but the death they predict is aided by Hester, a quick-thinking young woman who prefers to trust neither fate nor the Lord in important matters. The man fated to die is her father, Bulloch Williams, a murderer and a bootlegger. He cuts a new window into the front of his house to provide a view of anyone approaching, in spite of the superstitious warnings of his ill-treated wife. Death approaches in the form of God-fearing Simon, who comes to avenge the death of a friend. He kills Bulloch in a duel, not because of his prowess, but rather because Hester has blunted the firing pin on Bulloch's weapon.

---

52. Claude McKay, "If We Must Die," ll. 1–2, 13–14.

The new window symbolizes not only superstition but Hester's vision of the world, which implements and makes effective both her mother's superstition and Simon's trust in God. Hester's actions supplant neither superstition nor faith: the play allows the possibility that her actions may simply have been a working out of the omen, and of the divine plan. Thus, although at the immediate level of cause and effect, the universe of *The New Window* operates according to rational principles, the natural and supernatural levels of reality remain complementary; one does not negate the other.

Another play in the anthology, *Old Man Pete*, examines generational conflict, which is exacerbated by migration. In this play, an old couple from Virginia are transplanted to Harlem, their children's new home. Urbane and sophisticated, the children find themselves embarrassed by their parents' plantation dialect, "antique rags of the South," uncouth manners, and love of the Sanctified Church service. The old couple are crushed by a bitter quarrel that reveals the children's impatience. Having sold their farm in Virginia, they are homeless, but too proud to remain. They depart for the South on a bitter winter night and fall asleep on a park bench; in the morning a policeman finds them frozen.

The play attempts to be even-handed. Pete is a proud, irascible old man who advocates whipping his "flapper" daughter-in-law. On this issue, the audience's sympathy remains with him because he is so sentimentalized and she so unpleasant. However, the parents' complaints about their children's selfishness arouse no sympathy, for unlike King Lear's daughters, to whom the play makes graceful allusion, the children have made generous provisions for their parents, of which they are unaware.

The contrast between the generations is balanced in other ways as well. The marital relationship of the children and their spouses differs markedly from the loving, harmonious bond between Pete and Mandy. The values attributed to the Harlem sophisticates are in some ways progressive, but in other ways empty, in their focus on the pursuit of gaiety and excitement. Dramatically, the play belongs to Pete and Mandy. In the final scene, Harlem fades as Pete's closing speech makes vivid the sense of death as a "goin' home": "De sky is dark, Mandy; but down in Fuginia de sun is shining. Le's git in de sun. (A *brief silence, then he feebly continues.*) Wake up, Mandy! Ah heahs de horses neighing and de pigs is squealing. Dey is hongry, Mandy. Le's go feed de pigs."[53] Mutual intolerance causes Pete and Mandy's dispossession and death. Their transplanting may have been an error, but human weakness and not historical inevitability made it fatal.

Edmonds' *Nat Turner*, the play that won him a fellowship to Yale, draws on the best-known of the American slave revolts for its portrait of black heroism, a topic never treated by white writers of Negro folk plays. Scene 1 of the play mirrors faithfully the historical confession of Nat Turner, while Scene 2 selects detail in a manner revealing the playwright's concerns. Edmonds portrays Nat much as the historical Nat portrayed himself to Thomas Gray, his court examiner. Guided by visions and voices, obsessed with a desire to free his people, the charismatic, self-educated Nat Turner planned and organized an armed revolt that resulted in the death of almost sixty whites before his army of slaves was routed. Turner himself eluded capture for another eight weeks.

Scene 1 depicts a barbecue Turner arranged for his men before the revolt. With three exceptions, all the characters are taken from Nat Turner's actual account. Scene 2 depicts Nat after the revolt is defeated.

The historical confession reveals as unflinching Turner's belief in the rightness of his mission. Commenting on his approaching execution, he asks, "Was not Christ crucified?" Edmonds' Nat, like Jesus on the cross, wonders if God has forsaken him. In contrast with Scene 1, in which Nat enters to a community of his followers, in Scene 2 he enters to an empty stage, calling for his companions. He has arranged to meet Hark, his trusted right-hand man, but instead dying Jesse drags himself in to announce that Nat alone remains of the whole band. Lucinda follows Jesse, her boyfriend, and when he dies, she turns on Nat, castigating him for his "fine notions 'bout slaves should be free." Like other women in Edmonds' plays who advise caution because they do not wish to lose their loved ones, Lucinda prefers safety to freedom, and, distraught, she runs off threatening to reveal Nat's whereabouts. The final speech is from the Nat of Edmonds' creation: "Look at dat moon comin' back tuh light up de worl'. Hit is big and round and yellow. Hit done dripped out all hits blood. Ma hands is full o' blood, too. Will dey ever be clean? Was Ah wrong, Lawd, tuh fight dat black man mout be free? . . . Whut is Ah gwin tuh

53. Randolph Edmonds, *Old Man Pete*, in *Six Plays*, 49.

do now? . . . (*Shouting wildly as he goes out*) Sperit ob Gawd! Show me de way! Guide me! Lead me!"[54] This Nat is far from the dignified figure whose magnificent, terrifying presence so intimidated Gray.

Fanaticism is Nat's fatal weakness, according to Darwin Turner, but this "tragic flaw" is not the play's focus.[55] The historical Nat, about whom almost nothing beyond his confession is known, possessed the religious zeal of an avenging angel, and the impact of his bloody rampage shook the very foundations of slavery in America. He pleaded not guilty because, he said, he did not feel so, and if, as Edmonds' Nat states, the purpose of the revolt was to attract the world's attention to slavery and the determination of black people to be free, he succeeded.

Edmonds uses Nat Turner to raise specific questions about the role and meaning of religion in black life. The religious images in which the historical Nat expressed his confession remind one that the war over slavery included a war over biblical interpretation. Those images also evoke the militant religious tradition drawn principally from the Old Testament through which black slaves and succeeding generations expressed their yearning for liberation and understood the meaning of their condition. Moreover, through dramatic irony, Nat's final speech questions the very existence of the God in whose name he wreaked his vengeance. Yet, from a historical perspective, the despair in Nat's final speech is mitigated by ambiguity. Is his mission a working out of the divine plan for the end of slavery, or does it reveal a God who has turned his back on his prophet? Is it a monument to a religious tradition that has adequately expressed the black condition and shaped one of its most powerful revolts or to a tradition that mystifies its real nature? In *Nat Turner*, these questions remain unresolved.

The confusion of religious imagery throughout the play compounds this ambiguity, for Edmonds' Nat is simultaneously Old Testament prophet and Christ the Redeemer. The bloody vengeance Nat sought recalls the Old Testament and the wrath of the Lord Jehovah rather than the New Testament and the mercy of Christ. But comments by his followers and the final scene clearly depict him as a Christ figure. The same confusion exists in the historical confession, for at least according to Gray, Turner presented his mission through the language and images of both testaments.

54. Randolph Edmonds, *Nat Turner*, in *Six Plays*, 77, 82.
55. Turner, "The Negro Dramatist's Image of the Universe," 108.

In its exploration of the meaning of Nat Turner's rebellion in black history and more generally in its questioning of how the black condition manifests the divine plan, *Nat Turner* departs radically from the conventional treatment of black religion in the folk play. Moreover, this play and another in the anthology, *Bleeding Hearts*, specifically dispute the Negro folk play's usual treatment of religion in the black tradition—for example, the frivolous treatment of religion in Green's *The Prayer Meeting* and the depiction of religious hysteria in *Your Fiery Furnace*. And certainly both plays challenge the treatment of black religion in the play running concurrently on Broadway and elsewhere, *The Green Pastures*. Neither of Edmonds' plays attacks black religion; both sensitively explore how, rather than offering consolation for black suffering (as is usually depicted in folk plays), it instead raises painful questions and doubts to a devoted believer in the divine plan.

In its setting and some of its details, *Bleeding Hearts* bears closest resemblance to the plays in Paul Green's anthology *Lonesome Road*. *Bleeding Hearts* depicts a sharecropping family burdened by trouble. As the play opens, Miranda lies deathly ill, nursed by her daughter Carrie. Sister Jenny, a neighbor, has come to look in on her and diagnoses her pneumonia, which her white doctor had carelessly failed to identify. Miranda has asked for her husband, Joggison, and Carrie has sent her brother Buster to fetch him from the fields. But Buster returns instead with Marse Tom, the landowner, who has forbidden Joggison to leave his work and who speaks harshly to the sick woman.

A preacher arrives with a group of women to hold a church service for Miranda; this service constitutes most of the play and ends with Miranda's final ecstatic vision of life and her death. It provides comfort for the dying woman and accords her passing the meaning traditional in black religion—liberation: "Thank Gawd. Ah'se got a free soul, an' Ah'se gwine home tuh my Father! . . . (*Silence. Voices low and sweet, as if far off.*) Free at las' / Free at las' / I thank God I'm free at las'." However, Joggison's grief when he returns home to find "she passed away an' A wa'n't even heah tuh hold huh han'!" abruptly disrupts the harmony left by the service and the dignity of Miranda's death. The preacher offers his traditional consolation, "De Lord giveth an' de Lord taketh away," but Joggison curses the Lord, saying: "Now, what has Gawd done fah me. . . . Ma soul is . . . lost in hell—hell right heah on dis earth." Overwhelmed by rage, he declares his intention to go out and kill: "Ah'se gwin make others suffer lak Ah'se sufferin.'" When the preacher warns him that his family will suffer most from that course of action, Joggison responds: "Yuh is right, ag'in. Every-thin' Ah do is wrong. Everythin' is twisted into a knot, and Ah can't git hit untied. . . . Ah'll leave dis whole country, and go to whar Ah can be free. Ah'll leave de cotton in de fields. . . . Maybe den Ah won't turn ma back on de Lawd. Maybe den Ah'll be free." [56]

Joggison's tempestuous despair shatters whatever peace the church service created not only for the dying woman and her children but also for the audience. Even though he moves from blaspheming God to begging his forgiveness, and from murderous rage to his final vio-lent impulse to escape, too abruptly for adequate dramatic develop-ment, the final moments of the play are dramatic and powerful.

In *Bleeding Hearts*, religion and community dignify suffering. The hu-man caring revealed by the participants in the church service is as crucial as the religious service itself. Joggison, for reasons beyond his control, has been excluded from that experience, and through his turning from God finds himself turning from the family and commu-nity that can offer him sustenance. At the end of the play, the others are stunned by his vehement denial of the traditional source of sol-ace. But the audience sees the larger, more complex connections be-tween his faith, his community, and his powerlessness.

Bleeding Hearts suggests that Joggison's final position is that of his generation as well. When he briefly accedes to Carrie's appeal, the preacher praises him: "Den yuh done right, Joggison. Yuh done lak a real man." [57] But the preacher's idea of manhood, acceptance of suffer-ing in the name of the Lord, is not Joggison's final stance. His acces-sion is followed by murderous and ultimately self-destructive rage and then by his resolution to leave everything behind and face an un-known in which, as a free man, he may even turn back to God. Finally, *Bleeding Hearts* affirms the centrality of the religious experience to be-liever and nonbeliever alike while it poses radical questions about that religion's traditional orientation.

The play is significant in other respects as well. In none of Green's plays is there a black man of the simple stature and dignity accorded Joggison in his despair. *Bleeding Hearts* ends with his apparent resolve to abandon his family, but the context of the resolve makes clear that it emerges from the impossibility of caring for that family within an oppressive society. Moreover, the powerful presence of community in the play alleviates anxiety about the fate of his children should

56. Randolph Edmonds, *Bleeding Hearts*, in *Six Plays*, 121–22, 124, 125, 127.
57. *Ibid.*, 126.

Joggison leave them. The play neither applauds nor condemns his decision, which, in the context, is allowed the stature of a legitimate response to a real situation. In this, as well as in its portrait of the close-knit black family and community, the play departs from familiar stereotypes—for example, that of the profligate husband of Paul Green's *The Hot Iron*, who has abandoned his family from sheer irresponsibility. The portrait of the black family and community counters other of Green's portraits as well; in all of his plays the family is divided by strife, and the community, when depicted, is portrayed as backward and destructive of anyone who attempts to change or escape its petty concerns. Thus, in many ways, *Bleeding Hearts* corrects the conventional folk play and the plays in *Lonesome Road* in particular.

The two remaining plays in the volume, *Breeders* and *Bad Man*, also counter stereotypical characters and situations. In *Breeders*, a young girl poisons herself rather than accept the man chosen for her by her owner. Artistically, *Breeders* is the weakest play in the anthology, but it directly addresses the stereotypical portrait of the black woman as sexually loose in such plays as Green's *The End of the Row*, *White Dresses*, and *The Prayer Meeting*. Moreover, the play comments on the way slavery, callous of familial ties and even of life itself, debased black sexuality and made love a continual source of anguish. For example, Salem, the man chosen for the central character, Ruth, displays the boastful, cavalier attitude toward women typical of the black womanizer (he boasts that he manages to keep ten wives happy), and any humor is undercut by his blatant acceptance of his role as stud. Thus *Breeders* criticizes not only attitudes toward black women displayed in Negro folk plays but also the more general attitudes toward black sexuality.

As the play opens, Mammy is mourning the loss of her last son, killed escaping to freedom. Her daughter, Ruth, is apparently hardened to the vicissitudes of slavery, but, Mammy warns her, she is insensible because she has never had lovers or children to suffer for. Ruth does allow herself to be courted by David, although she resists giving in to her affection for him, thus betraying her fear of carrying the same sorrow as her mother. When David dies protecting her from Salem, she commits suicide rather than capitulate to the role ordained for her. In perhaps a deliberate echo of Maurya in Synge's *Riders to the Sea*, the play closes on Mammy holding her dead daughter and asking God when he will end black suffering.

As in *White Dresses*, the legacy shared by generations of black women is sorrow over love. However, in White Dresses, the heroine loves her employer's son, who, unknown to her until the final moment of the play, is her half-brother; and she despises the man whom her employer has encouraged to court her, not only because she already has a lover but because he is black. Indeed, the plot of Breeders severely rebukes the depiction of black women's sorrows in the Green play. In the final lines of White Dresses, Granny advises Mary, "I knows yo' feelings, chile, but you's gut to smother 'em in, you's gut to smother 'em in." What Mary must smother in is not only love but racial self-hatred. In Breeders, Edmonds describes Mammy thus: "Throughout the play, she gives the impression of grieving deeply, inwardly. Sometimes this inward grief flares out with more force than at other times; but it is always there eating away like a cancer." [58] That image is made vivid through Ruth's dying agony, her insides literally consumed by the poison she has taken. Moreover, in Green's play, the daughter repeats her mother's behavior. In Breeders, as in Bleeding Hearts, the younger generation rejects the passive suffering accepted by the older generation, although the price of choosing differently is equally high.

Bad Man explores aspects of black masculinity other than those in Breeders. In its chief character, Thea Dugger, to whom the title refers, figures from two folk traditions combine: the tough guy of Bret Harte stories and other western lore, who is prompted to noble acts by the touch of a good woman, and the black hero Stagger Lee. "He won't run from nobody. He ain't scared o' de debbil," Ted, another character in Bad Man, says of him admiringly. And he is wicked: "Dey say once when he was workin' in a steel mill in Birmingham, he went into a pool parlour where dey was gamblin'. One man started tuh pull a gun on him. He picked up a cue ball and hit him in de temple and killed him daid as a goat. Den he picked up de man's Smith and Weston and shot up de place. Everybody ran out in de street. Thea ran arter dem but didn't see nothin' but a mule. So he poured de lead into de mule." [59]

Bad Man is set in a sawmill camp, an environment familiar to the author from jobs held while working his way through school. A card game among the hands nearly leads to violence when Jack accuses Thea of cheating, but Ted's visiting sister, Maybelle, pacifies him. No sooner is peace restored, however, when the white foreman arrives to

58. Paul Green, White Dresses, in Lonesome Road, 68; Randolph Edmonds, Breeders, in Six Plays, 86.

59. Randolph Edmonds, Bad Man, in Six Plays, 16–17.

warn of an approaching lynch mob seeking the culprit of a local murder. Escape is impossible, and the foreman, wanting to protect his property and only secondarily his hands, bargains with the mob, offering the culprit for the lives of the others. Although innocent of this particular killing, Thea, six times a murderer and feared by every policeman in town, offers himself as victim. He gives as his reasons that, unlike the others, he has no family obligations and that as a wanderer, he was never meant to amount to much. The play ends as his companions helplessly watch his gruesome death: "We ain't nothin' but sawmill hands. All we is s'posed tuh do is to cut logs, saw lumber, live in dingy shanties, cut, fight, and kill each other. We ain't s'posed tuh pay no 'tention tuh a burnin' man . . . but ef de people wid larnin' can't do nothin' 'bout hit, 'taint nothin' we can do." [60]

Much is ironic about Thea's death. A gambling man, Thea refuses the luck of the draw offered by the others and insists on making the sacrifice. A bad man, he goes like a lamb to the slaughter. Ted, who gives the final speech, is Thea's special pet, and the link between them suggests the sacrifices of the older generation for the progress of the race. Since Ted is portrayed as aspiring after education and Thea as inarticulate and brawny, the link is also that of two aspects of black society; the sacrifice of one permits the other to move out of the sawmill and into the modern world, into the audience addressed by his final speech. More generally, Thea's sacrifice represents a deliberate abandoning of chance for choice, a movement from being victim of caprice—human or cosmic—to assuming some control over his destiny.

Other ironies concern the kinds of violence the play depicts. The cowardly behavior of Percy, one of the hands, suggests that he is the real murderer of the old white man who lived alone in the woods, and the manner of the murder, splitting the old man's head in two with an axe, is nasty in a way alien to Thea's violence. The parallels between the two crises in the play also reveal differences in the kind of violence in *Bad Man*. The first crisis occurs when Thea threatens to kill Jack and is prevented by Maybelle's pleading. The second occurs when the mob approaches and demands its victim. Thea's violence, revealed in his actions and words and also related by others, has none of the impersonal, brutal bloodlust that threatens from offstage. That the mob

60. *Ibid.*, 35.

does not appear onstage and that the play ends as Ted describes Thea's gruesome death leave the larger violence of the mob and of the society that produces such mobs still threatening the audience. The effect is that the black violence, which is the play's central subject, is not seen as simply destructive; the violence of the larger society forces the negative violence of black society to transform itself into positive energy.

The play also directly protests the social violence of lynching. Beginning in 1930, after about five years of relative quiet, lynch mobs again were ravaging the South. Thea's fate in *Bad Man*, although chosen by him, depicts the possible fate of all "bad men," for ultimately, the tough, defiant bad men of black folklore direct their challenge to white society, and that challenge is not countenanced.

The play also corrects earlier stage presentations of lynching. At the end of Green's Pulitzer Prize–winning *In Abraham's Bosom*, Abraham McCranie, the play's protagonist, falls victim to a lynch mob. That mob acts as judge of his fratricide and finally as his executioner. Although the play does not condone its bloody deeds, nor does it decry them. The mob functions as Abraham's approaching fate, its fury matched by the hysteria with which he begs for God's protection and then lapses into madness. The conclusion seems emotionally and aesthetically appropriate, and thus the nature of Abraham's execution is somehow mitigated. Therefore the final focus of *Bad Man*, the horror of lynching itself, must also be understood as responding to previous uses of lynching in drama wherein the lynching symbolized fate or appropriate retribution for human frailty. Thea's innocence is, of course, pointed. That he chooses his death to ransom others comments on the kind of inevitability that pervades white writers' depiction of the subject, as well as the usual passivity of the victim.

Edmonds' *Earth and Stars*, written in 1946 and revised in 1961, recapitulates much of the civil rights struggle in the postwar South. The earlier version focuses on the role of the church within southern black leadership after the war, while the later version is oddly prophetic of events during Rev. Martin Luther King, Jr.'s last years.

The entire play is set in the living room of the parsonage of a small southern city. The play's hero is Joshua Judson, a modern pastor, who has attempted to extend the jurisdiction of his ministry. He has formed an alliance with Reuben Mackey, the union leader, who is also involved in organizing a civil rights group similar to the Southern

Christian Leadership Conference (SCLC). Joshua plans to build a church hall with facilities for recreation, a nursery and child-care center, and a cooperative store. He clearly supports both a black union's strike in which his son Vernon takes part and the civil rights activities, and believes the church ought to be at the forefront of all civil rights battles. In addition, Vernon has organized a group of militant young people and invited freedom riders to stop in the city. The pastor's activities and stance bring him into serious conflict with his older, more conservative parishioners and ultimately with the white community. While both Anna and Wallis plead caution, Joshua remains committed to action.

Through Joshua, *Earth and Stars* advocates that the church must assume responsibility, along with labor and the press, for leading the struggle for civil rights. Various characters represent the forces of reaction. Jacob Washington, a deacon who owes his position as head of adult education for Negroes to white patronage, attempts to dissuade Joshua from his activism. He and Cora Wilkins, head of the Ladies Aid Society, prefer to build a new church, to refrain from secular concerns, and to let others, if they will, use the courts to pursue civil liberties— the path of the NAACP. Herbert Martin, a white moderate, appears late one night to beg Joshua to wait until the time is "ripe"; through this encounter, the play takes the southern moderates to task for their cowardice and procrastination. Rev. Junius Johnson, a bishop's representative summoned to investigate Joshua's unorthodox activities, demands that Joshua attend to the spiritual needs of his congregation and not attempt to lead its members into political action for which they are unprepared. And at one point, "Reb" Smith and "Woody" Hall, two stereotypical crackers, burst into the Judson home and use physical brutality to force Joshua and Reuben into submission.

A combination of various events—the strike, the civil rights organizing and the expected arrival of the freedom riders—produces a high state of tension in the town. As feared, unrestrained brutality meets the freedom riders, and in the ensuing demonstration, Vernon is murdered. While Anna and Wallis see Vernon's death as fulfilling their warnings about the dangers of activism, Joshua perceives the loss of his son as an indication that even more extreme action is required. He vows to go about the city preaching Christian brotherhood until the white community repents of its injustice to blacks. His subsequent martyrdom galvanizes his congregation into action. The play closes on the grief of the women, left widowed and orphaned through the courage of their men.

As in *The Land of Cotton* and *Nat Turner*, the women in *Earth and Stars* fear the militancy chosen by their men, and their foreboding is prophetic. At one point in the play, Curtis, Wallis' fiancé, promises Vernon to meet him later with the "usual southern ending—'if nothing happens'" and then teases Vernon for taking his remark so seriously. But of course something does happen, and, in this regard, the play mirrors events outside the theater. Artistically, *Earth and Stars* is a weak play, but its vision is clear. Anna, in her closing lament, unwittingly recapitulates the era that ended April 4, 1968:

> Wallis.   (*Soothing her*) Don't, Mother, don't! He just said a while ago never
>   to question the goodness and mercy of God.
> Anna.   I know and I'll try. I'll try and try again! But I haven't the spiritual
>   strength to sustain me.[61]

For Edmonds, when Paul Robeson performed *Othello*, a mutually legitimating process occurred: Robeson's genius brought black actors and actresses into their maturity and also made of Shakespeare's Moor a real black character. His *Gangsters over Harlem* is the other main work suggestive of his intentions. It shows that black actors and actresses ought to play any role that the stage encompasses—not because the audience is color-blind but because actors and actresses may don any mask they choose.

The approach Edmonds' work typified is one that is aware of the cultural tradition considered mainstream and seeks to enter it, to mold the black experience to what is perceived as universal. But as long as writers are overwhelmingly conscious of responding to a tradition to which they aspire, the idiom of that tradition will shape their idiom, and the forms of that tradition will dictate their forms.

The work of both Richardson and Edmonds typifies the first stage by which black dramatists laid claim to the theater. During this phase, the mere fact that realistic black characters inhabited the stage was a triumph, but the stereotypes they replaced cast long shadows, and thus these black characters were not always sure how to behave lest they be mistaken by the audience for their degrading antecedents. While the work of Richardson and Edmonds is interesting and valuable, their characters inhabit stages on which they are not really com-

61. Edmonds, *Earth and Stars*, in *Black Drama in America*, 416, 462–63.

fortable. They seem constantly to glance into the wings at the tradition preceding them or at the one they seek to enter.

Nevertheless, Richardson and Edmonds provided a base for subsequent black theater in several ways. They introduced to the stage a
variety of black characters from all walks of life: educated members of
the black middle class, hard-working and respectable poor black
families, black soldiers, rebellious slaves, and various historical figures, none of whom had ever been depicted before. Their plays dem-
onstrated clearly that black life in its infinite variety could be the subject of serious drama and that not only the pitfalls of stereotype but
also those of race literature could be avoided. Richardson, particularly, succeeded in portraying credible human failing in his characters
without resorting to controversial low-life depictions. In opposition
to race literature's idealizing tendency, Edmonds created plausible heroes and drama modeled on the Aristotelian formula, assuming long
before Arthur Miller that the common man and woman possessed
tragic stature.

Richardson and Edmonds did not, however, succeed in transforming the stage reality. Their plays are so intent on refuting a particular
tradition that the ultimate ground for what occurs on stage is the tradition being refuted. This allusion by negation indicates the double
consciousness of which Du Bois speaks in *The Souls of Black Folk*.
Double consciousness pervades the work of these playwrights; the
fact that neither develops significantly in spite of tremendous output
attests to its stultifying effect. Neither playwright can fully realize his
characters because he refuses to allow them real freedom of action
and expression. While this restraint in part reflects failure of imagination, more importantly, it expresses the radical insecurity of the black
figure on the American stage and suggests that a black stage reality
can occur only after the stage itself has been conquered.

TWO ❧
"IT'LL BE ME"
Langston Hughes

A striking aspect of the work of Willis Richardson and Randolph Edmonds is its almost unrelieved gravity, a response to the ubiquitous comic stage Negro and to the oppressive presence of the white world that ultimately determined the work's landscape, and a sign of the authors' intention that black drama be taken seriously. Aware in particular that both black and white audiences often responded to black folk culture with scorn or condescension, Richardson and Edmonds did not perceive that culture as capable of expressing serious concerns on stage.

Langston Hughes felt no such reluctance concerning either comedy or folk culture. Rather, he insisted that both the concerns of his works and the forms he used to express them be those of the ordinary black people he hoped would constitute his audience. Since black culture abounds in comic energy, Hughes wrote comedies; since black religion provides the language and experience through which black Americans historically have expressed their deepest longings, both social and spiritual, he wrote religious drama; since black folk culture is an oral tradition, he molded the forms of that tradition into theatrical scripts. Hughes wrote some conventional social drama as well; his first such play, *Mulatto*, first produced in 1935, held the record for the longest Broadway run of a play by a black American until it was broken in 1959 by Lorraine Hansberry's *Raisin in the Sun*.

Hughes's involvement with commercial theater began with *Mulatto* and lasted over thirty years. Although his response to that theater was mixed, his presence there was deliberate, as his poem "Note on Commercial Theatre" suggests.

> You've taken my blues and gone—
> You sing 'em on Broadway
> And you sing 'em in Hollywood Bowl,
> You mixed 'em up with symphonies
> And you fixed 'em
> So they don't sound like me.
> Yep, you done taken my blues and gone.
> You also took my spirituals and gone.
> You put me in *Macbeth* and *Carmen Jones*
> And in all kinds of *Swing Mikados*

And in everything but what's about me—
But someday somebody'll
Stand up and talk about me,
And write about me—
Black and beautiful—
And sing about me,
And put on plays about me!
I reckon it'll be
Me myself!
Yes, it'll be me.[1]

Like Richardson and Edmonds, Hughes wrote plays in response to white exploitation of black material. However, he was less concerned with countering stereotypes than with creating theater that embodied characteristic black forms of expression, for while he protested white exploitation, he understood the modern artists' attraction to the rich possibilities of black culture. His central impulse in the theater was always affirmation rather than reaction—a desire to give voice to the ordinary black folk, particularly those in Harlem. In "Note on Commercial Theatre," the voice of the people becomes the voice of the poet, and in this metamorphosis lies the crux of Hughes's art.

For over forty years a Harlem resident, Hughes observed his neighbors lovingly, knew their experiences intimately, and embodied those experiences and the ways his neighbors expressed them in all his writing. Although Hughes's characters dance, love, and sin much like characters in novels and plays by white writers exploiting black material, his characters also cry, hate, starve, and die. From both sets of experiences, Hughes weaves an integrated work that proclaims, at times protests, and at other times celebrates black American realities. When whites intrude into his work, they are perceived by his black characters as frequently vicious, often stupid and ridiculous, and always peripheral to the black experience except as oppressors. Hughes is the first black American writer to create an entire imaginative landscape that is strictly the domain of black people. In his drama, as in the rest of his work, there is no mistaking whose territory the audience is observing. In his best works, his fidelity to black life stems less from realistic detail than from the voices and context of the action. These move the audience to assent absolutely to the reality of what they perceive.[2]

1. Langston Hughes, *Selected Poems of Langston Hughes* (New York, 1970), 190.
2. The vividness of Hughes's recreation of black expression (by which I mean both voice and its context) is suggestive of the idea of "saturation" that

Hughes's compelling, authentic voices create a particular dramatic effect: they draw the audience to the speaker. Hughes is thus recreating the traditional relationship between black storytellers and their listeners, and between black preachers and their congregations. The storyteller's art rests less in the story itself than in the way it is told. The audience will listen to different versions of the same story to know the teller through the tale; likewise, a congregation will listen to different versions of the same sermon, not to discern the differences in content, but to know the preacher through the sermon.

Similarly, the Hughes reader or audience is always confronted by an embodied voice, by a person speaking. Black readers and audiences, particularly if urban, recognize the voice as familiar. White readers and audiences are forced to confront the black characters, not as projection of their needs or fantasies and not as social inferiors on the periphery of their experience, but rather as social equals who speak from their own vital social and cultural milieu. The power and assurance with which Hughes conveyed both voice and the landscape his characters inhabit created an important precedent for black American artists and clearly distinguished his work from that of his predecessors.

A writer nearly his whole life, Hughes composed in every conceivable genre: poetry, fiction, journalism, history, and drama. Born in Joplin, Missouri, in 1902, Hughes grew up in nine American cities, most in the North, and as a young man traveled extensively.[3] Tramp steamers brought him to Europe, Africa, and the West Indies. An invitation to join an ill-fated movie venture in Moscow resulted in fifteen months' travel in the Soviet Union during 1932 and 1933, and in 1937, he reported on the Spanish civil war for the Baltimore *Afro-American*.

Stephen Henderson develops in his critical anthology *Understanding the New Black Poetry* (New York, 1973), 10, 62–69. In his essay "expressive language," published in *Home* (New York, 1966), 171, LeRoi Jones describes a similar idea.

3. The main sources of this biographical information about Langston Hughes are his two autobiographical works, *The Big Sea* (New York, 1940) and *I Wonder as I Wander* (New York, 1956). Also see James Emanuel, *Langston Hughes* (New York, 1967); Donald C. Dickinson, *A Bio-Bibliography of Langston Hughes* (2nd ed.; Hamden, Conn., 1972); Milton Meltzer, *Langston Hughes: A Biography* (New York, 1968); Arthur P. Davis, *From the Dark Tower: Afro-American Writers, 1900–1960* (Washington, D.C., 1974), 61–73; Faith Berry, *Langston Hughes: Before and Beyond Harlem* (Westport, Conn., 1983).

His writing and dramatic activities led him all over the United States as well.

When Hughes arrived in Harlem in 1921 to attend Columbia University, he discovered home and the environment most congenial to his artistic talents and purposes. A central figure among the young talent that sparked the Harlem Renaissance, Hughes remained involved in the artistic life of that "Black Metropolis" until his death in 1967. Honored during his lifetime for his contributions to black American life and culture and as an important figure in American letters, Hughes encouraged countless young black writers who turned to him for guidance. Hughes's reputation as a writer both at home and abroad (his work has been translated into several dozen languages) rests primarily on his poetry, short stories, and four volumes of Jesse B. Semple columns; in spite of his importance for black theater, his dramatic work is not well known. Yet Hughes considered his plays his favorite and most important creations. In a 1939 radio interview in Beverly Hills, California, Hughes explained this preference by saying that he enjoyed seeing his characters embodied on stage, thought plays reached a wider audience than books, and believed that the American stage needed an accurate representation of the Negro's problems and achievements.[4] He hoped his own work would help fill that gap.

Hughes's plays may be divided into two general categories: those that rely on conventional stage realism and those that experiment with dramatic presentation. The first group includes comedies and social dramas in which character, setting, and situation are developed to tell a story. The second group, more significant in solving the problem of stage reality, includes all of the plays in which the dramatic form is dictated by a voice telling the story, usually that of a black Everyman figure or, in the gospel plays, a preacher.

Even Hughes's early, conventional plays are most eloquent when a character's soliloquy provides the emotional focus for the action. However, he gradually abandoned such conventional dramatic forms in his search for more appropriate ways to convey the black experience on stage. That Hughes began his artistic career as a poet in part accounts for his predilection for a single voice as dramatic focus. Moreover, his poetry readings influenced his dramatic experimenta-

4. This interview, for station KMPC in Beverly Hills, was given February 15, 1939 (Transcript, Langston Hughes Papers).

tion; for example, one of his most important plays, *Don't You Want to Be Free?*, which incorporates many of his already published poems and blues lyrics, personifies his poetic figures in a fashion he first employed in poetry readings. His experiments gradually extended beyond poetry readings and plays using his verse as he increasingly adapted the forms of black folk tradition to his plays—and his plays to them. Sermons, stories, spirituals, gospel songs, blues, and jazz finally provided both shape and subject for his dramatic work.

Hughes's formal experiments shed light on his purpose as a writer. In 1938, when Hughes formed his first company, the Harlem Suitcase Theater, he devoted his dramatic efforts to the bare stage of agitprop and to storytelling devices. The imaginative appeal of these forms for Hughes is clear. The black storyteller, preacher, and musician all perform theatrical acts, acts analogous to creating an imaginative world on a bare stage.

Not only Hughes's dramatic experimentation but also his attention to voice and his use of folk forms in all his writing reveal his sensitivity to the place of form in understanding and communicating a culture. Form both determines and reveals how a subject is apprehended. Marshall McLuhan's fundamental insight that "the medium is the message" pinpoints the relation. By using indigenous cultural forms, Hughes is insisting that his audience be informed by the black experiences depicted on stage, that it experience and understand the medium as well as what is said. For a white audience, the immediate effect is that of a powerful encounter with black America. For the black audience, the impact is more complex. The play, the poem, or the short story sharpens the black audience's awareness of the traditional form, making it vivid, and allowing it to be seen and understood anew. Thus, although imbedded in formal art forms, the traditional forms retain their original vitality and significance.

Hughes's development as a playwright, then, provides insight into his entire artistic career and clarifies the meaning of a term often applied to him—*folk artist*. In this, Hughes differs from Richardson and Edmonds, who wrote folk plays for the sake of realism rather than because, as dramatists, they particularly delighted in indigenous folk culture. Hughes's dramatic career reveals an original, fruitful resolution of the problems of molding the stage to the needs and visions of a black audience. Although many are now hardly known, soon after they were written Hughes's plays, like those of Richardson and Edmonds, were often produced by little theaters and amateur groups in the black community. Thus they had influence and established precedents. As well, several of his plays were produced in New York, and these especially influenced the relation of black theater to the wider context of the American stage.

Hughes's first published piece was a short children's play.[5] From 1928 on, he seemed always to have at least one dramatic iron in the fire. Discussions of his career as a playwright, however, generally begin with *Mulatto*, probably his best-known play and his first to be professionally produced. A resounding success, *Mulatto* opened on Broadway October 24, 1935, ran there for a year, and then toured for two seasons. The play has been translated into many languages and produced all over the world. There is even an operatic version, "The Barrier," which Hughes wrote with Jan Meyerowitz in 1948 and which has been produced at least seven times in the United States and abroad.[6]

　　Mulatto was an auspicious beginning to Hughes's career as a dramatist, but it was typical neither of his later plays nor of those representing the history of black theater. Broadway rarely offered plays by black playwrights: Doris Abramson records only nineteen as receiving professional productions in New York, on and off Broadway, between 1925 and 1959.[7] Until late in his career, Hughes usually had his work produced by small community theaters, notably Karamu House in Cleveland, or by companies he founded himself, the Harlem Suitcase Theater in New York, the New Negro Theater in Los Angeles, and the Skyloft Players in Chicago, which he founded in 1938, 1939, and 1941,

5. Langston Hughes, *The Gold Piece: A Play That Might Be True*, in *Brownies' Book*, II (July, 1921).

6. Langston Hughes, "The Barrier" (Typescript, Langston Hughes Papers). The "Barrier" file records productions in New York, 1950, 1953, and 1960; a broadcast of the Italian production in 1960; and another production at New York University in 1961. The file also records productions of the opera in Holland, 1954, and Italy, 1958. The original Broadway production played in Ann Arbor, Mich., before going to New York.

7. Abramson, *Negro Playwrights in the American Theatre*. Hughes has had work produced on and off Broadway more frequently than any other black American dramatist before Ed Bullins. See *I Wonder as I Wander*, 310–14, for Hughes's account of the Broadway version of *Mulatto*. A fuller account exists in Arnold Rampersad, *The Life of Langston Hughes, Volume 1, 1902–1941: I, Too, Sing America* (New York, 1986), esp. 311–18. There seems to be no trace of the script of *Mulatto* as produced.

respectively.[8] Moreover, *Mulatto*'s setting differs from Hughes's usual dramatic landscapes, for it is not black territory but rather a southern plantation house presided over by its white owner, Colonel Norwood, who lives in uneasy relation to his black housekeeper, Cora, and their four children. The setting is appropriate in a prophetic sense, for the central conflict in *Mulatto* is over the black characters' rights to that setting, expressed as Bert's claim to his father's house. Not only rightful place is at issue, but perspective as well. During the course of the play, Cora's view of the conflict gradually dominates, until finally the story is told, and its events explained, through her voice alone. Thus the house becomes hers, not only because as housekeeper, she has the keys, but because the audience comes to understand what has occurred through her experience of it. Her conquest of the stage, a pyrrhic victory at best, foreshadows elements in Hughes's later work and the conscious tactic of later playwrights, particularly Amiri Baraka.

A conventional play in many respects, *Mulatto* also is a work of some power and complexity, revealing a subtlety infrequently attributed to Hughes.[9] It is the story of a young man who kills his father and then, rather than die at the hands of a lynch mob, kills himself in his father's house. Although melodramatic, it is not more so than the history it conveys: Hughes sees miscegenation as epitomizing American race relations, particularly in the South. Moreover, his treatment of the "tragic mulatto" counters the conventional, popular characterization—specifically, Paul Green's racist treatment of the mulatto protagonist in his Pulitzer Prize–winning play, *In Abraham's Bosom*.[10]

8. Karamu House is the theater at a settlement house in Cleveland founded by Russell and Rowena Jelliffee in 1915 and later guided by them into prominence as an art center for young black people. Hughes himself attended the settlement house activities as a boy. Information concerning Hughes's connection with Karamu House is based primarily on Terence Tobin, "Karamu Theatre, 1915–1964: Its Distinguished Past and Present Achievements," *Drama Critique*, VIII (Spring, 1964), 87–91, and Reuben Silver, "A History of the Karamu Theatre of Karamu House, 1915–1960" (Ph.D. dissertation, Ohio State University, 1961).

9. Hughes treated the mulatto theme in several of his poems and short stories as well; it was a theme of great personal significance to him. See Arthur P. Davis, "The Tragic Mulatto Theme in Six Works of Langston Hughes," in Donald Gibson (ed.), *Five Black Writers: Essays on Wright, Ellison, Baldwin, Hughes and LeRoi Jones* (New York, 1970), 167–77.

10. The relation between *Mulatto* and *In Abraham's Bosom* is further suggested by the fact that Hughes began writing his play while staying at Jasper Deeter's Hedgerow Theater in Rose Valley, Pa. Deeter had directed the prizewinning

By making inheritance *Mulatto's* central conflict and by depicting the interracial family (rather than, as is usual, that of the black characters alone), Hughes challenges the assumed marginality of "tragic mulattoes," which usually determines their unhappy fate. Hughes depicts Bert as the mirror of his father in all but shade, equally proud, volatile, and stubborn, and equally torn by a hatred born of the need to deny an earlier love. Norwood hates Bert because Bert insists his father acknowledge him and because Bert publicly proclaims their relation. Bert hates Norwood for denying him and for the implications his father's denial has for his mother. In their final confrontation, this conflict emerges in the accents of the dozens.

> Norwood.   You're Cora's boy. . . . Nigger women don't know the fathers.
> Bert.   . . . You're talking about my mother.[11]

Cora had lived with Norwood for over thirty years "damn near like a wife," and Norwood had taken unusual measures to educate their children. Cora's soliloquies reveal that tenderness and intimacy did exist between them, but all loving expressions were private, carefully hidden from a white community that viewed the arrangement with alarm and did not interfere only because the Colonel "always [took] care of the folks on [his] plantation without any help." With his death, however, what fragile human bonds had existed vanished. "The Colonel didn't have no relatives," observes the undertaker. To the sheriff, Bert is simply "Cora's nigger."[12]

Although the play's events result in the death or dispossession of all the black characters, the interpretation of those events falls increasingly to Cora. In Act 1, many characters speak of the situation and impending conflict: Cora; her sons, Bert and Willie; and a black servant, Sam. Speaking for the white community is Higgins, who arrives to rebuke the Colonel for Bert's unseemly behavior in town and

---

production of Green's play. Beyond the mixed blood of the protagonist, the question of birthright is central to the dramatic action of both plays. *Mulatto* provides a precise rebuttal to several aspects of Green's work; for example, Cora is his response to Green's depiction of black women, particularly the black mother, and her relationship with Norwood counters Green's depiction of miscegenous relationships.

11. Langston Hughes, *Mulatto,* in Webster Smalley (ed.), *Five Plays by Langston Hughes* (Bloomington, 1963), 23. All drafts of *Mulatto* to which I refer are typescripts, Langston Hughes Papers.

12. Hughes, *Mulatto,* in *Five Plays by Langston Hughes,* 6, 28.

for the living arrangements that Higgins sees as its ultimate cause. In Act 2, after the fatal confrontation, Cora's voice predominates. Earlier she had reasoned with both father and son, pleading with them to avoid their impending conflict. Its aftermath drives her beyond reason. Spoken in acute distress, her first rambling soliloquy is a disjointed account of how she came to live with the young Norwood and of the harsh and tender moments of their shared lives. Her soliloquies also suggest the larger historical and even mythical context for what has occurred. Finally mad, Cora keeps insisting that the dead Colonel is out with the mob pursuing her son—a vision in which a terrifying historical cycle is seen clearly and in which the sequence of the oedipal story becomes fearfully confused. Father seeks to kill son while mother prepares a place for him in her bed, displacing the father and inviting the son to seek there his final resting place. Bert does die in Cora's bed, in his father's house, thus truly displacing the Colonel and laying claim to his inheritance. The play's ultimate impact arises from Cora's clear vision and the self-knowledge implicit in Cora's and Bert's final actions. Blind only is the mob that at last invades the house the Colonel kept so private. Because the members of the mob refuse to acknowledge the familial relations they find there, they cannot understand Bert's patricide, the crime that strikes at the root of all social bonding.

Hughes's drafts of Mulatto reveal that he only gradually discovered the dramatic possibilities and significance of giving the play over to Cora, of locating the meaning of Bert's fate in his mother's experience of it, of explaining it in Cora's voice. This discovery undoubtedly was influenced by his experience in reading his own poetry. As well, in 1931, while working on Mulatto, Hughes published his poem "The Negro Mother," in which he attributes to black women the burden of sorrow that is the black American legacy. It is likely, then, that his final centering of Mulatto's vision in the figure of Cora is a result of his meditations on the heritage of black women as well as of his developing sense of voice.

One of Mulatto's chief weaknesses is that the young Hughes is unsure of his focus. The play wavers between attending to Cora's experience and interpretation of the tragedy, and developing a more comprehensive portrait of the dual tragedy of father and son and the social context that makes their fates inevitable. This wavering reflects the play's concern with the distinction between public and private realities. It also is a function of addressing a double audience. The wider focus on father and son speaks more directly to a white audience, which must be made to understand the implications of its own behavior and racial attitudes. Cora's role embodies the struggle of a black audience wrestling with the meaning of its historical experience, and the implications of the choices it has made.

Thus *Mulatto* indicates one possible solution to the problem of double audience that has so constrained black playwrights. A white audience must be informed about things a black audience intimately knows. A black audience's self-understanding must be deepened. A resolution lies in Cora's voice, through which both groups may come to understand the significance of what has occurred.

Emperor of Haiti, Hughes's second social drama, is his only attempt at reconstructing a famous character in black history. In striking contrast to Richardson's history plays, whose landscapes are ultimately those of Western civilization, *Emperor of Haiti* depicts the Haiti from which all whites have been expelled. The play concerns the consequences of both literal and figurative conquest. It pursues this theme by examining the personal and social forces influencing the rise and fall of Jean Jacques Dessalines, the figure who presided over black Haiti's early attempts at self-government.

Hughes began toying with the idea of a musical play about Haiti as early as 1928. He wrote the dramatic version, *Emperor of Haiti*, during his 1936–1937 stay in Cleveland, and Karamu House claims the play's premiere.[13] As well, during the late 1930s, Hughes collaborated with William Grant Still on an operatic version, *Troubled Island*, which premiered in 1949. Hughes's imaginative attraction to Haiti stemmed from several sources. His great uncle, Mercer Langston, had been the American government's minister to the island, and Hughes himself greatly enjoyed his 1931 visit there. Moreover, Haiti has special significance to American blacks because its bloody revolution, which began with the 1791 slave revolt depicted in Act I, terrified American slave-holders and gave hope to their slaves. Hughes's choice of Des-

13. According to a note in the *Emperor of Haiti* file, Hughes began the play September 6, 1936, and completed it September 24, 1936, at the Majestic Hotel in Cleveland. The drafts are variously titled "Drums of Haiti," "Emperor of Haiti," and "Troubled Island," and the play has been produced under all three titles. See Therman O'Daniel, "Langston Hughes: A Selected Classified Bibliography," in O'Daniel (ed.), *Langston Hughes, Black Genius: A Critical Evaluation* (New York, 1971), 217.

salines as subject, rather than the more famous Toussaint L'Overture, suggests sensitivity to the Haitians' own sense of their history as well: " 'Whatever the means he employed to accomplish his ends,' remarks Louis Mercier, one of Haiti's foremost educators, 'Dessalines remains the most powerful spirit in our history. . . . One cannot be a real Haitian unless one is Dessalinian.'. . . The fact of the matter is that it was Dessalines who established Haiti's independence." [14]

Hughes's choice also suggests his didactic purpose. Dessalines, rather than Toussaint, was faced with the hard job of building political and economic structures in a country utterly unprepared for independence. His problems thus resemble those encountered by American blacks after emancipation, particularly those moving from a rural, illiterate life in the South to urban, industrial life in the North.

Although Hughes takes liberties with details, his portrait of postrevolutionary Haiti is basically accurate. He depicts the former slaves either as victims of exploitative landowners or as subscribers to the theory that freedom means liberation from work. In spite of his courage, noble ambitions, and military prowess, Dessalines cannot provide the needed leadership because the qualities of a nation builder are quite different from those required of a revolutionary leader. In Hughes's depiction, Dessalines and his associates succumb to behavior remarkably like that which Richardson castigates in the black bourgeoisie. They allow complexion, class, social and material ambition, and improperly valued education to disrupt solidarity and development.

Emperor of Haiti attributes Dessalines' fall to a combination of factors. The emperor's illiteracy makes him prey to mulatto treachery, and his decadence, reflected by his insistence on the pomp of a European court, creates resentment and alienation. His reliance on his physical and military prowess leads him to neglect the arts of government and diplomacy. His chief fault as depicted by Hughes is his move away from the common people, in whom, as the play describes it, the revolution was rooted.

An insistent theme in *Emperor of Haiti*, Dessalines' abandoning of the people is made particularly vivid through the depiction of the women he loves and the court he creates. Dessalines' black wife,

14. Langston Hughes and William Grant Still, *Troubled Island* (New York, 1949); Sheldon Rodman, *Haiti: The Black Republic* (New York, 1954), 15.

Azelia, his beloved companion in slavery and his trusted aide during the revolt, opens and closes the play. As emperor, Dessalines abandons Azelia for the mulatto Claire Heureuse, blind to the fact that she loathes him and loves instead his mulatto secretary, Vuval, whose treachery she abets. In Act 3, as the queen Claire Heureuse boards a ship for France, Azelia, a fruit vendor, discovers the emperor's dead body in the marketplace, stripped of its sword by his assassins and of its finery by ragamuffins. A figure reminiscent of Cora, Azelia, now mad, speaks of her continued love for Dessalines and identifies him to the people gathered around his body: "He was a slave . . . then a King!" [15]

The setting of the court banquet in Act 2, Scene 2, further elaborates the emperor's betrayal of the people. It is as though Dessalines literally has imposed on black Haiti—its mountains of Act 1 and seashore marketplace of Act 3—the landscape of European culture, a landscape so alien as to constitute in itself a violence to his revolutionary vision. Dessalines' simple, faithful followers become ridiculous when they are clothed in European court finery and accorded aristocratic titles. Hughes makes the scene into stock comedy, but he also uses it to show the discomfiture of the emperor's more clear-sighted followers. The scene's music heightens the conflict. As dancing girls sway to a "syncopated melody," the drums in the orchestra break into the music of a voodoo rite; then drums in the hills take up the beat, becoming more insistent as the scene progresses. The queen fears the drums, so Dessalines calls for a minuet, but he cannot still the drums in the hills, which symbolically threaten the trappings of culture and of power with which the emperor has deluded himself.

Hughes's pinpointing of Dessalines' failure in his abandonment of the people reflects not only his lifelong artistic principles and impulses but his ideological belief as well—essentially, the Marxist doctrine that both art and political action must be rooted in the culture of the masses.[16] Other, more general political implications emerge in Act 2, Scene 2, during a conversation between Dessalines

15. Langston Hughes, *Emperor of Haiti*, in Turner (ed.), *Black Drama in America*, 114. The text published in this anthology is the 1963 version, which Hughes began in 1960 as a revision of the 1936 text.

16. For a discussion of Hughes and the Communist party, see Young, *Black Writers of the Thirties*, 172–80, and Berry, *Langston Hughes: Before and Beyond Harlem*.

and his trusted advisor, Martel, who regrets but does not condemn the violence through which freedom has been achieved.

> Martel.   All my years, before our freedom, I too, never saw the sun rise but to curse it, but now free men can dream a bigger dream than revenge.
> Dessalines.   What dream, Martel?
> Martel.   A dream of an island where not only blacks are free, but every man who comes to Haitian shore. . . .
> Dessalines.   Too big a dream, Martel. If I could make Haiti a land where *black* men live in peace, I'd be content.
> Martel.   Yes, task enough, I know.[17]

The exchange reflects the continual debate within the Afro-American community over the politics of nationalism and those of assimilation; it alludes as well to the conflict on the left over the applicability of the class analysis to the American racial situation. The play illuminates Hughes's position on such issues, for as a whole, in it he sympathizes with Dessalines' nationalist and racialist position rather than with Martel's ideals. As well, Hughes blunts his analysis of the class interest that motivated the historical mulatto conspiracy against Dessalines by making his mulatto characters, Vuval and Claire Heureuse in particular, personally despicable. He portrays their hatred and scorn for the black characters as reflecting denial of their racial origins and arrogance based on their acquired education and other elements of culture, rather than as reflecting a desire to reassert the economic power and privilege their class had gained under the French. *Emperor of Haiti* thus emphasizes race rather than class as the source of community.

The play's treatment of the mulatto, in its American application, is more figurative than literal. It involves a condemnation of the bourgeoisie similar to that in Richardson's work rather than either a class analysis or an examination of the question of mixed origin. In this regard, *Emperor of Haiti* differs markedly from *Mulatto*, wherein mixed blood raises legitimate questions of inheritance, although like *Mulatto*, it challenges stereotypical white portraits of the mulatto that commonly attribute noble characteristics to the blood of whites and base characteristics to that of blacks.

While acknowledging that the character of Dessalines is "well-drawn, even in outline," one critic has found the play artistically flawed and historically inaccurate. He criticizes particularly Hughes's

17. Hughes, *Emperor of Haiti*, in *Black Drama in America*, 79.

use of "low comic relief while the plot lags."[18] Although justified, this remark, directed especially at the market scene in Act 3, requires comment in light of the bulk of Hughes's subsequent work in the theater. Hughes delighted most, at least in his conventional plays, in the depiction of folk and in comedy. His lingering with the common people and their banter, while at times self-indulgent, reveals his real interest in how the play's larger events are mediated through the experience of such characters.

The weakness of *Emperor of Haiti* is less its toying with history or its use of comedy than the inadequacy of its conception of Dessalines. For his portrait of the powerful hero in Act 1, Hughes draws on readily available historical and imaginative material; Dessalines' motive is shown to be his desire for freedom, and his personal magnetism an extension of his courage and authority. The portrait falters in Act 2, as Hughes minimizes the libertinism and tyranny that characterized the rule of the historical Dessalines in order to create a sympathetic hero. However, the emperor's fawning over Claire Heureuse, and his illiteracy and pretensions, make him appear something of a fool and diminish his stature established earlier. Hughes's Dessalines fails as a tragic hero because his hubris is inadequately understood and realized.

The last of Hughes's three forays into conventional social drama, "Front Porch," was written for the Gilpin Players of Karamu House in 1938 and performed by them the same year.[19] The play is Hughes's only explicit dramatic treatment of the black bourgeoisie. Its lower-middle-class family, the Harpers, lives in a white neighborhood. While all activity occurs on their front porch, whether that porch is black territory is doubtful, for Mrs. Harper constantly worries how her white neighbors will view what goes on there. Thus the color of the setting is also a theme in "Front Porch" and an interesting variant on the similar themes in *Mulatto* and *Emperor of Haiti*. It is the last time such a theme appears, which suggests that the son Cantwell's repeated pleading to return to a black neighborhood speaks for Hughes himself. Moreover, many of the play's shortcomings arise from Hughes's difficulty in finding appropriate language for his deracinated characters. This deficiency in language is less a failure of talent than an ex-

18. Darwin Turner, "Langston Hughes as Playwright," in O'Daniel (ed.), *Langston Hughes, Black Genius*, 94.
19. Langston Hughes, "Front Porch" (Typescript, Langston Hughes Papers).

pression of Hughes's discomfort with the setting, class, and politics he has chosen as the play's subject.

"Front Porch" is the love story of Harriet Harper and Kenneth, an idealistic union organizer whom she meets while innocently crossing his picket line. Mrs. Harper bars Kenneth from her house, for she favors Harriet's other suitor, J. Donald Butler, a stuffy graduate student so overblown as to constitute a caricature of bourgeois pretensions. Cantwell supports both Kenneth and his left-wing politics, and decries his mother's beliefs as those of a class whose days are numbered. When Harriet reveals that she is pregnant with Kenneth's child, Mrs. Harper forces her into an abortion, which is botched, and seals her fate by preventing Kenneth from supplying Harriet with the blood that would save her life.

The play's harsh criticism of the black bourgeoisie is mitigated only by a brief episode at the end of Act 2, wherein, in a monologue reminiscent of Cora's and Azelia's recounting of their sorrows, Mrs. Harper confesses that Kenneth recalls her dearly loved husband. His repeated failures, caused by racism, which crushed his sensitive, idealist nature, led to alcoholism and a premature death. In this moment, a more sympathetic and articulate Mrs. Harper emerges. Her flight from her roots is portrayed as a futile attempt to save her children from a legacy of sorrow. However, her eloquence in this scene is hard to reconcile with the pretensions of the woman who fawns over Butler and who deludes herself into thinking she is accepted in the neighborhood although, as Cantwell points out, only their Jewish neighbor is really friendly. At the play's conclusion, both personal and political hope have vanished. Having lost her daughter, Mrs. Harper withdraws into her house with her remaining children in a gesture borrowed from the final moments of Eugene O'Neill's *Mourning Becomes Electra*. The strike Harriet and Kenneth so strongly supported is broken.[20]

Obvious and melodramatic, "Front Porch" lacks the more convinc-

20. The files contain two versions of "Front Porch," identical but for the third act. In the alternate ending, to the typescript of which Hughes attached a scornful note, Harriet returns home having decided to keep the baby and is greeted by Kenneth and victorious strikers. Correspondence about the play in the Langston Hughes Papers (shown to me by Arnold Rampersad) reveals that Rowena Jelliffee wrote the second ending for two reasons: first, Hughes was so slow in completing the play that the company was in rehearsal without having received the third act; second, she realized Hughes had based the

ing characterization and sustained language that give the earlier plays their power and veracity; it lacks also the emotional clarity that mitigates their sentimentality. Its interest lies in the politics it expresses. Like *Emperor of Haiti*, "Front Porch" espouses racial rather than interracial class loyalty, despite its obvious political biases. For Hughes, Butler's posturing and Mrs. Harper's turning from her husband's bitter life ultimately constitute a rejection of their racial heritage rather than a political act. At the same time, Harriet's, Cantwell's, and Kenneth's racial loyalty is clearly more important than their fealty to the class struggle. Moreover, Mrs. Harper's forcing Harriet into an abortion violates what Hughes sees as a deeply held black reverence for life. In his short story of the same period, "Cora Unashamed," he denounces abortion as not only immoral but inimical to black views of the world.[21] Mrs. Harper's behavior, then, is much like Cora's; she aligns herself with the white world hoping thereby to create a better life for her children, and her self-delusion has similarly tragic consequences.

While not representative of Hughes's central dramatic purpose, his conventional social drama extends the work Richardson and Edmonds began. Like them, Hughes assumes the context of oppression and focuses on how his characters deal with its effects. As in classical tragedy, the denouements of his plays include some recognition by the characters of their choices within the sphere of their freedom. The plays do not simply honor their endurance of the things over which they have no power.

Viewed as commenting on stage reality, Hughes's social dramas all struggle with the problem of the black figure in a white ground. *Mulatto* makes two propositions in this regard. First, Bert's literal territorial challenge meets with defeat. Although at the beginning of the last scene the undertaker acknowledges black possession of the stage

---

play on the life of the man she had, completely by coincidence and without Hughes's knowledge, cast in the role of Kenneth, and she wished to conceal from him the use Hughes had made of his experience (Rowena Jelliffee to Langston Hughes, n.d., Langston Hughes Papers).

In light of Hughes's politics, it is interesting to note that he wrote Rowena Jelliffee that the labor theme in "Front Porch" was only incidental to the play and should be downplayed so as not to prejudice the audience (Hughes to Jelliffee, October 19, 1938, Langston Hughes Papers).

21. Langston Hughes, "Cora Unashamed," in Hughes, *The Ways of White Folks* (New York, 1971), 3–18.

when he says of the house, "Ain't nothin' but niggers left out here now," the lynch mob repossesses it minutes later.[22] Second, however, events acquire their final import from Cora's account of them, and thus she accomplishes her son's purpose; her voice establishes not simply a point of view on the stage reality, but at least momentarily that reality itself.

Emperor of Haiti begins with a black ground, and the failure to maintain it is essentially a failure of imagination. Dessalines crowns himself emperor and establishes for himself a European court because, finally, he cannot yet imagine either the form or the setting of post-revolutionary black power. The behavior of the historical Dessalines thus provides an analogy for the problem of the artist. Hughes's difficulty realizing Dessalines as emperor suggests both the limits of his talents and the lack of available models. Finally, "Front Porch" investigates an integrated landscape, but with little conviction. Those characters with bourgeois aspirations themselves imply that the setting is white; the others share the discomfort Cantwell expresses when he urges a return to a black neighborhood.

In Hughes's comedies, the conflict over territory subsides. Although conventional in form, Little Ham, "Joy to My Soul," Simply Heavenly, and the folk comedies Hughes coauthored with others establish a familiar black landscape that intrusions by whites fail to challenge. A completely black stage reality is not therefore achieved, however, for double consciousness intrudes by virtue of the stage tradition of the comic Negro, to which the comedies unavoidably, even deliberately, allude. The double consciousness is intended by the playwright partly as a challenge to his audience, one made possible because the plays' assurance rests on the black humor that is their subject and medium. Humor establishes its own territory; indeed, black humor historically has provided a ground by which blacks distance themselves from oppression, and it continues to do so.

All black humor, whether about whites or not, rests on shared assumptions about life. Outsiders may laugh for their own reasons, or may fail to see the humor at all. "Getting the joke" is a sign of oneness with the group. Humor's dynamic, then, helps establish the "blackness" of the setting, for humor is itself point of view.

22. Hughes, Mulatto, in Five Plays by Langston Hughes, 28.

However, the stage conventions Hughes employs allude to a tradition that subverts the assurance and security this ground provides. The comic Negro figures of minstrelsy, vaudeville, the musical comedy and revue, and all the forms they engendered are complex, particularly as viewed and enacted by blacks. Some recent critics have suggested that although these figures originated in the white racist imagination, they were taken over by black actors and writers.[23] In their hands, the image of the comic Negro was transformed and absorbed into black humor as an often bitter parody of the white mimicry of blacks on which minstrelsy thrived. For example, blacks as well as whites appreciated Stepin' Fetchit, but they understood him differently and laughed for different reasons.

In setting himself the task of writing comedy, Hughes challenged the tradition that ridiculed blacks. More than the social dramas, the comedies embody the process he described in "Note on Commercial Theatre": the reclaiming of the self whites had stolen, through the unselfconscious writing of plays about "me." Some critics have wished Hughes had been more reticent in this regard, and these he answered directly through a character in *Simply Heavenly*, first performed in 1957, who rages when rebuked for discussing watermelons: "Mister, you better remove yourself from my presence before I stereo your type! I like watermelons, and I don't care who knows it. That's nothing to be ashamed of, like some colored folk are. . . . I ain't no pretender myself, neither no passer."[24]

When evaluating whether or not comedy plays into racist stereotype, several distinctions are important. Is the figure being laughed at or with—is the joke, on some level, that the character is black, or is his race incidental, simply assumed, or, where observed, viewed from within the group? Is foolish behavior caused by the character's inability to measure up to implicit white standards of behavior and the audience's pleasure primarily an assertion of superiority, or is the character simply acting the fool and inviting the members of the audience while laughing to recognize themselves? Does the comedy of a particular form depend on an outsider's judgment, or are its origins in

23. For an excellent discussion and a review of the literature on this issue see Bernard Ostendorf, *Black Literature in White America* (Totowa, N.J., 1982), Chap. III.

24. Langston Hughes, *Simply Heavenly*, in Smalley (ed.), *Five Plays by Langston Hughes*, 125.

the humor of the people depicted? The differences can be subtle, particularly when the audience is struggling to distinguish between its own comic tradition and another, deceptively similar one, which has used similar forms to destroy the dignity of that audience. Hughes succeeded in sustaining the distinctions, for as Arthur P. Davis observes, his plays

> are written in the language of the "little" Negro of the urban North, the people he knew, loved, and understood best. They are also written *for* these folk, presenting ideas, themes, and situations which they understood. Given his objective, to write for a people's theatre, too much subtlety would be out of place. What he lacks in subtlety, however, he makes up in the understanding of these people and the tolerance and compassion he has for them. Perhaps his greatest gift is the gift of laughter—laughter *with*, not *at*, his characters. Deep down, Langston Hughes has a great faith in the essential worth and the indominatible spirit of the black man in the street and this faith comes through in his dramatic works.[25]

Hughes's first two comedies were written for and premiered by the Gilpin Players at Karamu House: *Little Ham* in 1936 and "Joy to My Soul" in 1937.[26] Both were hits. *Little Ham*, set in Harlem of the Roaring Twenties, depicts the adventures of Hamlet Hitchcock Jones, a sporty shoe shiner turned numbers runner, whose luck with both women and the numbers is the substance of the play. The program notes from the March 24–29, 1936, Karamu production describe *Little Ham* as exploiting the "comic contrasts and humorous moves" of the black belts of the northern cities, material that had previously appeared only in the musical comedy and revue. Chiefly, the notes continue, the play reveals "certain aspects of Harlem life centered around 'the numbers.' It is a play without a serious reason for being. It is just to laugh and in laughing to be happy." Both the Cleveland press and *Variety* reviewed the play favorably, although literary critics have damned it.[27] Certainly the play is slight, overwritten, and dependent on coincidence, but its joyousness and exuberance are engaging. Moreover, although it may have "no serious reason for being," *Little Ham* has resonance.

25. Davis, *From the Dark Tower*, 67.

26. Langston Hughes, *Little Ham*, in Smalley (ed.), *Five Plays by Langston Hughes*, and "Joy to My Soul" (Typescript, Langston Hughes Papers).

27. Program for *Little Ham*, Langston Hughes Papers; clippings, *ibid.* For negative comments see Turner, "Langston Hughes as Playwright," and Doris Abramson, "It'll Be Me: The Voice of Langston Hughes," in Jules Chametzky and Sidney Kaplan (eds.), *Black and White in American Culture* (New York, 1969), 380–90.

Little Ham's plot concerns the hero's separation from various old loves and his engagement with a generously proportioned new love, Tiny, who similarly quenches an old flame in order to take on Ham. Counterpoint to the love interest is the numbers game on which all the characters who wander through Madame Lucille Bell's Paradise Shining Parlors and Tiny's Beauty Shop pin their hopes. All is brought to bear on the choosing of a number—dreams, hymns called out in church, the address of a new girlfriend. Much as in Hughes's long poem "Montage of a Dream Deferred," published in 1951, but in a lighter vein, elusive dreams engage all the characters' imaginations, and these are both concretized and symbolized by playing the numbers. As luck would have it, and because Little Ham is a comedy, Ham and Tiny win at love, at numbers, at work, and at the Charleston contest with which the play concludes. Fortune smiles as well on Sugar Lou, the chorus girl who works in hit after hit; on Joe Louis, a passing celebrity in the action; and even on the janitor, who also plays Ham's winning number.

Other aspects of the play, however, remind both characters and audience that the smile of lady luck, like the spotlight in a theater, merely suspends troublesome realities. Only chance will release the inhabitants of the stage from the poverty and oppression that constrain them. Moreover, the delighted sense of proprietorship that many characters express about Harlem is ephemeral. As Ham and Tiny remark, although the world depicted belongs to colored folk, white folk run it. White detectives intrude in the first act, harassing Madame Bell, who collects numbers for her lover, Boss Leroy. By the act's end, he has been deposed by the new white mobsters, who have taken over the Harlem territory from the old white gang who gave him his power. Ham's winning number is only paid off because the newcomers wish to appear fair-minded. These intrusions suggest that just as black Harlem cannot control its destiny, good luck betokens no real change in fortune, and that comedy gives only a momentary release from a starker reality. Moreover, while the Roaring Twenties provides the play's atmosphere, its concrete details are those of the thirties. Its real theme is the Great Depression, and most of the characters are on relief.

If good fortune is gratuitous, so are the acts of generosity that characterize some of Little Ham's, Madame Bell's, and Boss Leroy's behavior, and so is the impulse to reconciliation that allows the characters to resolve the various love entanglements in the final scene. Small acts of generosity occur quite early in the play, as when Ham stops hustling long enough to give the Shabby Man a free shine so that he can use his last nickel to get to a prospective job downtown, or when Madame Bell gives free matches to the Old Lady, who has spent her last nickel on a number. However, comedy and carnival merely suspend chaos; they do not negate it. The mobster's gun in Act I is matched by Tiny's ex-lover's gun in Act 3. Neither is fired, but both could have been. In this setting, the spirit of comedy, like good fortune, is gratuitous.

Colloquially described as "laughing to keep from crying," the sense of comedy as respite from rather than negation of tragedy defines a crucial aspect of black humor. Thus although white intrusions and the oppression they represent elicit double consciousness, humor establishes a point of view that mitigates that consciousness's debilitating effects. Much of the play's humor lies in the playful, inventive, and combative qualities of black speech, whose brilliance is honed by awareness of audience. In *Little Ham*, more than in his later comedies, Hughes creates not only authentic black speech but also the characteristic contexts for its display. In the Paradise Shining Parlor and the beauty shop are appreciative audiences for the expressions of black speech. Thus the theater audience observes both the display and the appreciation on which the display depends. Finally, the play's comedy lies in apt imitation, not only of voice, but of types: the chorus girl, the West Indian, the deaconess, the hot stuff man, and so on. Delight in accurate imitation characterizes black humor. Thus in *Little Ham* black territory is maintained, not simply because the locale of the play is Harlem, but because black humor informs its action and vision.

Little Ham is certainly a flawed work. Perhaps its greatest shortcoming, as Darwin Turner has pointed out, is that while Hughes reproduces Harlem speech faithfully, the witticisms fail to generate larger meaning or to reveal the wisdom often embedded in folk expression.[28] Unlike Hughes's great creation of a few years later, Jesse B. Semple, whom he brought to the stage in *Simply Heavenly*, Ham has little to say, and thus, finally, the play fails to create a fully authentic voice. The vision that its use of black humor brings to bear on the question of stage reality is not extended to what the characters say about the world they experience.

28. Turner, "Langston Hughes as Playwright," in O'Daniel (ed.), *Langston Hughes, Black Genius*, 87–88.

"Joy to My Soul," Hughes's next comedy, extends aspects of *Little Ham* with an air of recklessness uncharacteristic of the author. First performed by the Gilpin Players in March, 1937, and revived by them ten years later, the play clearly follows on the success of the earlier work. Hughes called it a farce comedy; a production note suggests that all the characters be played in the exaggerated manner of Negro minstrel comedy—loud, gay, colorful, and overdone. Clearly, Hughes pursued in "Joy to My Soul" the attack on the comic tradition he had begun in *Little Ham*; in the later play comic types are exaggerated and even made grotesque. The play employs masquerade, but even when the mask is not literal, the characters often don behavior as though it were mask, much as in a minstrel show.

The plot concerns the fate of Buster Whitehead, a slow-witted, good-natured twenty-one-year-old country boy from Shadow Gut, Texas, who has gone to the Grand Harlem Hotel to meet his fiancée, Suzy Bailey, whom he contacted through a lonely-hearts column. Buster is a wealthy oilman, and much of the play depicts various characters' attempts to con from him as much money as possible during his stay. Suzy is large, ugly, and twice Buster's age. The night before their wedding Buster, high on reefers, runs off with Wilmetta, the cigarette girl, with whom he has fallen in love. Thus he saves her from two no-good stepfathers, who appear regularly to plague her for money. The next morning armed Suzy lies in wait for the newlyweds in the lobby, but shoots instead the mountain of luggage preceding them off the elevator. All is reconciled when they emerge: Buster gives Suzy "Oil Well Three" in gratitude for her having been the occasion of his meeting his true love.

Like that of *Little Ham*, the chief delight of "Joy to My Soul" is its display of types, which, in this play, range from ordinary folk, sometimes in postures of self-parody, to the truly grotesque—call girls, a boxer and his manager, gamblers, numbers men, an irate husband in search of his faithless wife, a medium, a midget, and her manager, who claims to be an Egyptian but is actually a local con artist. The Knights of the Royal Sphinx, whose convention is also at the hotel, march through the lobby in full regalia, playing a jazzed-up military march in the manner of the Sanctified Church, and when their music is not interrupting the action, jazz and blues float in from the hotel bar. A note in *The Big Sea* illuminates the parade and suggests Hughes delighted in aspects of Harlem as spectacle: "Once I saw such a lodge parade with an all-string band leading the procession, violins and mandolins and banjos and guitars in the street. It was thrilling and the music was grand." [29]

While the play's comic types and witty dialogue are often truly humorous and convincing, often the stage has so much activity that the pace becomes frenetic, and its madcap atmosphere acquires a note of desperation. This darker edge to the activity is certainly intentional: what was a parade of comic types in the Paradise Shining Parlor has become a freak show in the Grand Harlem Hotel. Little Ham and his chorus arise from the environment depicted in the earlier play, but in "Joy to My Soul" the sentimental central plot depicting the fate of innocents contrasts sharply with the bustling con game that serves as backdrop to their story. The play lacks a central controlling intelligence, and a point of view for its darker satire.

Reviewers were puzzled by the play, although audiences, according to one reviewer at least, loved it. The critics found it uncharacteristic of Hughes; *Variety* called it a "pot-boiler." [30] Certainly, because of its bizarre edge, "Joy to My Soul" occupies a peculiar place in Hughes's dramatic canon; it suggests his comic bent permitted a moment of madness—a direction he rarely pursued. [31]

Both *Little Ham* and "Joy to My Soul," whatever their flaws, are the works of an accomplished dramatist, their strength and novelty the assurance with which they stare minstrelsy down. To understand their genesis, we must turn to Hughes's first comedy, "Mule Bone," the play that he wrote in 1930 with his then good friend Zora Neale Hurston. [32] This comedy about a quarrel produced the quarrel about authorship that permanently disrupted their friendship of five years. In spite of the efforts of both their literary biographers, who wrote what of "Mule Bone" is as yet unclear; nonetheless, the collaboration had a profound effect on Hughes's later work.

By 1930 Hughes had written for the theater only his very short chil-

29. Hughes, *The Big Sea*, 274.

30. Reviews in the Langston Hughes Papers include Cleveland *News*, April 1, 1937; Cleveland *Plain Dealer*, March 28 and April 1, 1937; *Variety*, April 7, 1937, and one favorable review of the revival, Cleveland *Press*, March 25, 1939. The April *Plain Dealer* review reported that audiences loved the play.

31. Notably, Hughes's satirical short story "Rejuvenation Through Joy" in *The Ways of White Folk* and some scenes in his never-completed revision of "Cock o'de World" achieve some of the same quality.

32. Langston Hughes and Zora Neale Hurston, "Mule Bone" (Typescript, Langston Hughes Papers). Act 3 was published in *Drama Critique*, VII (Spring, 1964), 103–107.

dren's play and sketches of what would become *Emperor of Haiti*; "Mule Bone," then, was his first full-length theatrical piece. Hurston had published two short plays: in 1926, *Color Struck: A Play*, in *Fire!*; and, in 1927, *The First One: A Play*, in Charles S. Johnson's anthology of the New Negro writing, *Ebony and Topaz*, both works of some dramatic merit, and both rich in folklore detail.[33]

Working together, Hughes and Hurston wrote "Mule Bone" between March and June, 1930. They undertook the project as the first concrete step toward a plan they had discussed as early as 1926, originally formulated as an opera based on folk materials and later as a "*real* Negro art theatre," which would bring to the stage the folk tales Hurston knew and collected.[34]

The original tale on which "Mule Bone" is based concerns two hunters' fight over who had killed a wild turkey. In the tale, one knocks the other unconscious with the hock bone of a mule and is convicted because, as a minister tells the jury, if Samson slew three thousand Philistines with the jawbone of an ass, how much more lethal must be the more truly dangerous end of a mule. In the course of writing, Hurston and Hughes transformed the tale into a quarrel over a woman, but the trial retains the original argument. The play is replete with folklore material in much of the dialogue and detail—for example, the children's games in the first act and the traditional linguistic courting rituals with which Jim and Dave vie for the hand of Daisy.

Until Robert Hemenway's *Zora Neale Hurston: A Literary Biography*, published in 1977, only Hughes's rather self-serving account in *The Big Sea* testified to the manner of Hughes and Hurston's collaboration: "I plotted and typed the play based on her story, while she authenticated and flavored the dialogue and added highly humorous details. We finished a first draft before she went South again and from this draft I was to work out a final version."[35] Hemenway's account challenges Hughes's, claiming the play was not finished before Hurston

33. Zora Neale Hurston, *Color Struck: A Play*, in *Fire!*, I (November, 1926), 7–14, and *The First One: A Play*, in Charles Johnson (ed.), *Ebony and Topaz: A Collectanea* (New York, 1927).

34. Robert E. Hemenway, *Zora Neale Hurston: A Literary Biography* (Urbana, 1977), 115.

35. Hughes, *The Big Sea*, 320. See also 331–34 for Hughes's account of the quarrel; Rampersad, *The Life of Langston Hughes, Volume I*, Chap. 8, for his biographer's reconstruction; and Hemenway, *Zora Neale Hurston*, Chap. 6, for an account from Hurston's perspective.

left for the South in the summer of 1930; rather, she was to complete Act 2 during the summer and failed to do so. Hughes's biographer Arnold Rampersad surmises that Hughes was, at that stage, the more confident dramatist but that Hurston's contribution "was almost certainly the greater" since the folk materials that provide the play's substance and style were those of which Hurston "was absolute master and Langston no more than a sometime student." [36] Given Hughes's later work and the tenor of his imagination, it is likely, as he claimed, that he contributed the love triangle plot and the dramatic construction, while Hurston provided the original tale, "authenticated" the dialogue and details, and contributed much of the humor. It also seems likely that Hughes learned as much as he contributed and that from this collaboration came, for his own writing, a clearer, bolder sense of what it means to depict the folk and to use their characteristic expressions as authentic dramatic voice.

The quarrel erupted when Hughes learned the Gilpin Players had received a script of "Mule Bone" with only Hurston's name on it. The bitterness of the quarrel suggests that its roots lay deeper than Hurston's jealousy over the role of their typist, Louis Thompson, which she readily acknowledged, or even, as Rampersad suggests, the difficult relationship imposed on both of them by Charlotte Mason, their mutual patron. Hurston alone among the group which formed the Harlem Renaissance was a native of the rural South—as it were, a creature of the folklore she later collected. When she reached Harlem in 1925, by all accounts with immediate and enormous impact, she quickly gained popularity for her incessant recounting of the southern folklore that had shaped the world of her Eatonville, Florida, childhood. In a sense she embodied the artistic problem the young, dissident Renaissance artists were wrestling with: how to translate the vibrant culture of the folk into conscious artistic expression. None in the group was more concerned with this issue than Hughes—except, of course, Hurston, for whom the issue was intensely personal as well as artistic. Her early stories and plays, as well as her later work, depend heavily on the folk material that sustained her creative imagination. When she turned to anthropology as a student of Franz Boaz, she well may have, as Hemenway suggests, been seeking some

36. Hughes, The Big Sea, 138; Rampersad, The Life of Langston Hughes, Volume I, 184.

way to distance herself from the material that animated her, and until very recently her fame rested more on her anthropological work and less on her fiction.

In 1953, in a letter to Arna Bontemps, Hughes wrote concerning James Baldwin's *Go Tell It on the Mountain*: "If it were written by Zora Hurston with her feeling for the folk idiom, it would probably be a *quite* wonderful book. Baldwin over-writes and over-poeticizes in images way over the heads of the folks supposedly thinking them—often beautiful writing in itself—but frequently out of character—although it might be as the people *would* think if they *could* think that way. . . . I wish he had collaborated with Zora." [37]

This appears to be Hughes's first extended note about Hurston in his correspondence to his dear friend. Both the comment and its context suggest what Hughes learned from his collaboration with Hurston. In 1930 Hughes was still feeling his way, searching for the idiom that not only characterizes the folk but reflects what he later called the complexity of their simplicity. His early fiction embodies an authorial presence that extends beyond the consciousness of his characters, as does much of the poetry in his early volumes *The Weary Blues* and *Fine Clothes to the Jew*, except where he adopts the blues form. In none of the social dramas does he truly remain within the consciousness of the folk characters he depicts: Cora's soliloquy in *Mulatto* depends on a poetic license beyond what she might say, and in *Emperor of Haiti* only occasionally, in the preparation for the revolt in Act 1 and the market scene of Act 3, do folk characters express views credibly within the range of their experience and perception.

As Hughes wrote in *The Big Sea*, "Mule Bone" is the first genuine Negro folk comedy. Its authenticity rests both in its materials and in its attitude toward the folk. Unlike plays by white authors (notably *The Green Pastures*, which opened February 26, 1930), its figures are those of black folklore, not of white lore about blacks. Moreover, these figures do not symbolize a world view idealized and distanced from that of the audience; rather, their world is presented as a given—unsophisticated, even quaint, but real. The play is polished, well constructed, amusing, and appealing. Had Hughes and Hurston resolved their differences, the play might have realized the high expectations

37. Langston Hughes to Arna Bontemps, 1953, in Charles Nichols (ed.), *Arna Bontemps / Langston Hughes: Letters, 1925–1967* (New York, 1980), 302–303.

they had for it. Its strengths derived not only from Hurston's knowledge and materials but from what her very presence in the Renaissance represented.

This suggestion of influence may shed light, then, on the bitterness of the quarrel, which in a deep psychic sense concerned the territory both artists desperately strove to master. Personal and professional jealousy may have been conscious motives, but an unconscious motive may have been the necessary separation of two headstrong, highly creative people who, in searching for their own voices, had found that they had to part ways.

Hughes's quarrel with Hurston is all the more striking because throughout his career he collaborated frequently with a range of writers, both white and black. For example, during the 1930s, he worked with Ella Winter on a play about California farm workers, "Blood on the Fields"; with Kaj Gynt on a play about the adventures of a seaman, "Cock o'De World"; and with Clarence Muse on a revision of Arna Bontemps and Countee Cullen's *St. Louis Woman* and a film script, *Way Down South*, among others, although few of these projects were ever completed.

One that was completed and presented by the Gilpin Players in 1936 was "When the Jack Hollers," a folk comedy Hughes wrote with his lifelong collaborator on many projects, Arna Bontemps. Originally entitled "Careless Love," the play "When the Jack Hollers" is a love comedy constructed around the lore that the "holler" made by a Jack (according to Hughes, a mule used for breeding) in search of his mate makes a "woman's love come down." [38] Set in Mississippi Delta springtime, the play depicts a sharecropping community that consists of a large extended family and its neighbors. The chief characters are Mouse and his wife, Viney; Bogator, Mouse's brother; and Queen Esther, Viney's sister, who comes to visit from Memphis. She pursues Rev. Buddy Lovelady, the local preacher, whose eyes equally rest on women, money, and the Lord. Aunt Billie, midwife to an entire local generation and dealer in charms and magic as well, presides over the community.

While the Jack's hollering sets in motion the comic love theme in the play, the device has more serious thematic ramifications. Aunt

38. Langston Hughes and Arna Bontemps, "When the Jack Hollers" (Typescript, Langston Hughes Papers).

Billie speaks of her own hollering whenever she gets drunk, which releases the sadness she feels about the hollering black babies she
pulls "screaming out of their mothers' guts" and into the Delta. She
hints that she takes babies out of the world as well and does not
understand why this should be a sin, since "hard as this life is, it's
more of a sin helping people to get into this world than it is helping
them get out." [39] Aunt Billie's speeches contrast with the play's light-
hearted plot, and her eloquent, powerful voice ultimately provides the
ground for the play's action, rooting the depicted world in a traditionally articulated black world view. In so doing, Aunt Billie's voice
functions similarly to that of Cora in *Mulatto* and Mrs. Harper in "Front
Porch."

The poverty and oppression of Delta life counterpoint the play's
comic elements, although their cause, racism, is ridiculed. Viney and
Bogator poignantly long for a charm that would make white folks less
mean, and a white man, Sid Lowery, who abashedly approaches Aunt
Billie for an appropriate charm, becomes the butt of humor. Act 3 depicts a community fish fry that is disrupted by the Klan, whose members are unmasked when Lowery's cape is torn off by a thorn bush.
The blacks tell the Klansmen that they recognized all of them anyway.
In the discussion that follows, the white and black sharecroppers discover that their mutual enemies are the landowners and decide to
unite against them. Political issues resolved, the play ends with the
singing of "Careless Love," as all the couples united by the hollering
of the Jack embrace.

The end may seem unbearably sentimental and simplistic in its ideology; it is made convincing (if barely so) by the humor present in the
folk material, and in particular, that directed toward white oppression. The unmasking of the Klan concretizes the way humor can strip
aspects of life of their terror and thus of their danger, so that the resulting fearlessness is the first step to freedom. In "When the Jack
Hollers," the comic elements and the somber ones expressing the
cruelty and poverty of Delta life together create the tone and mood
underlying much of Afro-American folk culture. The real agonies are
not belittled: rather, triumphant laughter is simply the weapon chosen
and celebrated; the voice of Aunt Billie, whose cynicism, wit, courage,

39. *Ibid.*

and love embody all that allows her community to endure, finally controls the play.

The material on which "When the Jack Hollers" is based is clearly
Bontemps'. The play's setting and characters are similar to those in
his short stories set in the rural Alabama he came to know while
teaching in Huntsville, from 1931 to 1934. The play's dramatic form
and comic love theme, and possibly much of its humor, seem more
likely the product of Hughes's imagination, for while some of Bontemps' southern stories are humorous, they never possess the light-
heartedness that characterizes Hughes's comedy. The play's ideological resolution, its alliance of poor whites and blacks, might well have
arisen from Bontemps' observations, recorded for example in his
"Saturday Night: Portrait of a Small Southern Town, 1933," but again,
the humor with which it is depicted is clearly Hughes's.[40]

Hughes's contributions to the play, particularly the manner in which
the characters are delineated, reflect his work with Zora Neale Hurston.
As in "Mule Bone" and Little Ham, the characters are comic types,
rather than, as in Bontemps' comic stories, rural folk in comic situations. Richness of vision and significance emerge from the wisdom of
what they say rather than from their individual complexity. Even Aunt
Billie, the most complex of the characters, is a type, her several facets
less a matter of her individuality than a function of the world view she
articulates.

His joint ventures "Mule Bone" and "When the Jack Hollers," as well
as Hughes's own Little Ham and "Joy to My Soul," constitute a significant achievement, and one consonant with Hughes's dramatic purpose. They mark black dramatists' entry into Negro folk comedy, their
challenging and authenticating of the form. "Mule Bone" is essentially a folk tale rewritten for the stage and thus accomplishes what
Marc Connelly spuriously claimed for The Green Pastures. "When the
Jack Hollers," basically a conventional comedy in a folk setting, honors its material and does not compromise the folk world or use comedy to mitigate its portrait of southern rural life. Little Ham should
finally be understood as a folk comedy as well, although its folk are
urban, not rural. Their fish fry is a Charleston contest, and their con-
juring is all that is brought to bear on guessing a winning number.

What Hughes sought, although with mixed results, to bring to the

40. Arna Bontemps, "Saturday Night: Portrait of a Small Southern Town,
1933," in The Old South (New York, 1973), 157–69.

stage, as well as to the page in his poetry and fiction, was the rich, complex vision of the world he saw expressed daily in the speech, manners, and traditions of ordinary black people. In *Soul Gone Home*, written in 1936, he managed to realize that vision completely.

Soul Gone Home depicts the final argument between a mother and her son—final because the son has just died. The mother's rhetorical cry, "Come back from the spirit world and speak to me," is answered; her dead son, Ronnie, returns to berate her for her maternal failures. Information he gathered in his brief time in the spirit world has made clear to him exactly how bad a mother she has been. While Ronnie holds her at bay by rolling his eyes, she protests fearfully that she did what she could. They had no money, she explains, and thus Ronnie died of undernourishment (*undernourishment* is a word he learned in the spirit world and teaches her). He recalls always being hungry. Finally, he speaks to her gently: "We never had no money, mama, not even since you took up hustlin' on the street." But when she says her tears express her deep love, he retorts, "First time you ever did cry for me, far I know," and they are at odds with each other again.[41]

When the ambulance arrives to remove Ronnie's body, his mother becomes self-conscious. "Don't let them white men see you dead, sitting up here quarrelin' with your mother. Lay down and fold your hands back like I had 'em." He complies, first insisting on combing his hair and putting on his stocking cap. "I don't want to go out of here with my hair standin' straight up in front even if I is dead." While the body is carried out, Ronnie's mother simulates the hysterical grief she showed in the opening moments of the play, but as soon as the ambulance leaves, she prepares for the streets. "Tomorrow, Ronnie, I'll buy you some flowers—if I can pick up a dollar tonight. You was a hell of a no-good son, I swear!"[42]

The plight of the characters in *Soul Gone Home* is unmitigatedly tragic, although they and their situation are comic. Yet they are not simply comic types, for so daring is the dramatic situation created for them that it disrupts the stock images of cool delinquent and whore that might sentimentalize or otherwise shape our judgments. The re-

41. Langston Hughes, *Soul Gone Home*, in Smalley (ed.), *Five Plays by Langston Hughes*, 39, 41. The play was originally published in *One Act Play Magazine* (July, 1937). *Soul Gone Home* was written as an opera for Ulysses Kay in 1954 and performed by Universal Actors Co., Chicago, Spring, 1957. Harry Gaines directed.
42. *Ibid.*, 41, 42.

lationship between mother and child in *Soul Gone Home* is intimate and eloquent, and includes all the love and injustice that parents and children visit on each other, especially when the wrongs parents inflict on their children are beyond their control. Only through comedy can such painful insights be conveyed without destroying those who thus come to understand their own behavior. The play captures perfectly a moment of "laughing to keep from crying" and thus emerges as a powerful, lyric statement of the blues reality.

Soul Gone Home does draw on certain comic stereotypes. Ronnie's eye rolling and the belief in "haunts" that makes the play possible allude to the use of black superstition to motivate many a moment in Negro comedy. The play alludes as well to the wealth of folk tales and jokes that picture heaven as a troublesome place for black folks. The enlightenment Ronnie gains in his few moments in the netherworld provides him with a modern, secular explanation for his sufferings on earth, an explanation that goes beyond either his or his mother's way of understanding their situation. This modern view is subsumed into the folk perception when Ronnie adopts it as a weapon against his mother. Its presence in what is otherwise traditional folk discourse suggests that their plight is socially caused and not simply "the human condition."

Traditional depictions of the Negro also became the butt of Hughes's theatrical humor in three short, witty parodies, all written in the late 1930s. "The Em-Feuher Jones," based on O'Neill's popular work, makes of the hero an Aryan—or so he says, Hughes adds—who resembles Adolf Hitler and is terrified by the alien jungle setting. *Limitation of Life* reverses the roles in Fannie Hurst's popular *Imitation of Life*. In Hughes's play, a white servant parodies the obsequious attitude of the black servant in the original, obeying a black, middle-class mistress. In "Colonel Tom's Cabin," a parody of *Uncle Tom's Cabin*, Topsy rebels against the white folks and, much to Uncle Tom's dismay, wants to run off to Harlem.[43]

---

43. Langston Hughes, "The Em-Feuher Jones" (Typescript, Langston Hughes Papers), *Limitation of Life*, in Hatch (ed.), *Black Theatre, U.S.A.*, and "Colonel Tom's Cabin" (Typescript, Langston Hughes Papers). "Colonel Tom's Cabin" appears on a program for the Los Angeles production of *Don't You Want to Be Free?* by Hughes's New Negro Theater in Los Angeles. Hatch mentions "Little Eva's End" as on the program at the Harlem Suitcase Theater in his introduction to *Don't You Want to Be Free?* I suspect it is the same play as "Colonel Tom's Cabin."

These short pieces, along with *Soul Gone Home*, are the most blatant of Hughes's comic challenges to the genre of Negro comedy. His next full-length comedy, "Simple Takes a Wife," written in 1954, and the musical based on it, *Simply Heavenly*, written in 1957, reveal the limits of his sense of comic theater.[44]

The Simple plays are based on Hughes's great comic creation Jesse B. Semple, whose ruminations from his stool in Paddy's bar filled the columns of the Chicago *Defender* beginning November 21, 1942, and were later collected into five volumes. Jesse B. Semple, Simple for short, lives in Harlem, and through his voice the world of the average inhabitant of Harlem is articulated. His comments on politics, economics, law, love, marriage, family—and, continually, race—are alternately ironic, comic, serious. Whatever their mode, they always illuminate both the unique Afro-American experience and the human condition in general.

In Simple, Hughes found his perfect medium, for the sentiments expressed by Simple have their ultimate validation not in the principles that underlie them but in the humanity of the character who expresses them. Hughes is most compelling as a writer when his technique is most subjective—that is, when the world delineated exists as the extension of a persona, much as the folk tale hearkens back to the consciousness that articulates the world in the fashion of a story. When one reads Hughes, one first of all meets people and only secondarily gathers information or judgments about the world. This quality explains why his plays become most eloquent when he locates their vision in the voice of a central character.

Thus it was inevitable Hughes would adapt Jesse B. Semple to the stage. Hughes began his adaptation by simply selecting from the printed texts of *Simple Speaks His Mind*, published in 1950, and "Simple Takes a Wife" those episodes he felt suitable for the stage, and then

44. Langston Hughes, "Simple Takes A Wife" (Typescript drafts, Langston Hughes Papers). *Simply Heavenly* was originally presented by Stella Holt at the 85th St. Playhouse, N.Y. on May 21, 1957. Although plagued by financial and other problems, it played a total of 169 performances in New York. See O'Daniel (ed.), *Langston Hughes: Black Genius*, 217. Randolph Edmonds and the Florida A & M University Playmakers took the play on tour for the USO in 1963 but stopped performing it because both black and white troops saw it as racially controversial (Report, Randolph Edmonds to AETA Overseas Touring Committee, April, 1963, Langston Hughes Papers). "Simple Takes a Wife" has only been done abroad, notably in Prague. See Doris Abramson, "It'll Be Me: The Voice of Langston Hughes," 387.

modifying the dialogue. He selected as plot Simple's courtship of Joyce and as subplot, illustrating Simple's infidelities, his disastrous trip to New Jersey with his girlfriend Zarita, which ended in a car crash that landed him in the hospital and in trouble with Joyce. His friend Melon's pursuit of Mamie and the marital strife of Archie and Bodidley serve as minor love motifs. His drafts show that Hughes had special difficulty restricting himself to a manageable plot outline. The early versions of "Simple Takes a Wife" include several scenes between Simple and his young cousin, who is also his boarder, F. D., that Hughes was loath to strip from the final version; and many of Simple's choice monologues, included in earlier drafts, he also reluctantly discarded. The final version of "Simple Takes a Wife" retains only Simple's discourses on leading white troops from Mississippi and on Aunt Lucy's last whipping.

As Darwin Turner has pointed out, in the Simple stories, Jesse is a "folk hero . . . his foibles never detract from his dignity; for like the Greek Gods and the heroes of various myths, he is larger than life . . . he . . . is remembered primarily as a voice." Since the plays consist largely of action, Simple philosophizes little, and the activities that in the stories are simply the occasions for his reflections assume major proportions. Thus he becomes merely a "Harlem barfly," rather than "the embodied spirit of the Negro working class." [45]

Hughes's own likening of Simple to Charlie Chaplin's tramp suggests the problem of expression in the Simple plays as well. Chaplin's tramp accomplishes through the eloquence of gesture what the original Simple accomplishes through his voice. Without the stature provided by eloquence, Simple and Chaplin's tramp are sentimental, even ridiculous. Both "Simple Takes a Wife" and Simply Heavenly are charming, well-controlled, and engaging, but disappointing when compared to their brilliant source. Without Simple's monologues, his satirical bite and his insight are lost.

Hughes's comic genius is indisputable; however, it is not best displayed in stage comedies. As his theatrical experiments, his comic poetry, and his Simple stories reveal, his major talent is, ultimately, projecting the collective voice of the black folk, not creating characters who provoke interest because of their complexity or individual uniqueness. As he promised in "Note on Commercial Theatre," his

45. Turner, "Langston Hughes as Playwright," in O'Daniel (ed.), *Langston Hughes, Black Genius*, 91.

stage comedies attack and reclaim stereotypes white audiences have laughed *at*, transforming them into comic types a black audience can laugh *with*. Certainly the comedies pave the way for a play like Ossie Davis' wonderfully outrageous satire on plantation stereotypes, *Purlie Victorious*, first performed in 1961, and for the unabashed hamming that enlivens Richard Maltby, Jr.'s acclaimed revue *Ain't Misbehavin'*. However, plotted comedy based on types is a limited form, and Hughes's understanding of it is by and large conventional.

Between 1930 and 1938, Hughes completed seven full-length and several one-act conventional plays and worked on at least three or four others. However, his more original and significant dramatic work was yet to come, grounded in his experience with conventional theater but shaped by his poetry readings and a new influence: his encounter, both in the United States and in Russia, with agitprop and other kinds of radical theater.

In 1923 Hughes gave the first public reading of his poetry; in 1927 he inaugurated the form of dramatic reading he later made famous when he read his poems at Princeton University to the background singing of the Lincoln University Glee Club. By 1931 Hughes, an accomplished reader of his work, had developed a technique that he described in *I Wonder as I Wander* as to begin with comedy and then to move to those poems that explored the painful aspects of the black experience. In 1931 Hughes published *The Negro Mother*, a collection of six long poems, each spoken by a different member of the black community: the Colored Soldier, the Black Clown, a dejected unemployed worker, the Big-Timer, the Negro Mother, and the Dark Youth of the U.S.A.[46] Included in the volume are marginal notes for dramatic recitation instructing that each poem be read to music and in appropriate costume. Thus, by 1931, Hughes had begun to realize the dramatic potential of the poetry reading, a medium he would later develop into a complex dramatic form.

In the same year, to raise money for the Scottsboro Defense Fund, Hughes also wrote his first verse drama, *Scottsboro Limited*. Agitprop, introduced to New York by the Poletbuehne in 1930, provided, rather than Hughes's poetry readings, the model for this work. Douglas McDermott's description of a typical Poletbuehne performance might

46. Hughes, *I Wonder as I Wander*, 56–60, and *The Negro Mother and Other Dramatic Recitations* (1931; rpr. Freeport, N.Y., 1971).

equally describe the style of *Scottsboro Limited*: "A puritan simplicity
. . . was evident in the staging of agit-prop skits. The goal was to share
the play with its spectators. . . . The principle was that 'settings, costumes, make-up, lights are to be done away with as far as possible.'. . . Simplicity was reinforced in most productions by musical
accentuated words and rhythmical movements . . . [and words] were
snapped out swiftly and rhythmically." [47]

In Hughes's play, a series of short scenes recapitulates the story of
nine black youths summarily condemned to death for the alleged
rape of two white women. The boys, the eight white workers who appear at the end of the play, and, at times, the voices of the mob speak
in poetry; the various white characters in prose. The play is structured
by its rhythm as well as chronology; for example, Hughes dictates
that the trial be "conducted in jazz tempo: the white voices staccato,
high and shrill; the black voices deep as the rumble of drums." In the
play's final moments, the eighth boy proceeds to the electric chair, but
then breaks his bonds, saying:

> Burn *me* in the chair?
> NO! . . .
> Let the meek and humble turn the other cheek—
> I am not humble!
> I am not meek!
>
> . . . .
>
> All the world, listen!
> Beneath the wide sky
> In all the black lands
> Will echo this cry:
> I *will not die!*

As the boys smash the chair, they are encouraged by the "Red voices"
and joined by the eight white workers, who assure them they are no
longer alone. Finally, actors and audience join in a cry of "Fight, Fight,
Fight!" [48]

A stirring piece of propaganda, *Scottsboro Limited* equally pleads the
case of the Scottsboro defendants and publicizes the work of the
Communist party, which was providing the youths legal assistance
and had made of the case an international *cause célèbre*. Following the
1932 publication by Golden Stair Press of a small pamphlet entitled

47. Douglas McDermott, "Agit-prop: Production Practice in the Worker's
Theatre, 1932–1942," *Theatre Survey*, VII (November, 1966), 120–21.
48. Langston Hughes, *Scottsboro Limited: Four Poems and a Play* (New York,
1932), 12, 16–17, 18.

Scottsboro Limited, which contained the play and four poems, Hughes's international reputation was enhanced. The play was performed in Moscow and Paris as well as the United States, and the pamphlet translated into many languages and widely distributed.

While artistically slight, *Scottsboro Limited* uses techniques Hughes later employs in more complex and subtle ways. In this work he experiments with the conveying of information through brief dialogues, with the dramatic effects of rhythm and choral speech, and with the use of a single white figure in a series of roles, not only as dramatic economy, but also as a statement about white oppression. In *Scottsboro Limited*, the white figure plays interlocutor, judge, sheriff, jail keeper, and preacher, his metamorphoses suggesting the pervasiveness of oppression and that racism is a way of behaving that individuals can choose or reject.

Another agitprop play, "Angelo Herndon Jones," which Hughes wrote in 1935 for a *New Theater* competition, is in the style of *Waiting for Lefty*, Clifford Odet's famous work of the same year.[49] Having more of the characteristics of social realism than of agitprop, the play's staging draws on the theater Hughes encountered during his trip to the Soviet Union in 1932–1933. There, he reports in *I Wonder as I Wander*: "The theatre that fascinated me most of all was Oklopkov's Drasni Presnia, the most advanced in production styles of any playhouse I have ever seen. Arena staging was the least novel of its innovations. . . . From the young Oklopkov and the older Meyerhold, both of whom were kind enough to talk with me and to invite me to attend rehearsals, I acquired a number of interesting ways of staging plays, some of which I later utilized in my own Negro history play, *Don't You Want to Be Free?* done in Harlem without a stage, curtains, or sets."[50]

His earlier venture, "Angelo Herndon Jones," employs a simple set. A wall in the center of the stage bearing a poster announcing an Angelo Herndon meeting divides the stage into three playing areas; lighting indicates scene changes. Short dialogues delineate the poverty-stricken lives of the main characters, Lottie and Sadie Mae, two prostitutes; Buddy Jones and his pal Link; Buddy's pregnant girlfriend,

49. Langston Hughes, "Angelo Herndon Jones" (Typescript, Langston Hughes Papers). According to Malcolm Goldstein, "Angelo Herndon Jones" won the competition because it was the only stageable play received. See *The Political Stage: American Drama and Theatre of the Great Depression* (New York, 1974), 161–63.

50. Hughes, *I Wonder as I Wander*, 199–200.

Viola; and her mother, Ma Jenkins. When Ma Jenkins and Viola are evicted, Viola finds Buddy at the Angelo Herndon meeting and begs for help. He brings the whole meeting to battle successfully against the eviction. The play concludes as Buddy decides to work with Herndon and to name his and Viola's child Angelo Herndon Jones.

"Angelo Herndon Jones," like *Scottsboro Limited*, is narrow in scope and intention; its purpose clearly is to support the kind of interracial political coalition typified by Herndon's organization. However, while the *Scottsboro Limited* characters are highly stylized and undifferentiated figures, those in "Angelo Herndon Jones" speak and behave realistically. Only the voices of the idealized brotherhood of workers lack all veracity. Moreover, the Scottsboro boys are literally imprisoned in and by the white world, and the play affords them little ground of their own, in either setting or language. "Angelo Herndon Jones," however, depicts characters not only from but in the black community, and when black and white workers arrive to fight the eviction, the white workers are absorbed into that community, this sense reinforced by the fact that they are sent by a black leader. Hughes quickly abandoned the highly stylized form of Poletbuehne agitprop, for it necessarily restricted how his characters could express themselves.

However, stage reality is not simply a matter of what occurs on stage; it also is a function of what the play shares with and demands of its audience, and agitprop particularly attends to that interplay. In *Scottsboro Limited*, Hughes has the central white character, as well as the mob and the "Red voices" at the end, arise from the audience, which joins in the final cry of "Fight!" "Angelo Herndon Jones" employs no such devices, but this aspect of agitprop clearly intrigued Hughes, for both his chronicle and his gospel plays include the audience in the event. The former are essentially stories told to the audience; the latter make of the audience a congregation, a role more complex than that of mere spectator. From his poetry reading and his early agitprop, Hughes evolved his most original and significant theatrical work.

In 1938 Hughes founded his first theater group and wrote for it *Don't You Want To Be Free?*, which ran on weekends for a total of 135 performances in a loft on West 125th Street in Harlem. A striking departure from his previous work, *Don't You Want to Be Free?* draws on his own poetry, his readings, his experiments with agitprop, and his increasingly precise sense of what he wished to accomplish in theater. *Don't You*

Want to Be Free? succeeds in projecting the collective voice of black people and in creating the relationship between play and audience crucial to transforming both a black audience's relation to theater and a white audience's relation to plays about blacks. Indeed, it finally resolves the problem of establishing a black stage reality. For this reason, *Don't You Want to Be Free?* became the prototype for much of Hughes's dramatic work over the next fifteen years and influenced his gospel plays as well.

In *Don't You Want to Be Free?* the characters are deliberately representative rather than individual. The narrator is simply the Young Man, and other characters are A Girl, A Boy, and so on. The story is that of black Americans, and it is told directly to the audience, which, at various points, is invited to share and to respond. Most important, it establishes its setting through the narrator's voice. Like the storyteller or preacher, whose words evoke a landscape and fill in its details, the narrative voice performs an imaginative act; the landscape evoked and depicted is that of the black imagination, which reveals black history as it is recalled by black people.

Hughes subtitled *Don't You Want to Be Free?* "From Slavery Through the Blues to Now—and Then Some! with Singing, Music and Dancing." The play chronicles black American history by focusing on how black people have experienced and been affected by oppression. The play's substance is Hughes's own poetry, mostly gathered from two collections, *The Weary Blues*, published in 1926, and *Fine Clothes to the Jew*, published in 1927. His poems flow naturally from the characters, lending perspective and form to the situations that occasion them. Principally, the poetry attends to the emotional impact of various events. For example, a lynching gives rise to the following lines, spoken by the victim's lover:

> Way down South in Dixie,
> (Break the heart of me!)
> They hung my dark young lover
> To a cross road's tree.

A journey north is accompanied by Hughes's blues lyrics.

> Goin' down de road, Lawd,
> Goin' down de road,
> Down de road, Lawd,
> Way, way down de road.
> Got to find somebody
> To help me carry dis load.

Traditional material is included as well: for example, this spiritual is an old woman's response to the narrator's account of various slave revolts:

> Oh, nobody knows
> The trouble I've seen
> Nobody knows but Jesus.[51]

The play opens on a bare stage, "except for a lynch rope and an auction block. No special lighting. Only actors needed—and an audience." The Young Man steps forward and invites the audience to share in the play: "It's about me, except that it's not just about me now standing here talking to you—but it's about me yesterday, and about me tomorrow. I'm colored. . . . Well, this show is about what it means to be colored in America. Listen." Then, as prologue, the narrator recites Hughes's poem "I Am a Negro."[52]

The first sequence depicts the period from African origins to the Civil War. Central to each episode is its rhythm: an intensification of oppression creates conflict, which in turn gives rise to revolt. In the early episodes the revolt is by a single character and is cruelly repressed. In later scenes depicting contemporary Harlem, all the characters rise to recreate the Harlem riots of 1935.

As in Hughes's earlier works, one white character plays all the white roles; toward the end of the play, his role changes every few minutes. The increasing pace of the changes lends him the aura of a devilish trickster figure: in every situation portrayed he attempts to inflict yet another hardship on the black characters. The Young Man, who serves as combination narrator, raisonneur, and spokesman when he is not directly involved in the action, provides continuity of a different kind. It is his story: he is the young man who attacks the overseer for cheating him of money due on his crop—an assault for which he is lynched. The same actor, in the next scene, exposes another type of victimization through his dialogue with the Mulatto Girl, who becomes a prostitute rather than earn two dollars per week in a white family's kitchen. Their interchange is adapted from Hughes's poem "Ruby Brown." Bitterly, the Young Man turns away from her and heads north, singing, "Goin' down the road." During the next sequence, he steps out of the action and becomes narrator again. While the many roles given the

51. Langston Hughes, *Don't You Want to Be Free?* in Hatch (ed.), *Black Theatre, U.S.A.*, 268, 269, 266.
52. *Ibid.*, 263.

white character lend him a devilish aura, the many roles and resurrec-
tions of the central black character suggest and celebrate the indom-
itable spirit of black Americans, who continue to survive the various
torments inflicted upon them.

Hughes's poem "Bound No'th Blues" introduces "what came to be
known as the Blues Sequence of the play. . . . Pianist Carroll Tate
rocked the piano in the old fashioned blues tradition and the audience swayed with it laughing, crying and pounding its feet rhythmically." [53] The sequence is a discourse on and demonstration of the
blues: weary blues, family blues, loveless blues, left-lonesome blues,
morning-after blues. While some of the material is traditional, most
of the lyrics are Hughes's own, and each is accompanied by an appropriate dramatic situation.

The succeeding scenes, incorporating some of Hughes's favorite
poems ("Brass Spitoons," "When Suzanna Jones Wears Red," and "The
Negro Mother"), suggest aspects of the black experience in the North.
The pattern of the early scenes continues with an important new element. When the Landlord comes to evict Mother and Son, the Young
Man, as the Son, challenges him: "You don't live in [this house]! We
live here! This is Harlem." His comment marks a change in attitude;
until this episode, the Young Man's refrain and that of other characters
was individual—"I am tired." Now, finally, the refrain is collective—
"This is Harlem speaking now. . . . Harlem is tired"—and the pace of
the play accelerates until the tiredness erupts into rage and riot.[54]

But riots solve nothing, a member of the audience points out. The
Young Man agrees and observes that the solution is to organize. He
concludes the play with a short lesson on workers' solidarity.

> *Member of the audience.*   You mean organize with that white waiter who won't
>   serve you? Organize with him?
> *Young Man.*   Yes, I mean with that waiter, too. His problem's the same as
>   ours—if he only knew it.

Finally, actors and audience join hands, singing, "Who wants to come
and join hands with me? / Who wants to make one great unity?" [55]

This joining of actors and audience, for white members of the audi-

---

53. Mitchell, *Black Drama*, 104–105. Hughes extracted the blues sequence
and extended it into a short play, "Blues Sketches," for separate production
(Typescript, Langston Hughes Papers).
54. Hughes, *Don't You Want to Be Free?* 273, 276.
55. *Ibid*, 276, 277.

ence, requires moving from their territory into the black territory created by the play. It demands that the white audience not simply see the black world but see themselves as the black world sees them—that is, as white figures in a black ground and a black landscape. In making this demand, *Don't You Want to Be Free?* moves beyond the dramatic conclusion of *Scottsboro Limited*, for the political unity on which the later play insists also asks the white members of the audience to shift their ground. The shift is subtle but important, for it is unprecedented in drama. It also counteracts the difficulty Hughes has with the political implications of his invitation.

A contemporary review of *Don't You Want to Be Free?*, part of an article on Hughes appearing in the *Crisis*, suggests that the play runs into difficulty when the poet turns from what he feels to what he thinks: "Langston Hughes *feels* the oppression, the pain and misery, the greatness and beauty of his race; but he only *thinks* (in this play, at least) that they should organize with the white worker to promote their betterment. . . . He *feels* the Negro as his race, but only *thinks* himself (at least, in this work) a member of a white and black working class."[56]

One might quarrel with McLeod's statement as a generalization about Hughes's poetry, but it is a useful comment about his plays. When Hughes pursues the logic of emotion, his sense is unfailing; when he employs leftist rhetoric, his work often falters.[57] More accurately, this play and other of his works as well falter when they move from the articulation of the folk. The revolutionary sentiments spoken do not come from existing people or circumstances, and Hughes consistently fails as a propagandist because he is unable to find the voice of humanity. *Don't You Want to Be Free?* in particular fails when it strays from the folk vision that informs it, which the critic George Kent describes this way:

56. Norman McLeod, "The Poetry and Argument of Langston Hughes," *Crisis*, XLV (November, 1938), 359.
57. This is not always true in his writing, however. McLeod cites "A Revolutionary Ad for the Waldorf Astoria" as an example of Hughes's work in which the revolutionary sentiment is felt and successfully articulated. According to Hughes, the poem contributed to Hughes's break with his patron, Mrs. Rufus Osgood Mason (whose name he never revealed but whose identity became public after his death). It addresses the opening of the famed Waldorf Astoria in the midst of the Great Depression. See *The Big Sea*, 320–24, for the poem and his patron's comments, and Rampersad, *The Life of Langston Hughes*, Volume I, 193, for some contradictory comments.

From the animal tales to the hipsterish urban mythmaking, folk tradition has *is-ness.* . . . Things are funny, sad, tragic, tragicomic, bitter, sweet, tender, harsh, awe-inspiring, cynical, other-worldly—sometimes, alternately expressing the conflicting and contradictory qualities; sometimes, expressing conflicting qualities simultaneously. . . . Thus, upon entering the universe of Langston Hughes, one leaves at its outer darkness the *type of rationality* whose herculean exertions are for absolute resolution of contradictions and external imposition of symmetry. . . . In Langston Hughes's vision, both in regard to the folk and to himself, the most nearly consistent focus is upon a life-manship that preserves and celebrates humanity in the face of impossible odds.[58]

It is not that work embedded in a folk tradition cannot embody elements of ideology. Kent continues: "Folk vision could suddenly shift from tenderness to biting cynicism and . . . within its womb a pragmatic embracement of ideological impulses that promised survival was a secure tradition." But the ideological sentiments expressed in *Don't You Want to Be Free?* are articulated in the idiom of the left that generated them. This use of a borrowed language confirms McLeod's conclusion that Hughes thought rather than felt their validity.[59]

The tension between the awkwardness of Hughes's ideological statements and the eloquence of the rest of his material decreased in the later versions of *Don't You Want to Be Free?*, not because Hughes had found an artistic resolution to the problem, but because he stopped expressing his political and social beliefs in an overtly Marxist fashion. He reworked the play at least six times during the next sixteen years; each version updates the material and reflects the immediate political situation.[60] The 1944 version includes scenes depicting segregation in the army and the exclusion of black workers from a war plant; the play decries "dividedness at home" as hindering the war effort. It omits the Harlem riot and ends with a plea for unity in the war effort. The 1946 version concludes with the insistence that, the war over, democracy must be ensured at home. The 1952 version follows the Harlem riots with a conversation between the Young Man and a Dixiecrat about the number of black Americans who died over-

58. George Kent, *Blackness and the Adventure of Western Culture* (Chicago, 1972), 53, 54.

59. *Ibid.*, 56. Hughes's blues opera "De Organizer" (Typescript, Langston Hughes Papers), written from 1939 to 1941, articulates political sentiments more successfully.

60. There are six versions of the play in the Langston Hughes Papers, dated 1938, 1944, 1946, 1949, 1952, 1963; my discussion is based on these texts.

seas and in the riots at home. It clearly equates the riots with the black fight for freedom, and ends with the spiritual "O Freedom." Reflecting the conservative political climate, the camaraderie between black and white workers depicted in earlier versions is cut from the 1952 revision, and the play urges integration as its sole political goal rather than class struggle.[61] For the centennial of emancipation in 1963, Hughes made a final revision. Not much is changed except that when the audience member asks the Young Man what to do, he advises him of the activities of such organizations as the NAACP and the Congress of Racial Equality (CORE).

Hughes borrowed the form and much of the material of Don't You Want to Be Free? for other plays. "For This We Fight" shapes the material in Don't You Want to Be Free? for a different narrator, a black father in uniform explaining why he has enlisted to his son, who has heard a classmate say blacks ought not to join the war effort.[62] Historical sequences in this play are more detailed than in its prototype; it is replete with the names of black heroes, leaders, and artists. The play clearly equates the enemy overseas with repression at home, and expresses the hope that defeat of the enemy will affect domestic fascism.

In 1955 and 1956 Hughes also adapted the form of Don't You Want to Be Free? to two occasional pieces. The first, "St. James: Sixty Years Young," celebrates the history of St. James Presbyterian Church; the second, "The Ballot and Me," was commissioned by the church for its voter-registration campaign.[63] Subtitled "The Negro's Past in Suffrage: A Historical Sequence," the latter recounts the history of black enfranchisement since the American Revolution, crowding the stage with important historical figures, including all blacks who held federal electoral office since Reconstruction.

Finally, in 1964, Hughes returned once more to the format and some of the material of Don't You Want to Be Free? for his acclaimed

61. In 1953 Hughes was summoned before Senator Joseph McCarthy, and during the McCarthy era he was a target of the political attitudes that era reflected. See Berry, Langston Hughes: Before and Beyond Harlem, particularly the epilogue.

62. Langston Hughes, "For This We Fight" (Typescript, Langston Hughes Papers).

63. Langston Hughes, "St. James: Sixty Years Young" and "The Ballot and Me" (Typescripts, Langston Hughes Papers).

"Jericho-Jim Crow," which celebrates the civil rights struggle.[64] As in *Don't You Want to Be Free?*, in "Jericho-Jim Crow," one character plays all the white roles, and a boy, a girl, an old man, and an old woman depict a series of black characters whose experiences symbolize the history related. To the blues and spirituals used in the earlier play, Hughes added gospel songs and a full choir; in the style of his later work, the play recreates the atmosphere of a church meeting.

Like that of *Don't You Want to Be Free?*, one purpose of "Jericho-Jim Crow" is to encourage those engaged in political struggle and to urge others to join them. The play's melding of religious, political, and social material reflects the actual role of the black church in the postwar civil rights fight and recalls the critical role of the church in the freedom struggle throughout Afro-American history. Moreover, the religious material provides both the conviction and the dramatic energy that the ideological material in the earlier plays intended but failed to provide. "Jericho-Jim Crow" does not falter as did the earlier pieces from which it is derived. Its sustained conviction reveals again that Hughes is most at home when using the forms of American black expression. Although Hughes was not, in the conventional sense, a religious man, he understood fully the place of black religion in the black imagination. Because of that understanding, he frequently depicted black religion and employed its forms in his drama.

For Hughes the 1960s was a period of renewed dramatic activity, and all his plays from that time focus on music and religion, subjects that bring together the concerns of his entire dramatic career. The form that most nearly realizes what Hughes wanted to accomplish in the theater is the gospel play. His use of the storyteller and of music in the chronicle plays sheds light on his turning to religious themes and on the gospel play as the almost inevitable result of his earlier experimentation.

The storytellers and their art are central to all folk culture, and what John Donald Wade writes of southern humor obtains for all tellers and their tales: "Somehow the story itself is not primarily the thing one laughs at. If that were true, a story read or told by a radio-entertainer or by a boresome man with a good memory would be as

64. Langston Hughes, "Jericho-Jim Crow" (Typescript, Langston Hughes Papers).

amusing as the one heard acceptably. The important part of a story is the effect it has on the teller, and one must naturally know the teller to perceive what that effect is. . . . For the initiated understand well enough that the teller, in telling, is himself the main point of his story."[65]

The Young Man in the prologue of *Don't You Want to Be Free?* presents himself in just this fashion: he advises the audience that hearing his story requires coming to know him. Moreover, by telling his story, he comes to know himself, for in his various roles, he explores the historical postures of the black man in America. Hughes's use of the storytelling technique is most obvious in his poetry, wherein speakers frequently become known through the sentiments they express.

The process set in motion by the device of storytelling creates a novel, challenging social situation. Coming to know the speaker requires that the audience offer him a hearing. This is an obvious but not generally acknowledged aspect of the relationship between storyteller and audience. The type of respectful attention in, for example, *Don't You Want to Be Free?*, wherein the actor and stage reality are black, is an exceptional social gesture in America. For the black audience, the resulting situation redeems the degrading history of the stage Negro. For most whites, the situation is rare inside the theater and outside it.

The situation established by this dramatic relationship is analogous to the relationship between preacher and congregation in the black church, to which Hughes finally turned for the form and substance of his theatrical work. In *Black Preaching*, Henry Mitchell equates storytelling techniques with those of a good preacher. His comments clarify why Hughes was attracted to the black sermon as a theatrical event:

> As is true with all good storytelling, the Black Bible story must first of all be a work of art in its own right. The teller must tell it as if the telling were an end in itself, even though he may intersperse asides to sustain the obvious relevance of the action in the story. At any time while the story is being told, the teller must be caught up in it as if he had seen it happen. . . . He must so communicate the story as to cause his audience to feel as if they, too, are at the scene of the action.
>
> And yet the story must never be told for the sake of mere entertainment. . . . The response so often and so freely generated by this great art

65. John Donald Wade, "Southern Humour," in W. T. Couch (ed.), *Culture in the South* (Chapel Hill, 1935), 625–26.

must be focused beyond the teller to the source of the message, and to his will for the worshipper.[66]

What congregations want to know from preachers is what God told them through their encounter with the Word—the impact of the story on the teller. A good black sermon moves the congregation to dialogue, to a call-and-response antiphonal exchange with the preacher. This dialogue springs from the emotions generated by the sermon, by the preacher's fervor, and by the intensity of communication achieved.[67] Much of what Hughes wanted to accomplish with his art is captured perfectly in Mitchell's description of the climax to a black sermon: "In a black climax at its best, the idea—the point which has been made—is embraced and celebrated. It is, as it were, burned into the consciousness of the hearer."[68]

If black religion is one cornerstone of American black culture, black music is the other, and the two are not really separable. Black music, both religious and secular, was Hughes's lifelong passion. In addition to reading his poetry to music, he wrote lyrics for blues, gospel songs, operas, and popular music.[69] However, his use of songs in musical comedies or operas differs radically from his use of black music in his chronicles and gospel plays. For example, there is a crucial difference between his use of music in his musical *Simply Heavenly* or his conception of the music in *Street Scene*, and music as it occurs in *Don't You Want to Be Free*? In the last play, blues and spirituals not only provide musical background and bridges for the action but are the characters' responses to events. For example, when an old woman covers the bodies of the dead after a revolt at the auction block, singing "nobody knows the trouble I've seen," the spiritual, or "sorrow song" as

66. Henry H. Mitchell, *Black Preaching* (Philadelphia, 1970), 133–34, 122.
67. For much of this discussion I am indebted to Bruce A. Rosenberg, *The Art of the American Folk Preacher* (New York, 1970).
68. Mitchell, *Black Preaching*, 195.
69. In addition to the lyrics written for his own plays using music, Hughes completed four opera libretti, *Troubled Island*, "The Barrier," "Esther," in 1957, and "Port Town," in 1960. He also provided the lyrics for Elmer Rice's *Street Scene*, with music by Kurt Weill, and for "Just Around the Corner," from a book by Abby Mann and Bernard Drew, and music by Joe Sherman. All these works were produced. Typescripts in the Langston Hughes Papers also include "De Organizer," music by James P. Johnson, which has never been produced; "Soul Gone Home," written for Ulysses Kay and performed in Spring, 1957; and six or seven other musical works in various stages of completion.

W. E. B. Du Bois called it, is her response to three hundred years of slavery. Similarly, in the "Blues Sequence" of the play, the blues are the life experiences of the characters expressed in verse and song. Each performance is a reincarnation of the experience that originally inspired the blues, and the form itself a reminder of how Afro-Americans have transcended suffering. Ellison's well-known definition of the blues is illuminating here: "The blues is an impulse to keep the painful details and episodes of a brutal experience alive in one's aching consciousness, to finger its jagged grain, and to transcend it, not by the consolation of philosophy but by squeezing from it a near-tragic, near-comic lyricism. As a form, the blues is an autobiographical chronicle of personal catastrophe." [70]

In musicals, songs may express a character's emotions, but the plays typically are not about music as part of the fabric of the world portrayed. A character may even tell his life in song, but the form of that song does not arise from a cultural ritual and mode of expression to which the audience responds almost instinctively, knowing the shape of what will follow. Hughes described the usual reaction to the blues in his definition prefacing Fine Clothes to the Jew: "The mood of the Blues is almost always despondency, but when they are sung, people laugh." [71] While some musicologists have taken issue with Hughes's observations, his suggestion is important: the laughter is a recognition of, and an assent to, the entire reality evoked by the opening chords on a blues singer's guitar.

In discussing Hughes and the folk tradition, George Kent comments that Hughes "seldom takes up a form that could not express the folk or that expresses forms of response to existence that are foreign to their sensibility." [72] The forms of response to existence finally become Hughes's subject, and therefore, in the chronicle and gospel plays, music is an integral part of the work. Moreover, the conventional play is about a people or an event; form and content are discrete. In the chronicle and gospel plays, the play is the event and in some sense an expression of the actors themselves; thus the distinction between form and content is eradicated.

Hughes's first play with a religious theme, The Sun Do Move, pub-

70. Ralph Ellison, Shadow and Act (New York, 1964), 78.
71. Langston Hughes, Fine Clothes to the Jew (New York, 1927).
72. Kent, Blackness and the Adventure of Western Culture, 59.

lished in 1942, is subtitled "A Music Play." Divided into prologue and three acts, the play is episodic, reflecting the influence of Hughes's chronicle plays and his brief Hollywood experience in 1939 with Clarence Muse, writing the scenario and some songs for a movie entitled *Way Down South*. In his production notes for *The Sun Do Move*, Hughes recommends: "Production without scenery in the simplified manner of OUR TOWN or WAITING FOR LEFTY. The play may be done in the style of a motion picture or radio drama with no break in continuity, no intermissions, the spirituals between scenes serving as transition music during the blackouts."[73]

The Sun Do Move employs a conventional plot to recount the story of slavery. Principally, the tale concerns Rock, who is sold away from his wife, Mary, just after his son, Little Rock, is born. He vows to escape, return for his family, and bring them north. His first attempt results in recapture and the death of his companion, Frog. His second attempt, seven years later, succeeds. He returns for Mary, and together, with the help of the underground railroad and the Quakers, they safely reach freedom. But Little Rock is not with them, for sold away from his mother, he has died. The play ends as Rock joins the Union army to fight in the Civil War.

The Sun Do Move uses spirituals and other traditional music extensively to express the emotions of individuals and of the whole community. The music becomes the fabric of the play, evoking both the historical period and its meaning to black people. Yet, as the title of the play suggests, *The Sun Do Move* makes a more complex use of both the forms and the substance of black religion. The title is taken from a famous sermon, "The Sun Do Move," first preached by John Jasper of Richmond, Virginia. Hughes may have had the original preaching in mind when Rock's grandmother, Grandma Lanthie, says about freedom, "I know it'll come, chile, sure as the sun do move," for the play is set within the time of John Jasper's preaching career.[74]

The sermon is principally concerned with resolving the conflict between the Lord's word and scientific teaching that the sun stands still. The first part of the sermon takes as text Josh. 10:13: "So the sun stood still and the moon halted until a nation had taken its ven-

73. Langston Hughes, *The Sun Do Move* (New York, 1942). The original title for the play was *Sold Away*.
  74. Ibid., 13.

geance." Noting that the text suggests "de Lord God is a man of war,"the preacher disclaims any knowledge of how the sun actually behaves but asserts that his trust is in the word of the Lord.[75] The thematic complexity of the sermon resides in the juxtaposition of the recounting of Joshua's triumph over the Amorites with the assertion that the power and the word of the Lord is the ultimate truth. Thus, while ostensibly the argument concerns the mechanics of natural phenomena—if the Lord could stop the sun, then, that implies, it was moving—the deeper concern is with the power of the Lord that is not seen, that resides in faith only, and with its triumph over secular knowledge based on logic and on empirical evidence.

The play is almost an exegesis of the sermon. Only Rock and Mary's faith in themselves and in freedom, of which empirically they know nothing, makes freedom possible. Most of the other slaves in The Sun Do Move are portrayed as lacking the faith and vision to dare freedom. None of them know where the North is; only Rock says he will find out. None believe escape from the quarry of Rock's second owner possible except Rock, who, seeing David as emblem for his action, uses a stone to strike the guard and escape.

Both the presentation of the desire for freedom as constituting a triumph of human spirit and imagination and the play's constant use of spirituals and Old Testament motifs suggest the presence of an apparent contradiction similar to that in the sermon "The Sun Do Move." In the play, escape to freedom becomes the triumph of faith and imagination over empirical situation and historical fact. The portraits of the other slaves, sometimes comic, sometimes compassionate, suggest that they are blind, whereas Mary, Rock, and Grandma Lanthie see clearly with the light of faith and heightened understanding. Their clear vision defies the empirical, "secular," logical givens of their situation by transcending them, just as the preacher in "The Sun Do Move" defies the secular interpretation of natural phenomena rather than denying it.

The prologue to The Sun Do Move provides a delicate, poetic statement of the play's intention. A sweeper enters and explains to his companion, Joe, that he is sweeping away "Monday, Tuesday, Wednesday, Thursday, Friday . . . everything but yesterday."

75. John Jasper, "The Sun Do Move," in Arna Bontemps and Langston Hughes (eds.), The Book of Negro Folklore (New York, 1958), 228.

Joe. Then I guess I got to take off these drapes cause they won't be
  stylish. . . .
Sweeper. Don't worry. You don't need no drapes in Africa.

They step into the African past, into an Ashanti scene interrupted by
the arrival of slavers, who carry off King Ebewe, Queen Melanthie, and
their people. The scene shifts to the Middle Passage and the death of
King Ebewe, portrayed in song and dance. Joe and the sweeper appear
again, now dressed in the garb of 1800. The scene suggested is the
New Orleans slave market, and the sweeper is now "sweeping away
blood and tears. . . . The white folks don't like to walk in that stuff—
not here in New Orleans. The fine ladies might get blood . . . on their
slippers." [76] The slave Melanthie, Grandma Lanthie of the later scenes,
is auctioned off.

The sweeping motif concludes the play as well. Mary's final speech
as Rock goes to war recapitulates what has occurred: "While you're
gone, I'll keep the doorstep clean. I'll sweep away yesterday. There
won't be no more slavery time sorrows no where when you come
back. . . . (*as the cast moves onstage behind her*) I look back and I see all the
miseries of slavery time . . . . Then I look ahead—and see my race
blossoming like the rose. . . . I see my people everywhere, all over
America, all over the world taking part in the making of a new life.
Folks, the sun do move!" [77]

The sweeping motif comments eloquently on what the play has accomplished. Rather than sweep a painful past under the rug, *The Sun
Do Move* allows that past to be reknown, reexperienced, and assimi-
lated as painful heritage made triumphant through faith and thus
transformed into a foundation for the future. The name Rock boldly
suggests an equation between the church and the slaves of the past,
and Mary's final vision, ending "Folks, the sun do move!" is a triumph
of faith. Hughes's stirring, idealistic, but ultimately sentimental conclusion is qualified by its allusion to the sermon that provides the
play's central motif. For although the sermon celebrates the triumph
of faith and the power of the Lord, it also acknowledges the powerful
obstacles placed in the path of faith.

The form of *The Sun Do Move* lies between the form of the chronicle
plays and the sermon form to which it alludes through title and

76. Hughes, *The Sun Do Move*, 1, 3.
77. *Ibid*, 46.

theme. While it takes religious material as its inspiration and includes the spirituals as expression of the slave experience, finally, its
dramatic form is more conventional than that of Hughes's chronicle
plays. The form of *The Sun Do Move* remains in evidence in the early
drafts of Hughes's first gospel play, "Black Nativity." [78]

"Black Nativity" tells the Christmas story in song, dance, and mime.
Its form is a black church meeting, which concludes as a church service. The narration is taken from the gospel of Luke and from poems
written by Hughes for the play. A choir accompanies the retelling of
the Christmas story by the narrator.

Although spirituals had long been used in folk plays about black
people, "Black Nativity" marks the first use of gospel music on stage.
Hughes described gospel music as the freewheeling, free-swinging
original of the spirituals, deeply rooted in the culture of the Negro
masses—"happy songs, celebrating the greatness and glory of God
and affirming his ways with men." [79] But the play is considerably more
than a gospel concert. The drafts of "Black Nativity" reveal clearly the
purpose informing Hughes's writing.

Early versions of "Black Nativity" use the form of the chronicle play.
A narrator introduces the action, and the play unfolds as a series of
vignettes. Through succeeding drafts, the role of the pilgrims seeking
Christ gradually increases, and their discussion about religion finally
becomes a church meeting. The speech of King Balthazar gradually
assumes the shape and rhythm of a black sermon; as a sermon, it is
given to an elder, and the pilgrims become the congregation of the
church meeting with which the play concludes. The vignettes lose their
dialogue and become mime and dance; finally, all dialogue in the play
is spoken by the narrator, who is also exhorter. In other words, the
narration becomes a sermon, and the play, a church service.

The transitions in the various drafts make clear Hughes's artistic
commitment to exploring the way knowledge and faith are experienced and made vital by black culture. In a sense, "Black Nativity" and
the other gospel plays become hermeneutic events; "Black Nativity"
celebrates the Savior's birth by exploring and celebrating its meaning

78. Langston Hughes, "Black Nativity" (Drafts and typescript, Langston
Hughes Papers).
79. From an article written by Hughes for the Spoleto Festival of Two
Worlds's program notes for "Black Nativity" (Typescript, Langston Hughes
Papers).

in a particular tradition. Finally, the play does not simply depict the Christmas story or even a black church service. Rather, it gives its audience an experience of black religion, of the special meaning and significance black culture has given to the Bible stories.

An immediate success, "Black Nativity" opened in New York in 1961, traveled to other cities in the eastern United States, and then to the Spoleto Festival of Two Worlds in Italy and throughout Europe. Finally, it returned to New York for another run and closed there in January, 1964.[80]

Hughes's focus on the black church service became even more precise in his next gospel play, "Gospel Glory." A note from Hughes attached to a typescript instructs that the play must relate its material as though it is told by an elder of the church and sung by brothers and sisters in the choir. No settings or costumes other than choir robes are to be used.[81] "Do you know your Bible?" the elder asks the choir, and the play is their response: it relates the life of Christ from the Nativity to the Ascension into heaven. Tableaux and mime act as figuras for certain events: the Nativity, the healing of the blind man, the meeting of the woman by the wayside, the enlisting of black Simon, and the mourning of Martha and Mary.

Hughes's third gospel play, *The Prodigal Son*, is even more precisely structured as a sermon. The earliest drafts, like those of "Black Nativity," tell a biblical story through a series of vignettes, in this play portraying the stages of the prodigal son's journey into sin. The prodigal son's employer finally brings the repentant son to a camp meeting, where he is saved before returning home. In the final version, the narrator has become exhorter and the play a sermon.

In selecting the story of the prodigal son, Hughes chose, according to Bruce Rosenberg, the topic of one of the most popular folk sermons in America, and his use of the biblical material is also traditional. In *Black Preaching*, Mitchell explains the relation of the text to the sermon as follows: "In the first place, the story should include, without alteration, every possible aspect of the Bible account. . . . The written account, is a condensation which requires reconstitution, just like dried milk or dehydrated soup if one is to have a full meal."

---

80. The production information for "Black Nativity" and the other gospel plays is from O'Daniel (ed.), *Langston Hughes, Black Genius*, 218.
81. Langston Hughes, "Gospel Glory" (Typescript, Langston Hughes Papers).

Like a good black preacher, the exhorter in The Prodigal Son moves in and out of the story to make its meaning clear to a contemporary audience. As he speaks, the story unfolds through dance, mime, and the songs of the choir. Moving away from the text, he rushes over to save the prodigal son from Jezebel's lovemaking, saying: "Listen, son! Listen! Sin will gangrene your body and putrify your soul. You can't be wishy-washy about sin. Look sin in the face and stare it down. . . . So stand up and look sin in the face and conquer it."[82] He includes in his list of temptations not only loose women but heroin as well. While the exhorter's narration comes directly from Luke, his pleas to the prodigal son derive from traditional sermon rhetoric.

Hughes intended the atmosphere of his gospel plays to be one of reverence, wonder, and joy. He once admonished a cast for acknowledging applause after individual numbers: the show was to be a church meeting, never a concert.[83] Reviews of the play suggest his casts created the atmosphere he desired.

Hughes's gospel plays constitute a particular and exciting response to the demands of black theater. They offer both black and white audiences a satisfying experience and easily address their differing interests, for the plays inform a white audience of the black religious tradition and simultaneously provide a black audience with a theatrical celebration and reexperience of a familiar, crucial part of their heritage. The plays are also appropriate in the parish halls, schools, and community centers where they have been performed. In a sense, their meaning varies according to the setting for the performance. The context of theater adds an element of artifice that a community production, possibly within an actual church setting, would avoid. The gospel plays are both plays and religious expressions. In this versatility is

82. Rosenberg, Art of the American Folk Preacher, 29; Mitchell, Black Preaching, 138; Langston Hughes, The Prodigal Son, Players, XLIII (October–November, 1967), 19. This is the version performed in 1965 at Greenwich Mews Theatre, N.Y., on a double bill with Bertolt Brecht's Exception to the Rule. Apparently, some controversy accrued over the final version. A letter to the producers from a member of the cast, G. Jeanette Hodge, claims that the staged version was a community project and that the play was merely "retold" by Hughes. But the earliest draft in the Langston Hughes Papers is dated 1963. The Prodigal Son opened May, 1965, in New York and then toured Europe in Fall, 1965.
83. A note Hughes wrote to the producers of "Black Nativity" after he saw the London production in 1963 insists that the cast maintain a religious atmosphere, and such notes exist in the files of all the gospel plays in the Langston Hughes Papers.

also their limitation; the closer they come to being what they depict, the less able they are to comment upon what they celebrate, to provide a new perspective on the experience.

Perhaps because he sensed this problem, Hughes, in his last full-length play, *Tambourines to Glory*, returned to the form of conventional stage realism to examine aspects of black religion and black music. Indeed, *Tambourines to Glory* in part addresses the entire phenomenon of staging a religious experience and thus comments ironically on his gospel plays.

Tambourines to Glory was first produced in Westport, Connecticut, in 1960 and on Broadway in 1963. While it combined two forms in which Hughes had recently achieved popular success, the gospel play and the musical, *Tambourines to Glory* was not received well. After the Westport tryout, Hughes suggested to the producer that the play fell between the two stools of the musical and the gospel play. He attributed the problem to the way songs were sung, but the fault lies rather in the play's entire conception.[84]

Hughes's note to *Tambourines to Glory* sums up much of his dramatic work as well.

> *Tambourines to Glory* is a fable, a folk ballad in stage form, told in broad and very simple terms—if you will, a comic strip . . . about problems which can only convincingly be reduced to a comic strip if presented very cleanly, clearly, sharply, precisely and with humor.
> *Tambourines to Glory* is, on the surface, a simple play about very simple people. Therefore, all of its performers should be sensitive enough to appreciate the complexity of simplicity. . . .
> Much of the meaning of *Tambourines to Glory* lies in its songs. . . . When the curtain falls, the final effect must be that of having heard a song—a melodic, likable, dramatic song.[85]

Hughes ends with the comment that the audience ought to be encouraged to sing along with the temple choir during the scenes depicting religious services. As his author's note suggests, Hughes tried to include in *Tambourines to Glory* almost every successful aspect of his literary and dramatic career; he succeeded in realizing none of them.

Some of the play's difficulties arise from Hughes's attempt to draw upon a multiplicity of forms. As in the gospel plays, the structure of the church scenes and their compelling music invite the audience to

84. Hughes, note, Langston Hughes Papers.
85. Langston Hughes, *Tambourines to Glory*, in Smalley (ed.), *Five Plays by Langston Hughes*, 184.

participate in the fervor of the church service. Other scenes, however, demand a different reaction from members of the audience—to observe and evaluate the actions of characters as they might in a conventional drama. Moreover, a basic concern of the play is charlatanism in the church. Thus the question is inescapable: is the church service to which the audience is asked to respond the expression of Essie's faith or of Laura's cynicism? Finally, the prologues to the first and second acts, spoken by Buddy Lomax, encourage the audience's critical perspective: "You think I'm who you see, don't you? Well, I'm not. I'm the Devil . . . in this play, according to the program, you might think I'm Big-Eyed Buddy Lomax—if I didn't tell you in front, no. . . . Watch me this evening. I'll find work for idle hands—stage hands—to do. Unemployed actors, too. The Theatre Guild put me up to this. On with the show . . . Laura, are you in the wings?"[86]

Although clever and amusing, the prologues undermine the theatrical illusion Hughes intended, according to his notes. That the audience knows Buddy is the devil is important to complete the play's conceit. Moreover, the kind of devil he is, arising from the trickster devil of black religion, is certainly appropriate to the play's morality structure. But the implicit acceptance and faith that folk forms demand as responses, and the act of celebration they embody, rarely can exist simultaneously with manipulation of the dramatic perspective and a plot that concerns misrepresentation of the image portrayed.

The story of *Tambourines to Glory* concerns two women, Essie and Laura, who, beset by poverty, decide to establish a church. The church is extremely successful—largely due to the assistance of Buddy Lomax, Laura's lover, who urges such dubious schemes as selling Jordan water and giving out lucky numbers during the sermons. Laura invariably persuades honest Essie to go along with each new gimmick. When Buddy mistreats Laura and turns to a younger lover, she kills him. Laura briefly pins the murder on Essie, who is arrested, but then repents and returns to her church to be saved.

The duel between good and evil in the play is expressed musically as well as thematically. The language of the church is gospel music; the language of the world is the blues encountered in the Harlem bars that are Buddy Lomax's favorite environment. This dichotomous attitude to black music is traditional. The blues were regarded as sinful,

<hr>

86. *Ibid.*, 188.

partly because they originated in bars and other places of ill repute, but also because they spoke of earthly trials without reference to the God who rewards his children's suffering and because they celebrated erotic love rather than divine. Gospel music confines itself to praising the Lord, who is often addressed as "lover of the soul."

Of course, finally, gospel music and the blues are simply two sides of the same coin, and Laura's murder of Buddy realizes this two-dimensionality as well. In a blues or ballad tradition, if a man mistreats a woman who has fight in her, she pays him back. Thus, on the secular, blues level of the play, Laura reenacts an archetypal pattern of the blues story. On the level on which *Tambourines to Glory* is a morality play, Laura's action is equally necessary, for her sin is literally loving the devil—exactly what the exhorter suggests of the prodigal son when he tries to tear him away from Jezebel. To be redeemed, Laura must triumph over the devil, and so she does. When, in the final church service, Laura enters and sings her repentance, the two aspects of reality, sacred and secular, are united. Hughes is obviously delighted by his effecting of this theatrical reconciliation. Unfortunately, the dramatic working out of the play's thematic concerns does not succeed as he intended.

In his 1926 literary manifesto "The Negro Artist and the Racial Mountain," Hughes asserted that choosing the life of black folk as subject for his art was also a way of choosing himself—a way of possessing himself through the rhythms and traditions of black people.[87] In creating black theater, and particularly in creating a black dramatic landscape, Hughes also constructed a place in which to situate himself as artist, a context from which he could speak about what interested him to those he wished to address.

Hughes's response to the problem he raised in his 1939 radio interview—that Negro problems and achievements had not yet received accurate representation on the American stage—extends the meaning of representation beyond that conceived by Richardson or Edmonds. "Representation" does not mean, for Hughes, only plays about black people that mimetically suggest their lives. The forms through which they articulate their experience must also be represented: the people must not merely be spoken about; they must speak. Hughes was sen-

87. Langston Hughes, "The Negro Artist and the Racial Mountain," in Addison Gayle, Jr. (ed.), *The Black Aesthetic* (Garden City, N.Y., 1972), 167–72.

sitive to who was speaking in all artistic forms—a question the dominant culture often takes for granted when responding to artistic expression. While Richardson and Edmonds had the same uneasiness
about who was speaking, they felt compelled to speak in a way acceptable to the dominant culture in order to gain a hearing. Hughes
insisted that he be met on his own terms and on his own turf, both by
his white audience and by those members of his black audience who
expressed discomfort with his art.

Hughes explored the gamut of appropriate ways to let the voices
of his people be heard. The content and language of Cora's speech
achieves the kind of lyricism that grows from the black tradition,
but the soliloquy form is not indigenous to it. This tension between
voice and form occurs in all his conventional plays, from *Mulatto*
to *Tambourines to Glory*. In the chronicle and gospel plays, however,
Hughes discovered uses of the theater that permitted folk forms full
expression.

Nevertheless, Hughes's particular resolution to the problem of
creating a black stage reality, which is most effective in his gospel
plays, while important, is limited and particular. As George Kent suggests about Hughes's blues lyrics, his gospel plays may be too close
to the folk forms that give rise to them. Kent points out that the artist
using folk forms must capture the spirit of the art and add to the folk
elements a fuller articulation of assumptions that the folk artist has
to merely hint at because his audience is closely akin to him.[88] Hughes
certainly intended and usually realized that fuller articulation. As he
indicated in his "Note on Commercial Theater," he celebrated the folk
tradition by translating it into formal art so that it might assume a
contemporary vitality. Thus he perceived himself as an artist using
folk forms rather than simply as a folk artist whose world view is completely congruent with that of his audience. Furthermore, his audiences were diverse, both racially and nationally, a fact of which he
never lost sight. In most of his work, Hughes played with, rather than
assumed, the folk artist's congruence with his audience. In his gospel
plays, however, the distinction is almost purely theoretical, so close is
he to the folk form the play emulates.

Hughes understood completely the difficulties confronting black
theater as it emerged from a hostile, racist stage tradition, and his

88. Kent, *Blackness and the Adventure of Western Culture*, 160.

resolution of those difficulties is gentle. He prefers to conquer the stage by eliciting assent from his white audience rather than by threatening it. Moreover, he provides it with a rich experience of black culture, thus forever superceding such parodies of the culture as *The Green Pastures*.

Hughes's legacy to black theater was finally what he intended. He brought to the stage figures from the black experience that had been stolen and abused by white artists in a racist stage tradition. His work was ultimately that of rehabilitating the stage for black audiences, completing the work Richardson and Edmonds had begun. His un-selfconscious display of every aspect of black folk expression created a vital black stage reality. The characters he depicted were ultimately benign. With LeRoi Jones, a new black character entered the stage; his presence forever altered the American imaginative perception of the black experience.

THREE ∽

"NO ONE WILL TURN TO THAT STATION AGAIN"
LeRoi Jones

When *Dutchman* opened at the Cherry Lane Theatre, March 24, 1964, it signaled a new era in Afro-American drama. Jones's allegorical tale of relationships between blacks and whites in America neither protests social injustice nor proposes solutions. Rather, *Dutchman* describes those relationships as a ritualized reenactment of a script written by history and by an innately corrupt white society—a script in which both blacks and whites are captive actors riding a doomed ship. Certainly no black or white American sensitive to the implications of American culture and history learned anything new from the play, but *Dutchman's* forthright antagonism to and informed hatred of the society that created the tortured consciousness of "the American Negro" shocked its audiences. Not only white audiences were dismayed by Jones's vehemence. Hughes began his review of Jones's *The Slave* and *The Toilet* as follows: "It is the fashion for young authors of Negro plays nowadays to make their heroes all villains of the darkest hue, or crazy, living in crazy houses. The whites are for the most part villains or neurotics, too, so I gather that contemporary Negro playwrights do not like anybody anymore—neither their stage characters, their audiences, their mothers, nor themselves. . . . Certainly times do change, as the saying goes." [1]

Hughes objected to both the violence and the language in the plays, adding, "What all this does for race relations (as if it mattered at this late date) I do not know." He suggested to the producers of *The Slave* and *The Toilet* at St. Mark's Playhouse that "for the sake of today's sensitive Negroes and battered white liberals," both plays ought to be double cast and the performances alternated racially: "To reverse the complexions on stage every other night by alternating casts would make for very intriguing theatrical evenings. Black would then be white—and white, black—which alternately would cancel out each

---

1. Langston Hughes, "That Boy LeRoi," in Lindsay Patterson (ed.), *Anthology of the American Negro in the Theatre* (New York, 1967), 205.

other—since some critics claim that LeRoi Jones may not really be writing about color at all, but instead is concerned with no group 'smaller than mankind.' God help us all."[2]

Clearly, Hughes did not share Jones's sensibility or his sense of decorum; however, he neither denigrates Jones's talent nor rejects the meanings of the plays. Younger black writers responded to Jones wholeheartedly, for they saw in his autobiography, as expressed in his writings, a kind of *Bildungsroman* for the Black Arts Movement. So powerful was his influence, particularly in the latter half of the 1960s, that, to many, the name Jones chose to symbolize his commitment to the spiritual and cultural life of black people when he became a Kawaida minister seemed absolutely appropriate. The name, Imamu Amiri Baraka, means Spiritual Leader (Imamu) and Blessed Prince (Amiri or Ameer Baraka).[3]

Jones's radical, articulate analysis of the issue with which the Black Arts Movement was centrally concerned is the source of his tremendous impact on his contemporaries. His own work, both theoretical and artistic, provided a base on which others could build or against which they could react while freeing themselves from the forms and aesthetic standards of white culture and developing forms and standards appropriate to their own heritage and concerns. A succinct statement of the core of his theoretical position appears in *Blues People: Negro Music in White America*, Jones's provocative, influential work on black music; it is particularly relevant to his conception of theater and of the black stage reality.

> Music, as paradoxical as it might seem, is the result of thought. It is the result of thought perfected at its most empirical, *i.e., as attitude,* or *stance.* Thought is largely conditioned by reference; it is the result of consideration or speculation against reference, which is largely arbitrary. There is no *one* way of thinking, since reference (hence value) is as scattered and dissimilar as men themselves. If Negro music can be seen to be the result of certain attitudes, certain specific ways of thinking about the world (and

2. *Ibid.,* 206.
3. After his play *The Slave* (1965) Jones began using either Jones and Baraka or Baraka alone on some of his publications—if not on the title page, then in the preface. I begin calling him Baraka in my discussion of plays following *The Slave* because these works express the beliefs and sensibility that his new name symbolizes.

only ultimately about the *ways* in which music can be made), then the basic hypothesis of this book is understood.[4]

Thus, for Jones black theater is ultimately a stance, an attitude; its "reference" is the world as it appears to black Americans. During the height of the Black Arts Movement, there was considerable debate over which plays satisfied this criterion, but some assumptions were shared by all who identified themselves with the movement. Black theater addresses black audiences. It employs forms that arise directly from African and Afro-American culture. It embraces both "Black Revolutionary Theatre" and "Theatre of Black Experience"—the former, political and clearly didactic in its orientation, and the latter, depicting and exploring the lives of black people in America. Finally, black theater takes its standards from the black aesthetic. Larry Neal's introduction to the *Drama Review* issue on black theater defined both the Black Arts Movement and its aesthetic principles.

> The Black Arts Movement is radically opposed to any concept of the artist that alienates him from his community. Black Art is the aesthetic and spiritual sister of the Black Power concept. As such, it envisions an art that speaks directly to the needs and aspirations of Black America. In order to perform this task, the Black Arts Movement proposes a radical reordering of the western cultural aesthetic. It proposes a separate symbolism, mythology, critique and iconology. The Black Arts and the Black Power concept both relate broadly to the Afro-American's desire for self-determination and nationhood. Both concepts are nationalistic. One is concerned with the relationship between art and politics; the other with the art of politics.[5]

All members of the black theater movement ascribed to Neal's manifesto to some degree, although individual writers' distance from Western cultural aesthetics and choice of "symbolism, mythology, critique and iconology" varied. All agreed that the validation of their art must come from its reception by the black community and not from the reactions of white critics and audiences. Thus they explicitly rejected the notion of a "double audience." When asked if whites would be given permission to produce his plays, Jones replied:

> I don't care, but I think its value is sort of mitigated in terms of the circumstances or its environment. I know that a group of white people seeing *Slave Ship* doesn't begin to have the *registration*, in terms of life-needs. If it doesn't come out of actual life-tone, that has been manifested by some-

4. LeRoi Jones, *Blues People: Negro Music in White America* (New York, 1963), 152–53.
5. Larry Neal, "The Black Arts Movement," 29.

thing that exists, that is real, then it's not the same thing. It's the difference between a duck and one of those whistles that sounds like a duck. They might sound the same, but it's a whole different structure being represented.[6]

Ultimately, Jones's artistic journey "home" was a Bildungsroman for black theater and the entire Black Arts Movement because it involved a conscious, carefully articulated search for the structures that informed his personal history and for the forms that truthfully expressed, first, his own experience and, second, collectively, the experience of his people.

The complex model Jones proposed for black theater developed from his own preoccupations. In his early poetry he conducts a fruitless search through Western culture for images of his identity and concerns, images adequate to his personal sense of dislocation and despair. He grows to understand his failure to find them not simply as a matter of the culture's well-mystified ethnocentrism, but rather as a matter of cultural genocide—an extreme conclusion, perhaps, but one that is a logical extension of his understanding of art and of the relation of a people to its culture. Following the dictum of his early associate Charles Olson, Jones understood form as simply an extension of content. Form that does not flow from the experience it seeks to express falsifies that experience and violates it. Thus, in his essay "Myth of a Negro Literature," he accuses Afro-American writers of betraying themselves and their people by yoking their experience to bourgeois forms of art.[7] Thus also he comes to understand and argues in Blues People, published in 1963, that jazz and all other black music is the language Afro-Americans developed to give uncensored accounts of their experiences. The language imposed by the slave master, he concludes, was and is the slave master's most effective form of control.

It is ironic that Jones, more vehement than any of his contemporaries in his rejection of white culture, derived so many of his insights from his association with the avant-garde white poets of the 1950s and early 1960s. As editor of several small journals and of the Totem-Corinth Press, which he founded with Theodore Wilentz, Jones num-

6. Saul Gottleib, "They Think You're an Airplane and You're Really a Bird," Evergreen Review, XI (December, 1967), 53.

7. LeRoi Jones, "Myth of a Negro Literature," in Home: Social Essays (New York, 1966), 105–15.

bered among his associates such writers as Allen Ginsberg, Gregory Corso, Hugh Selby, Gil Sorrentino, and Diane DiPrima, as well as members of the Black Mountain School, notably Charles Olson, Robert Creely, and Edward Dorn. Jones's anthology of the avant-garde, *The Moderns*, published in 1963, is still highly regarded, and according to Wilentz, Jones was a "brilliant editor."[8]

Jones was closely associated with the avant-garde in jazz as well, Ornette Coleman, Don Cherry, and Thelonius Monk, in particular. These two groups of associations gradually assumed a symbolic dimension, for Jones later saw them as projections of the "double consciousness" in which he increasingly located his conflict as a black American questioning his relation to the rest of American society. Indeed, so extensively did Jones explore the metaphor of "double consciousness" that his work may have finally laid it to rest.

In his two early volumes of poetry, *Preface to a Twenty Volume Suicide Note* and *The Dead Lecturer*, published in 1961 and 1964, respectively, Jones is unable to locate himself in the landscape he examines, except perhaps in the following lines:

> My silver bullets all gone
> My black mask trampled in the dust
>
> & Tonto way off in the hills
> moaning like Bessie Smith.
> ("Look for You Yesterday, Here You Come Today," ll. 97–100)

In the last poem of the earlier volume, he dismisses what he would later call home.[9]

> Africa
> is a foreign place. You are
> as any other sad man here
> american
>   ("Notes for a Speech," ll. 38–41)

The idea that form which falsifies content is violation is central to all of Jones's work. His early, loosely autobiographical fiction; *The System of Dante's Hell*, an extended narrative; and *Tales*, a collection of short stories, examine how the tenor and concrete detail of lower-class black and integrated neighborhoods, poverty, and urban blight affect the medium of a highly literate and poetic language. The effect is a

8. Quoted in Theodore Hudson, *From LeRoi Jones to Amiri Baraka: The Literary Works* (Durham, N.C., 1973), 16.
9. LeRoi Jones, *Preface to a Twenty Volume Suicide Note* (New York, 1961), and *The Dead Lecturer* (New York, 1964).

dense, vivid prose, visceral and violent: "I am myself. Insert the word disgust. A verb. Get rid of the am. Break out. Kill it. Rip the thing to shreds. This thing, if you read it, will jam your face in my shit. Now say something intelligent!"[10]

Jones's intention in these works is not simply to shock but to inflict on his readers the experience of violation central to his own and, later, all black people's experience of American life and culture. Double consciousness in his work emerges as a kind of masochism, for his attraction to both black and white culture is laced with pain. By negating him, white culture so succeeds in destroying his sense of himself that he cannot affirm himself in black culture. Jones's first extended poem about a black figure, in *The Dead Lecturer*, is appropriate to his later work in the theater. Jones depicts the actor Willie Best first as a crucified Christ.

> A cross. The gesture, symbol, line
> arms held stiff, nailed stiff, with
> no sign, of what gave them strength.
> The point, become a line, a cross, or
> the man, and his material, driven in
> the ground. If the head rolls back
> and the mouth opens, screamed into
> existence, there will be perhaps
> only the slightest hint of movement—
> a smear; no help will come. No one
> will turn to that station again.
> ("A Poem for Willie Best," ll. 38–48)

By portraying Best thus, the poet himself crucifies him, but other passages contain tentative images of affirmation.

> At the cross roads, sits the
> player. No drum, no umbrella, even
> though it's raining. Again, and we
> are somehow less miserable because
> here is a hero, used to being wet.
> . . . .
> This is the dance of the raised
> leg. . . .
>   As a dance it
> is obscure.
> . . . .
> A renegade
> behind the mask. And even
> the mask, a renegade
> disguise.
> ("A Poem for Willie Best," ll. 49–53, 90–91, 96–97, 157–60)

10. LeRoi Jones, *The System of Dante's Hell* (New York, 1966), 15.

Jones's play with language and image revealed to him that his isolation and alienation were cultural and racial rather than personal, and this realization led him to redefine his sense of the poet's task. He observed in 1964:

> I write poetry only in order to feel, and that, finally, sensually, all the terms for my life. I write poetry to investigate my self, and my meaning and meanings. But also to invest the world with a clearer understanding of itself, but only by virtue of my having brought some clearer understanding of myself into it. I wrote in a poem once, "Feeling predicts intelligence." . . . The point of life is that it is arbitrary, except in its basest forms. Arbitrariness, or self imposed meaning, is the only thing worth living for. It is the only thing that permits us to live.

In the same year, he wrote: "What is called the imagination (from image, magi, magic, magician, etc.) is a practical vector from the soul. It stores all data, and can be called on to solve all our 'problems.' The imagination is the projection of ourselves past our sense of ourselves as 'things.' Imagination (Image) is all possibility, because from the image, the initial circumscribed energy, any use (idea) is possible. And so begins that image's use in the world. Possibility is what moves us." [11]

To make meaning of the arbitrariness of meaning, the individual must transform old forms into new ones and invest old images with new meanings. Artists must do the same for their people; only then do they fulfill their responsibility. Jones's vehement attack on white culture, then, is the extension of his earlier, more personal and narrowly literary concerns.

Jones's investigation of his experiences and his making them symbolic of the condition of black people in America is most fully realized in his plays, for therein he externalizes his conflicts and brings them to a resolution. The process he dramatizes so eloquently requires a theater of exorcism—an idea of the theater and its possibilities he encountered in Antonin Artaud.

Jones first mentions Artaud in "the revolutionary theatre," an essay that reveals his profound understanding of and affinity with Artaud's thought and style. [12] In the *Theatre and Its Double* Artaud writes: "*Theatre*

11. Imamu Amiri Baraka, "GATSBY'S THEORY OF AESTHETICS!" in Baraka, *Black Magic: Poetry, 1961–1967* (New York, 1969), 41, and "the revolutionary theatre," in Jones, *Home*, 213.

12. During his Air Force years in the mid-1950s, Jones read extensively. He seems then first to have encountered Artaud's work (Diane Dippold, "A Tramp with Connections" [Ph.D. dissertation, University of Maryland, 1971], 71).

of cruelty means a theatre difficult and cruel for myself first of all . . .
[Its cruelty is the] much more terrible and necessary cruelty which
things can exercise against us. We are not free. And the sky can fall on
our heads. And the theatre has been created to teach us that first of
all." Artaud's vehement attack on Western culture and on language for
its ability to falsify or deny experience, and his desire to use the theater to enable man to contact "Danger," closely parallel Jones's own
concerns.[13]

A critical difference between Artaud and Jones is that Artaud wel-
comes the chaos and destruction hidden beneath the veneer of Western culture, seeing it as constituting a positive metaphysics, while
Jones fears it. In his early work, he too senses that "the sky can fall on
our heads," but his fear of the danger is only exorcised when he connects his fear and insecurity to that experienced by all blacks in
America.

Generally, however, the two writers' views of art and other aspects
of culture are similar. For example, in Artaud's preface to his own *The
Theatre and Its Double*, the likeness to Jones is unmistakable: "What is
most important . . . is to extract, from what is called culture, ideas
whose compelling force is identical with that of hunger. . . . Either
these systems are within us and permeate our being to the point of
supporting life itself . . . or they do *not* permeate us and therefore they
do not have the capacity to support life. . . . This said, we can begin
to form an idea of culture, an idea which is first of all a protest."[14]

Such cultural alienation is, most precisely, a rupture between things
and those words, ideas, and signs that are their representation. Jones's
insistence that black music is the only truly indigenous aspect of
Afro-American culture is tied to his idea that the music constitutes
the only language solely developed by Afro-Americans, and is the
only language that is validly descriptive of their experience. When
used by black people, white language and other aspects of white culture, because imposed, create a rupture between things and their
representations.

In "No More Masterpieces," Artaud makes a statement clarifying
Jones's frequent insistence that his own works are "less literary": "Let
us . . . recognize . . . that a form, once it has served, cannot be used
again and asks only to be replaced by another, and that the theater is

13. Antonin Artaud, *The Theatre and Its Double* (New York, 1958), 79, 42.
14. *Ibid.*, 7–9.

the only place in the world where a gesture, once made, can never be made the same way twice. If the public does not frequent our literary masterpieces, it is because those masterpieces are literary, that is to say, fixed; and fixed in forms that no longer respond to the needs of the time." In "hunting is not those heads on the wall," Jones makes a similar point by distinguishing between "noun" and "verb" to express two concepts of the nature and function of art. The former concept equates culture with completed artifacts and denies the importance of "process," which "only can transform and create, and its only form is possibility." The latter concept is "*verb process*, the doing, the coming into being, the at-the-time-of. Which is why we think there is particular value in live music, contemplating the artifact as it arrives, listening to it emerge. . . . Formal art, that is, artifacts made to cohere to preconceived forms, is almost devoid of this verb value." [15]

Functional art, that is, art not "separated from some natural use," preceded art produced for its own sake, and since its meaning is connected to its use, it retains its "verb" value. The secularization of culture and objectification of knowledge in the West contributed to the worship of the artifact. Jones argues that the naming of gods beyond the concept of God as "the force out of which the world and life issued" resulted in the substituting of god-as-artifact for god-as-process.[16] He implies that a culture in which process acquires central importance (hunting as opposed to those heads on the wall) perceives art and the artistic process as sacramental; that is, the importance of the artifact lies in its relation to that which it makes manifest. In a spiritual culture, the artist becomes priest or magician. Jones, like Artaud, calls not merely for a different culture but for a more organic relation between people and culture, and also between symbols and what they signify. While the relationship between musician and music is a paradigm for and, in a sense, the purest version of the relationship between artist and art that Jones seeks, the relationship between dramatist and the theater has a similar form. The kind of theater that aspires to the sacramental function is ritual theater, one type of which is the theater of cruelty as Artaud defined it.

In including process in his theory of art and in placing emphasis on the act of creation, Jones, like Artaud, is attempting to reconstruct

15. *Ibid.*, 75; Jones, "hunting is not those heads on the wall," in Jones, *Home*, 174–75.
16. Jones, "hunting is not those heads on the wall," in *Home*, 176, 177.

a spiritual basis for meaning; he is attempting to recall the gods by invoking them. Theater becomes a central art form for culture because the form implies and includes audience. Total theater, or ritual theater, is ceremony rather than spectacle; the audience, which, both for Artaud and for Jones, is a collective, is crucial to the creation of the event.

Four aspects of Artaud's approach to theater are important particularly for Jones's later work: the concept of theater as alchemy, the primacy of *mise en scène*, the secondary importance of text, and the concept of the theater of cruelty. Of alchemy and the theater, Artaud writes: "The theater must be considered as the Double, not of this direct, everyday reality of which it is gradually being reduced to a mere inert replica . . . but of another archetypal and dangerous reality, a reality of which the Principles, like dolphins, once they have shown their heads, hurry to dive back into the obscurity of the deep." [17]

For Artaud, both alchemy and true theater employ matter and symbol to purify ordinary reality and states of consciousness. The goal of alchemical theater is to create "states of an acuteness so intense that we sense, beyond the tremors of all music and form, the underlying menace of a chaos as decisive as it is dangerous." Thus, it is the function of theater to destroy all that holds people back in their encounter with the ground of being. The kind of theater in which this is possible Artaud calls "poetry in space": "This very difficult and complex poetry assumes many aspects: especially the aspects of all the means of expression utilizable on the stage, such as music, dance, plastic art, pantomime, mimicry, gesticulation, intonation, architecture, lighting and scenery." [18]

Language must be kept to a minimum: the theater of *mise en scène* addresses the senses rather than the intellect. *Mise en scène* hovers on the border between prearticulation and language. It turns ordinary language against itself, using it primarily as incantation; it is directed toward exorcism, toward "mak[ing] our demons flow." [19]

Finally, Artaud's concept of cruelty is complex. It includes all that is cruel in the ordinary sense, especially as cruelty in the world exists in the individual. But, more exactly, it concerns the positive cruelty that is birth or becoming: "Effort is cruelty, existence through effort is a

17. Artaud, *The Theatre and Its Double*, 48.
18. Ibid., 51, 38, 39.
19. Ibid., 60.

cruelty. Rising from his repose and extending himself into being, Brahma suffers, with a suffering that yields joyous harmonics perhaps, but which at the ultimate extremity of the curve can only be expressed by a terrible crushing and grinding." [20]

People are so degenerate, Artaud feels, that only through the skin can metaphysics reenter their minds. The true purpose of theater is "to create Myths, to express life in its immense, universal aspect, and from life to extract images in which we find pleasure in discovering ourselves." [21] This self-discovery through contact with the ground of being, accomplished by shattering our ordinary defenses, especially our use of language and reason to categorize experience and thus to hold it at bay, Artaud calls cruelty. Jones's later plays move exactly in this direction.

The theater of cruelty concept lies at the root of what Jones wishes to accomplish. The creation of new cultural forms requires a radical purging and reordering of primary ways of experiencing the world and a rebuilding of articulation about experience. Thus Jones's artistic journey home is not merely a turning to the original forms of black cultural expression. The old forms express historical experience; the new ones must be made appropriate to present consciousness. Jones discusses the dynamics of this remaking most frequently in his writing on contemporary jazz, contained in the volume *Black Music*. For Jones, this music is the primary black theater of cruelty: "The content of the New Music, or the New Black Music, is toward change. It is change. It wants to change forms. Freedom and finally Spirit. . . . There is the freedom to exist (and the change to) in the existing, or to reemerge in a new thing." [22]

The above is taken from the article "The Changing Same (R & B and the New Black Music)," in which Jones argues that both the new black music and contemporary rhythm-and-blues, especially as sung by James Brown, are radical not merely in their attention to change but also in their return to African and American roots. The paradox in the article's title is analogous to the paradox in the two senses of the word *radical*. When the musicians go back to the roots of experience for appropriate forms and place them in a modern context, the forms

20. *Ibid.*, 103.
21. *Ibid.*, 99, 116.
22. Imamu Amiri Baraka, "The Changing Same (R & B and the New Black Music)," in *Black Music* (New York, 1967), 199–200.

are changed and given new meanings. What is produced is radical both in the sense of departing from the mainstream and in the sense of returning to roots.

Thus Jones is complex not only in his movement away from white culture but also in his understanding of what it means to come home to black culture. In that home he wishes to build a new edifice, or, as he began calling his home town, New-ark. The materials had always been available to Jones, but his understanding and use of them are new, and through this new use the materials themselves are transformed.

Jones's plays, particularly those written between 1960 and 1967, dramatize the intellectual and other personal conflicts of which his poetry and fiction speak more intimately and about which his essays theorize. By projecting his conflicts onto the wide canvas of the stage, Jones literally externalized them and allowed them to play themselves out. In doing so, he enacted for himself and for his audience the cruelty of which Artaud speaks—cruelty that is also intrinsically becoming. Coincidentally, he created a revolution in American theater, and explored grounds and provided models for the emerging new black theater.

Jones's plays fall into two groups: those that are pre–theater of cruelty and those that are distinctly expressions of the mode. The pivotal play in the former division is *The Slave*, which both reviews Jones's earlier work and anticipates the plays in the latter division, which culminate in *Slave Ship*. During his later phase, Jones, now Baraka, completes the process of transforming both the language and the landscape of black theater, not so much providing it with models as acting as a catalyst for its firmly grounded artistic freedom and assurance. It is in this sense and as a tribute that a version of the comment Jones ascribed to Willie Best applies to his own artistic autobiography as *Bildungsroman*: No one need turn to that station again.

Jones's earliest extant play, *Dante*, later called *The Eighth Ditch*, appears as a chapter in his autobiographical fiction, *The System of Dante's Hell*, where it is called *The Eighth Ditch (Is Drama*.[23] Jones has described it as

23. According to both Theodore Hudson and Diane Dippold, two earlier works were written, although no manuscript for either remains. An advertisement in *Yugen*, the journal Jones edited with Hettie Cohen (later Hettie Jones), announced that "A GOOD GIRL IS HARD TO FIND" was to be presented by "The

a "sort of dramatization of the False Comforters theme." A short piece, the play depicts a homosexual encounter between 46, a "middle class Negro youth . . . in the boyscouts," and 64, "an underprivileged negro youth [also] in the boyscouts," which takes place one afternoon in an army tent. As 46 lies on his cot reading, 64 harasses him, challenging the young man's knowledge of black ghetto life, or "the streets."[24] He ends by taking him sexually but protecting him when a third character, 62, enters and wants to join in. That night, 64 approaches 46 again, mounts him, and as he reaches climax, others enter, cheering him on. The play ends inconclusively; a melee encircles the couple.

An inspiration for this play may have been the relationship between a black intellectual, who is also a writer, and an earthy exponent of "soul" that is portrayed in the writings of Claude McKay, the Harlem Renaissance writer. In *Home to Harlem* and *Banjo*, intellectual Ray believes his education has exiled him from the instinctual, spontaneous manner of life that he observes in, and occasionally enjoys with, his friend Jake. Jones frequently uses the name Ray for himself in *The Toilet* and *Tales*. In the latter, he writes of "Ray, a name I'd already saved for myself, sailing around the stupid seas with a 'wistful' little brown girl waiting for him while he masturbated among pirates . . . dying from his education. Shit. It's too stupid to go into."[25]

Like Ray, what 46 finally wants of 64 is knowledge of the "funky blacks facts of life." Like Ray, he has been both voyeur and occasional participant in that life. And also like Ray, he is a writer who wishes to describe black life in his stories. 46 allows himself to be violated by 64 without resistance and afterwards fears only that he will become pregnant. He submits because, he says to 64, "you say it's all there is . . . I guess."[26] While the play depicts a dialogue between the middle-class persona for the poet and a black man from the street, it

Troupe" at Sterington House, Bloomfield, N.J., August 28, 1958 (Dippold, "A Tramp with Connections," 30; Hudson, *From LeRoi Jones to Amiri Baraka*, 147). Hudson mentions "Revolt of the Moonflowers" as having been written by 1959 and as the play often said to have been Jones's first. For production information on *Dante* and *The Eighth Ditch*, see Dippold, "A Tramp with Connections," 91, 169. The play originally appeared in *Floating Bear*, No. 9 (1961), a journal published by Diane DiPrima and LeRoi Jones.

24. Hudson, *From LeRoi Jones to Amiri Baraka*, 147; LeRoi Jones, *The Eighth Ditch*, in Jones, *System of Dante's Hell*, 85, 80.

25. LeRoi Jones, *Tales* (New York, 1967), 96.

26. Jones, *The Eighth Ditch*, in *System of Dante's Hell*, 89.

becomes richer when seen as an internal dialogue between the poet who has entered the white world and his black roots.

46's life on the border of the black experience has left him unsuited for dialogue with his roots, but as 64 warns him, he cannot escape them. What those roots demand of him is to "narrate the sorrows of my life. . . . My inadequacies . . . and yr own. I want to sit inside yr head & scream obscenities into your speech. I want my life forever wrought up with yours!" 64 accuses him: "What do you know? You sit right now on the surface of your life. I have, at least, all the black arts. The smell of deepest loneliness." He promises that when 46 does write his life, he will be "a . . . foil." The portrait 64 paints of himself as he proceeds to rape 46 caricatures Jones's early poetry and Clay's speech in *Dutchman*, for all 64 has to offer 46 is the blues: "Steam-shovel blues. . . . Abstract expressionism blues. . . . Existentialism blues. . . . Kierkegaard blues . . . the blues blues. . . . Bigot blues, White friend blues, Adultery blues. . . . Kafka blues." [27]

The image of the homosexual encounter vividly portrayed in *Dante* describes exactly the effect of turning away from roots. Since 64 penetrates 46 from behind, 46 merely submits. In no sense does he embrace his black heritage—rather, he is violated by it. 64 mocks the dilettantism of 46 in whatever aspects of black culture he claims, primarily his skill at dozens and his love of whitened jazz (as opposed to 64's love of rhythm-and-blues and the belly rub). No real knowledge of the other can be gained through this homosexual encounter, as the play's circular structure emphasizes. The play begins and ends at night: "This is the first scene. Tho it is the end. Show it first, to give it light. As it shd be seen (BEFORE) as some justification. Some mortal suffering; slant the scene towards its hero's life. His black trusts. Together, we look in." [28]

As 64 first covers 46, the narrator interrupts with words that look forward to the prologue of *The Slave*: "The mind is strange. Everything *must* make sense, must *mean* something some way. Whatever lie we fashion. Whatever sense we finally erect . . . no matter how far from what exists. Some link is made. Some black gesture towards light. . . . This is a foetus drama. Yr hero is a foetus. Or if we are to remain academic . . . he is a man dying." [29] Because 46 has turned to the white

27. *Ibid.*, 82, 83, 84, 85, 86, 87.
28. *Ibid.*, 79.
29. *Ibid.*, 84.

world and refused to embrace the black, he will be violated by what he has refused to acknowledge in himself. What the play clarifies for the audience is only the darkness of his night.

Disturbing images of sexuality abound in Jones's work. As symbols, they suggest the possible uses and abuses of one's creative energy, as well as of one's relation to self and others.[30] For Jones, heterosexual relations between black men and black women represent not only love and creation but self-acceptance; and relations between black men and white women signify a lack of self-knowledge and self-acceptance, stymied or misappropriated creative energy, narcissism, and self-degradation. Masturbation implies a self-involvement from which the individual can find no release in creativity or in relation of any kind. Moreover, creative energy in Jones's schema may be expressed as violence, and if violence is not used to destroy one's oppressors, it is internalized and becomes self-destructive.

The pervasiveness of sex in Jones's work shocks, as intended, but that is not its sole purpose. Rather, it makes explicit his insistence that American race relations constitute a violation of personal integrity, a distortion of humanity, and an obscenity, for which explicit, distasteful sex is the most emotionally effective image. In Jones's early work, such sex symbolizes the energy of the ghetto world; in his later work it is attributed to Western civilization and American society in particular. Whether the image is attributed to blacks or to whites, it is always emblematic of self-hatred and the perversion of one's energies. Jones's early work is sympathetic to those trapped in the world it represents, but his later work scorns them.

Dante is concerned primarily with homosexuality as self-hatred; 46's fear and rejection of what 64 represents results in his violation. The entry of onlookers who want to participate emphasizes the humiliation of discovered homosexuality—"his black trusts," as the narrator calls it. Of course, the audience has observed him all along; what he wishes to keep hidden has not ever been so. Moreover, the phrase "black trusts" is ironic: the obscenity lies not in his roots, which deserve and require his trust, but in how he feels about them. Thus he is the author of his degradation. Both he and his roots are marked by the deforming effects of racism.

Jones's next play, *The Toilet*, also uses homosexuality as its central

30. Hudson, *From LeRoi Jones to Amiri Baraka*, 73.

metaphor. Written in 1961, the year that *Dante* was first produced, it was first performed in 1962 by the Playwrights' Unit of Actors' Studio at an off-off-Broadway house. Of his early plays, Jones prefers *The Toilet*: "I like it best . . . it came so much out of my memory, so exact. Just like I was a radio or something and zoom didn't have to do any rewriting."[31]

The Toilet takes place in the men's washroom of a high school. William Karolis, a white boy, has sent Ray Foots, a black, a love letter; and Foots's gang has arranged to bring Karolis to the washroom to fight its leader. As the play opens, some members of the gang are away capturing Karolis; others loiter in the washroom, playing the "dozens" and waging mock and real battle among themselves.

One of the black gang members, George Davis, brings a white companion, Donald Farrell, to the washroom for the confrontation. When Farrell protests the plan, Ora, the most violent of the gang, punches him in the stomach. Once all are assembled, Farrell is forced to leave. Karolis has arrived already badly beaten, and Foots refuses to fight him in that condition. But Karolis, unashamed, acknowledges the letter and, with unsuspected strength, attacks Foots, strangling him. The members of the gang rush to protect their leader: Ora jumps Karolis, and the entire group beats him severely. The boys revive Foots and take him with them, leaving Karolis badly hurt, possibly dead. As the play ends, Foots returns: "He stares at Karolis' body for a second, looks quickly over his shoulder, then runs and kneels before the body, weeping and cradling the head in his arms."[32]

Of the end of the play, Jones has commented: "When I first wrote the play, it ended with everybody leaving. I tacked the other ending on; the kind of social milieu that I was in, dictated that kind of rapprochement. It actually did not evolve from the pure spirit of the play. I've never changed it, of course, because I feel that now that would only be cute."[33] In his biography of Jones, Theodore Hudson suggests that this comment is self-serving; however, it is probably true. The omission of Foots's return is more in keeping with the tenor of *The System of Dante's Hell*, from which the play's characters come. In the prose work, there is no such rapprochement between the hero and the violence in himself or in his environment.

31. Quoted in Hudson, *From LeRoi Jones to Amiri Baraka*, 158.
32. LeRoi Jones, *The Toilet*, in *The Baptism and the Toilet* (New York, 1966), 37.
33. Quoted in Hudson, *From LeRoi Jones to Amiri Baraka*, 159.

The play's central conflict resides within the two sides of the gang's leader, symbolized by his two names, Ray and Foots. The black characters know him as Foots, and both the white characters call him Ray. In his rage, Karolis screams at Ray: "That's who I want to kill. Foots. . . . Are you Ray or Foots, huh? Right here in this same place where you said your name was Ray. . . . You stupid bastards. I love somebody you don't even know."[34]

But Farrell says to Ray, when he finds out about the letter, "A letter? . . . Oh, Ray, come on. Why don't you come off it," suggesting that he, as well as Karolis, knows the Ray side of Foots's personality.[35] The insinuation of Farrell's comment is lost on the other, but the play clearly indicates (even without the final tableau) that "Ray" exists. Upon his entrance, he is described as "nervous but keeps it hidden by a natural glibness and a sharp sense of what each boy in the room expects, singly, from him. He is the weakest physically and smallest of the bunch, but he is undoubtedly their leader." Foots has been spotted as "promising." He remarks: "That goddamn Van Ness had me in his office. He said I'm a credit to my race. . . . He said I'm smart-as-a-whip . . . and should help him to keep all you unsavory elements in line." When he notices Karolis slumped in the corner, he reacts with "horror and disgust . . . but he keeps it controlled as is his style. . . . He goes over to Karolis and kneels near him, *threatening to stay too long*," and when he hears that Ora is responsible for Karolis' injuries, he "looks at Ora quickly with disgust but softens it immediately to comic disdain."[36]

In the brutalized environment of *The Toilet*, elaborated in *The System of Dante's Hell* and the earlier stories in *Tales*, Foots, not Ray, survives, for this environment produces and requires brutality. The tragedy for Ray Foots is that the Ray part of his personality can only be shared with whites, a sharing that takes the shape of an obscene interaction. The homosexuality itself is less at issue than the trappings of the encounter, for homosexuality is simply the converse of the macho dozens games played by the black gang members. Neither the activities of Foots and his gang nor Ray's private acts are a model for the expression of humanity.

Most critics who favored the play insisted—like Hughes, with his

---

34. Jones, *The Toilet*, in *The Baptism and the Toilet*, 59–60.
35. *Ibid.*, 56. See Dippold, "A Tramp with Connections," 106.
36. Jones, *The Toilet*, in *The Baptism and the Toilet*, 51, 52, emphasis added.

facetious suggestion of switching the racial identities of the characters—that the play's meaning lay in universal truths about the degen-
eration of the humane impulse in a brutalizing world. However, in an
introduction to the play, Jones emphasizes its particularity, saying it is
about "the lives of black people" and "about love." He describes Ray
as unable "(because he is a victim) to explain that he is something
stranger than the rest even though the blood and soul of him is as
theirs." [37] *Dante* caricatures the plight of the intellectual black who denies his roots; *The Toilet* describes the limbo of marginality of a black
character who functions in both the white and black worlds but can
express himself totally in neither.

Jones's next play, *The Baptism*, which opened March 23, 1964, takes
sexual behavior of various kinds as its principal metaphor. A satire both on religious hypocrisy and on the sexual hypocrisy it can
engender, in form, *The Baptism* combines a burlesque of a Black
Mass with that of a passion play. The theme plays on the idea of the
second coming, for its Christ figure is a fifteen-year-old boy who confesses to having masturbated 1,095 times in the last year—every time
he prayed. "I could not help it. Thinking of God always gives me a
hard-on." [38]

The play's setting is "an almost well-to-do arrogant Protestant
church, obviously Baptist." *The Baptism* opens as the minister and a
homosexual (who may represent the devil) meditate on love. They are
interrupted by the young boy who has come to be baptized. An old
woman accuses the boy of masturbating each time he prays, but a
chorus of women enter and greet him as their saviour: "He is the Son
of Man. The big stroker of the universe. It was he who popped us. . . .
Our holy husband." The boy denies he is Christ: "I am a whole and
ignorant youth. I thought I might save the girls by telling them I was
related to God. I didn't say Son. They only assumed." Upon discovering that they have been violated by a false messiah, the women turn
on him, and the minister prepares to sacrifice him "to cleanse the
soul of man." He is the Son of God, the boy then proclaims, and slays
the minister and women with a silver sword because they have "no
charity! No love! . . . There will be no second crucifixion." A messenger on a motorcycle appears to inform the Christ, called Percy,

37. LeRoi Jones, "Introduction by the Playwright," in Otis L. Guernsey (ed.),
The Best Plays of 1964–1965 (New York, 1965), 244.
38. Jones, *The Baptism*, in *The Baptism and the Toilet*, 17.

that his father wishes him to return home, for the world is to be destroyed that night. Percy protests that he wishes to save mankind, but the messenger forcibly removes him. Only the homosexual, knocked unconscious by the women while he was defending the boy, survives; he leaves to cruise the bars, wondering what happened "to that cute little religious fanatic."[39]

Essentially, *The Baptism* attacks pseudolove, and especially pseudo-eroticism, in all its guises, and thus may be seen as an outrageous, comic version of *The Toilet*. The Christ figure wastes his love by spilling his seed, and punishes the members of the congregation because they have no charity. The minister's purported meditation on love is really on "our cloak of color, our love for ourselves and our hymns. . . . Not Love. (*Moans*) Not love. The betrayed music." The homosexual echoes him: "Not love. (*Moans*) Not Love. The kneeling is only suppliant. Tarzan of the apes of religion. . . . That thin Jewish cowboy." The minister "fuck[s] no one who does not claim to love me" and accuses the homosexual of being "less selective." While the minister confines his relations to "the mystical body," the homosexual embraces the body politic: "I want it all. I want nothing to pass me. . . . Let no one say we have not fucked everything and everyone we could." But the homosexual's love for the people is as perverse as the minister's for God or the women's wholly erotic love for Jesus. The Christ must kill them, for they have neither true *caritas* nor *eros*. As Hudson observes, "God does not consider the modern world worth His passion, and He forcibly rescues His Son, the agent of love, from a meaningless crucifixion."[40]

The Baptism seems an anomaly in the Jones canon.[41] Jones's humor, never completely absent, is rarely this outrageous and does not become so again until, in his later plays, he turns the weapon of ridicule on white society. The play savagely attacks Christianity and possibly the black church in particular for its impotent mixture of messianic

39. *Ibid.*, 11, 24, 25, 29, 32.

40. *Ibid.*, 11, 19; Hudson, *From LeRoi Jones to Amiri Baraka*, 162.

41. Two images in *The Baptism* do reappear in other works. The minister's pose as he dances in the opening minutes, employing a "slow dance step with leg raised," appears in "A Poem for Willie Best" as the posture of the minstrel. The homosexual calls for his father's friends with their bowling bags—an image that reappears in connection with the father in *Great Goodness of Life: A Coon Show*. In that play, the father's name, Court, suggests Jones's father's name, Coyt, and the play is dedicated to him. In *The Baptism*, then, Jones may connect himself with the homosexual.

dreams and political conservatism. The satire is often acute. However, the tone and vehicle are thoroughly Greenwich Village bohemian and thus finally inappropriate to the subject, the church of the black bourgeoisie.

Radically different in its focus is the play that opened the day after *The Baptism* and that turned Jones into a celebrity over night, *Dutchman*. Like all Jones's plays, its plot is simple. Clay, a middle-class young black man, is approached on the subway by Lulu, a white woman. She baits him seductively and finally enrages him. When he reveals his true feelings toward her and whites in general, she kills him. As the play closes, Lulu moves toward her next victim.

The scene is set in "the flying underbelly of the city. Steaming hot, and summer on top, outside. Underground. The subway heaped in modern myth." In this modern Flying Dutchman ("Give the sense of speed"), Lulu and Clay engage in what Jones sees as the true dialogue underlying race relations in America. There is no escape from the allegorical world of *Dutchman*; no one can claim historical innocence in its post-Edenic world, though Lulu and Clay attempt it briefly. Lulu says: "And we'll pretend the people cannot see you. That is, the citizens. And that you are free of your own history. And I am free of my history. We'll pretend that we are both anonymous beauties smashing along the city's entrails. (*She yells as loud as she can*) GROOVE!"[42]

Interpretations of *Dutchman* abound, and the play admits of many levels of meaning. Three in particular are germane: first, the play as amplification of the dialogue within the poet's persona, the subject of Jones's earlier plays and poetry; second, the play as a historical and cultural analysis of American race relations; third, the play as a meditation on the relation between language, art, and act in the process of liberation, a concern of much of Jones's theoretical writing as well as of his poetry and fiction.

Dutchman is the first of Jones's plays extant that chooses a heterosexual theme, but sexual and emotional "normalcy" are not therefore implied. In *The Dead Lecturer*, published the same year, Jones finally locates his relationship to and rejection of white culture in the symbol of the white woman, and *Dutchman* completes this metaphor.[43] In this play, the "white" speaker is externalized and the dialogue within

42. LeRoi Jones, *Dutchman*, in *Dutchman and the Slave* (New York, 1964), 3, 21, hereinafter cited parenthetically by page number in the text.
43. William C. Fischer, "The Pre-Revolutionary Writings of Imamu Amiri Baraka," *Massachusetts Review*, XIV (Spring, 1973), 228–29.

Jones's psyche played out, its deadly implications clarified by Lulu's knife. More clearly than in the poetry, in *Dutchman* and the play that directly followed it, *The Slave*, the internal dialogue is understood ultimately as arising from a particular sociohistorical context and as determining a set of alternatives now defined clearly as life and death.

Two settings and logics govern the world of *Dutchman*. The first setting and its logic is historical and mundane: the setting is the New York subway during the late fifties or early sixties, and the logic that of simple seduction, which, like dialogue, invites a movement from ignorance or innocence to knowledge of the other. The second setting and logic, symbolized in Lulu's apple, is mythical and archetypal: the place is Eden and the logic is that of the Fall, a movement from innocence and ignorance through knowledge to death. The logic of the Fall rather than that of normal sexuality predominates because the woman is sexually perverse, deceptive, and bent on destruction. Lulu is both serpent and Eve: although she claims to offer knowledge, nothing can be learned from her because she "lies a lot"; and her knowledge of Clay ("you said you know my type") is not genuine—although sufficient for his destruction. Lulu's seduction is a power game, and because she takes the initiative, she wields the power. Her knowledge of Clay's type is extensive because she has created it. When she accuses Clay of staring at her "ass and legs" through the window, he responds: "Oh boy. Wow, now I admit I was looking in your direction. But the rest of that weight is yours" (7).

As a member of the black bourgeoisie, Clay speaks Lulu's language and shares her ambitions. By believing he is a "black Baudelaire," Clay accepts responsibility for the cultural malaise that Lulu believes is her own "novel form of insanity." By responding to her advances, Clay affirms her perverse sexuality; by accepting the lines she feeds him, he gives her power over him. The stereotype that Lulu imposes upon Clay is not, however, entirely to her satisfaction; his passivity and seriousness make him too much like "all those Jewish poets from Yonkers, who leave their mothers looking for other mothers, or others' mothers, on whose baggy tits they lay their fumbling heads. Their poems are always funny and all about sex" (28).

Moreover, he refuses to become the mouthpiece for her impotent rage.

> Lulu.   Be cool. Be cool. That's all you know . . . shaking that wildroot
> cream-oil on your knotty head, jackets buttoning up to your chin, so full

of white man's words. Christ, God. Get up and scream at these people.
Like scream meaningless shit in these hopeless faces. . . . Clay, you got
to break out. Don't sit there dying the way they want you to die. Get up.
Clay. Oh, sit the fuck down."

(31–32)

Clay does eventually express his own rage, and his lengthy denunciation of Lulu and all she represents is, in a sense, an orgasm evoked
by Lulu's verbal seduction. Not only does Lulu elicit the orgasm, but
she predicts its content, as she warns Clay in the first act: "May the
people accept you as a ghost of the future. And love you, that you
might not kill them when you can. . . . You're a murderer, Clay, and you
know it (*Her voice darkening with significance*). You know goddamn well
what I mean." Clay responds, "I do?" (21). Her metaphorical orgasm
follows his, as she stabs him with her knife.

Heterosexual encounter is a sharing of life-force and, in Jones's
metaphorical system, symbolic of healthy human interaction. Only
death, however, can result from a union between diseased people.

Lulu. Into my dark living room. Where we'll sit and talk endlessly, endlessly.
Clay. About what?
Lulu. About what? About your manhood, what do you think we've been
talking about all this time?
Clay. Well, I didn't know it was that. That's for sure. Every other thing in the
world but that. . . .
Lulu. I'll make you a map of it. Just as soon as we get to my house. . . .
One of the things we do while we talk. And screw.
Clay. (*Trying to make his smile broader and less shaky*) We finally got there.
Lulu. And you'll call my rooms as black as the grave. You'll say, "This place
is like Juliet's tomb."
Clay. (*Laughs*) I might.
Lulu. . . . You'll say, even whisper, that you love me.
Clay. Maybe I will.
Lulu. And you'll be lying. . . . It's the only kind of thing you will lie about.
Especially if you think it'll keep me alive.

(25–27)

Lulu knows she bears death, but Clay ignores her warnings to the
fatal end. "I lie a lot," she says. "It helps me control the world. . . . You
tried to make it with your sister when you were ten. . . . But I succeeded a few weeks ago" (9). When Clay asks "in honor of whose God"
they will act, Lulu answers, "Mine" (23). And after Clay's outburst,
Lulu remarks, "I've heard enough" (37).

Seduction of a black man by a white woman resulting in the man's
death replays historical fact, and the subway passengers in the sec-

ond act, whose presence is suddenly revealed as purposeful, evoke the righteousness, if not the frenzy, of a lynch mob. Both Lulu's whorishness and her contempt for "long walks with deathless intelligent lovers" suggest elements of that archetypal scene in American mythology of the white woman, starved for sex by the impotence of her own men, seeking the virility of the black man (28). In liberal New York society, the taboo against interracial union is not as stringent as in the South of the archetypal scene (though Clay's reluctance to look at Lulu through the window recalls southern mores), but the result is the same because the woman is insane and bent only on destruction. She has nothing to give and wants not sex but life itself.

The encounter between Clay and Lulu is also doomed precisely because they contact each other through the stereotypical roles they reenact and because Lulu's understanding of Clay's stereotype is better than his of hers—were he closer to his southern roots, he would have understood the danger immanent in the encounter. Clay reveals his ignorance of her role in his surprise at the dwelling to which Lulu imaginatively takes him.

Clay.   You live in a tenement?
Lulu.   Wouldn't live anywhere else. Reminds me specifically of my novel
    form of insanity.

(24)

For Jones, stereotype is a weapon white America uses to control its black citizens; in Dutchman, he suggests that stereotyping is a particularly deceptive form of untruth because the stereotype has just enough valid characteristics to enable its creators to predict the actions of those it purports to describe. Lulu knows almost everything about Clay, and what she does not know about his "pumping black heart" will not hurt her unless he acts on its feelings. What makes the stereotype doubly dangerous for the black man is that he is tempted to hide behind it: "Don't you tell me anything! If I'm a middle-class fake white man let me be. And let me be in the way I want. . . . Let me be who I feel like being. Uncle Tom. Thomas. Whoever. It's none of your business. You don't know anything except what's there for you to see. An act. Lies. Device" (34). Demystification of the stereotypes is thus important not only for the whites who create them but also for the blacks who may be tempted to hide behind them rather than to express themselves truthfully. Therefore Dutchman purposefully exposes the treacherous nature of stereotyping, as do some of Jones's later plays in a more comic mode.

Lulu controls Clay both through her knowledge of his type and through her manipulation of language. She initiates their encounter and from her first "hello" orchestrates the ritual in which Clay will be victim. The script is hers: "Now you say to me, 'Lulu, Lulu, why don't you go to this party with me tonight?' It's your turn, and let those be your lines" (16). Moreover, she constructs a pageant within the play: in most of the dialogue she gradually reveals details of the evening they will spend together, which ends at her house, where they will "screw." The audience learns of Clay's own plans for his evening through Lulu: she guesses them correctly, and he merely confirms her suspicions. The impact of Lulu's guessing game about Clay's life and immediate plans is that Clay materializes in *her* voice and language. Clay just corrects her when she is wrong about a detail. When she states, "Your grandfather was a slave, he didn't go to Harvard," he remarks, "My grandfather was a nightwatchman" (18). Clay rarely expresses himself, for as Lulu knows, his mask cannot express his black humanity. Lulu remarks: "Everything you say is wrong. . . . And why're you wearing a jacket and tie like that? Did your people ever burn witches or start revolutions over the price of tea? Boy, those narrow-shoulder clothes come from a tradition you ought to feel oppressed by" (18).

Her savage attacks on Clay's bourgeois self-portrait contain elements of truth. In assuming a bourgeois role, he assumes with it a history, culture, and despair that are not his. His comparatively laconic responses to Lulu's flood of words indicate his self-restraint, as does his cautious and uneasy physical response to her flagrant sexual display. As soon as spectators enter the car, Lulu accuses him of being out of place:

Lulu.   Do they frighten you?
Clay.   Frighten me? Why should they frighten me?
Lulu.   'Cause you're an escaped nigger.
Clay.   Yeah?
Lulu.   'Cause you crawled through the wire and made tracks to my side.
Clay.   Wire?
Lulu.   Don't they have wire around plantations?
Clay.   You must be Jewish. All you think about is wire. Plantations didn't
        have any wire. Plantations were big open whitewashed places like
        heaven, and everybody on 'em was grooved to be there. Just strummin'
        and hummin' all day. . . . And that's how the blues was born.

                                                                    (29–30)

These lines set off Lulu's frenzied dance that culminates in Clay's furious denunciation, for which Lulu murders him. The images each chooses in the repartee above suggest that the masked Clay deceives himself, and that Lulu's vicious distortions are closer to the truth. Clay *is* out of context, not so much because he is associating with her publicly as because his public face denies his true self. As a figure without his own historical and social ground, Clay becomes mere symbol, the symbol the Negro is to the white world; Lulu's image of the plantation warns of a possible political reality for that symbol, which Clay refuses to contemplate.

The above passage also serves as ironic counterpoint to Clay's long speech that follows: "You don't know anything except what's there for you to see. An act. Lies. Device. Not the pure heart, the pumping black heart. You don't ever know that. And I sit here in this buttoned-up suit, to keep myself from cutting all your throats. I mean wantonly. . . . Old bald-headed four-eyed ofays popping their fingers . . . and don't know yet what they're doing. They say, 'I love Bessie Smith.' And don't even understand that Bessie Smith is saying, 'Kiss my ass, kiss my black unruly ass'" (34).

Clay goes on to argue that black art forms, especially blues and jazz, acquire their energy from the black man's deathly rage. He thus speaks of the impact of *Dutchman* itself and of the play's concern with the relationship between language and action. Clay observes the impact of his rage on his own art: "And I'm the great would-be poet. Yes. That's right! Poet. Some kind of bastard literature . . . all it needs is a simple knife thrust. Just let me bleed you, you loud whore, and one poem vanished. A whole people of neurotics, struggling to keep from being sane. And the only thing that would cure the neurosis would be your murder. Simple as that" (35).

Like the art that results from black rage, Clay's speech replaces action and would be unnecessary if he simply killed Lulu. It also substitutes for the physical orgasm never achieved, just as Lulu's description of their assignation substitutes for the real thing. However, if, within the context of Jones's play, to abandon language for action is to achieve sanity, Lulu's "novel form of insanity" is exorcised by her murder of Clay. Lulu chooses life by choosing action, while Clay chooses death by being content with words. The expression of Lulu's sanity reveals something of the rationality delineated by Clay in the last part of his speech:

> One more thing. And you tell this to your father, who's probably the kind of man who needs to know at once. So he can plan ahead. Tell him not to

preach so much rationalism to these niggers. Let them alone. Let them sing curses at you in code and see your filth as simple lack of style. Don't make the mistake, through some irresponsible surge of Christian charity, of talking too much about the advantages of Western rationalism, or the great intellectual legacy of the white man, or maybe they'll begin to listen. And then, maybe one day, you'll find they actually do understand exactly what you are talking about, all these fantasy people. All these blues people. And on that day, as sure as shit, when you really believe you can "accept" them into your fold, as half-white trusties late of the subject peoples. With no more blues, except the very old ones, and not a watermelon in sight, the great missionary heart will have triumphed, and all of those ex-coons will be stand-up Western men, with eyes for clean hard useful lives, sober, pious and sane, and they'll murder you . . . and have very rational explanations. Very much like your own.

(36)

Lulu must kill Clay because she has goaded him into admitting that he wants to kill her. Thus, her murder of him is a form of self-defense. She is sane in the sense that she performs a rational act; Clay admits that his retreat into language is not rational. However, the cyclical and sexual nature of the play indicates the nature of her deeper, continuing insanity; Lulu murders to gratify a desire that can never finally be satisfied. The murder of which Clay speaks would be a move toward sanity because it would symbolize refusal to continue internalizing pain by turning it into artistic expression. The source of his pain is clear; Clay's murder of Lulu would end the pain and free him. Lulu's murder of Clay, however, in no sense liberates her. Like the captain of the Flying Dutchman legend, she is condemned to a cycle of killing until one of her victims frees her by refusing to be content with words. Lulu both desires Clay and fears him; he is her "Christ," but to be redeemed she must die, for the world she controls is "like Juliet's tomb"—death to both life and love (20).

Since the play moves its audience from innocence to experience by demystifying its stereotypical encounter, one might argue paradoxically that the work of art is in itself liberating and can engender liberation in others. The play ends as a black conductor walks through the car after the passengers who have disposed of Clay's body have disappeared. He greets the young man destined to be Lulu's next victim. Jones believed that his presence suggests that "there were black people in the world willing to guard other black people." [44] However, the conductor, who enters "doing a soft shoe, and half mumbling the words

44. Edward Parone to author, October 24, 1974.

of some song," leaves the car after greeting the "brother" (37–38). Edward Parone, the director of the first production of *Dutchman*, persuaded Jones that the conductor did not convey what he intended, and omitted the character. Nevertheless, it is important that Jones believed that the action of *Dutchman* was not necessarily cyclical. Having witnessed Lulu's deadly ritual, the black community and audience of *Dutchman* could put it to an end.

Thus the play makes explicit the death white America holds for the black man innocent of its corruption. Filled with references to Afro-American social history, the play outlines the shape of that history in several ways. Lulu's pretence that a relationship between her and Clay is possible comments particularly on the egalitarian game playing of the northern liberal, whose attention to the Negro, like Lulu's invitation, is verbal only, and who recoils or becomes vicious when honestly confronted with the black experience. (A survey of white critical reaction to both *Dutchman* and *The Slave* certainly exemplifies this syndrome.)[45] More generally, Lulu's behavior recapitulates the entire history of white behavior toward blacks in America: she forces herself on Clay, impels him to use her language, and alternately rewards and ridicules his attempts to imitate her. Finally, she goads him into a demonstration of his manhood so that metaphorically she can castrate him more precisely. The apple Lulu offers Clay suggests the archetypal fruit of the Tree of Good and Evil; it also symbolizes the American Dream through its allusion to the Big Apple, New York. Lulu's offer of the apple and her interference when Clay tries to eat it encapsulate much of American race relations.

Dutchman's handling of the relation of language, art, and action is more difficult to delineate, for the play both affirms and denies the validity of art in the process of self-liberation. In his later, often quoted poem "Black Art," written in 1965, Jones insists:

> Poems are bullshit unless they are
> teeth or trees or lemons piled
> on a step. Or black ladies dying
> of men leaving nickel hearts
> beating them down. Fuck poems
> and they are useful, wd they shoot

45. Two interesting articles in *American Imago* analyze *Dutchman* from psychological perspectives. More interesting is that the authors of the articles initiated their studies to account for the critical furor stirred up by the play. See Diane Weisgram, "LeRoi Jones' *Dutchman*: Inter-racial Ritual of Sexual Violence," *American Imago*, XXIX (1972), 215–32, and George Adam, "Militant Black Drama," *American Imago*, XXVIII (1971), 107–28.

come at you, love what you are
breathe like wrestlers, or shudder
strangely after pissing . . . .
                    We want poems
like fists beating niggers out of Jocks
of dagger poems in the slimy bellies
of the owner-jews. . . .
                    We want "poems that kill."
Assassin poems, Poems that shoot
guns. . . .
Let there be no love poems written
until love can exist freely and cleanly.[46]

Certainly Clay's poems, as he admits, are not of this variety, although, in a sense, his speech is; neither are the jazz and blues of which he speaks explicit in the way "Black Art" demands. However, in *Dutchman* Jones does not say that black art is only an expression of rage. More precisely, he says that the energy so admired by white audiences is directed at them, and that much of black creativity has been channeled into finding codes or veils for hatred. Thus, what whites admire in black art is primarily a self-destructive repression of hatred and pain, while black art ought to be an expression and celebration of life.

For Jones, when form is not expressive of content, violation has occurred. The essential formlessness of Clay's long outburst is in marked contrast to the controlled quality of the rest of the play, which like Clay's three-button suit, comes from Lulu's world, not Clay's. Although she says she lies, Lulu speaks truthfully about herself, and the play's form is hers; Clay prevaricates except in his final speech, which is, essentially, the material from which life-giving black art will come, and which is as yet unshaped. Analogously, language and action must be unified; deceit occurs when a dichotomy exists between the two. In *Dutchman*, Jones advocates art and violence—not art as a substitute for violence.

However, he also suggests, both in *Dutchman* and in the poem "Black Art," that art in itself can be a form of violence. The impact of his own creations is searing for black and white audiences alike. His images are rarely aesthetically pleasing unless concerned, in his later work, with psychologically free black people. His language, often obscene and violent, creates images that must be contemplated as though they are the things themselves, and that give psychic shocks only slightly less brutal than the machine guns he believes may fol-

46. Imamu Amiri Baraka, "Black Art," in *Black Magic: Poetry,* 1961–1967 (New York, 1969), 116–17.

low. As *Dutchman* makes obvious, for Jones there is little distinction between cultural and physical genocide. Therefore, there is little distinction between the role of the artist and the role of the revolutionary. Clay's mistake is that he believes words will save him from action. He does not realize that his words have sufficed as "action"—they force Lulu to kill him. True expression is finally itself an action on which further action can be predicated. Clay may deny this, but *Dutchman's* audience, Jones hopes, will not. His next play, *The Slave*, elaborates this discussion of art and action, as well as other themes contained in *Dutchman*.

Premiered December 16, 1964, on a double bill with *The Toilet*, *The Slave: A Fable in a Prologue and Two Acts* opens on an old field hand alone on the stage. His ruminations lead directly into the play, wherein he becomes Walker Vessels, a black revolutionary who leaves battle to visit Grace, his former white wife; their two daughters; and her second husband, a white college professor called Brad Easley. As explosions rock the house and Walker drinks himself almost into a stupor, the three adults debate the kind of man Walker has become and the nature of the revolution he has instigated. Walker claims that he has come for his children, asleep upstairs. Easley attempts to kill Walker, but Walker kills him instead; an explosion in which Grace is mortally wounded then destroys the house. Dying, Grace pleads with Walker to save the children, but, he answers, they are already dead. Also hurt in the explosion, he crawls away, reverting at the end of the play to the posture of the field hand of the prologue, and children are heard crying in the background.

One of the ambiguous aspects of the play is the fate of the children. Optional stage directions suggest that a child's cry can open the play as well as close it. If the option is not taken, the end suggests that the children are alive. If it is taken, the crying may merely symbolize the new order to which the play looks forward. The fate of the children may be ambiguous because it lies beyond the knowledge of the playwright himself.

The Slave is less a depiction of actual revolution than an exploration of the consciousness of the black revolutionary.[47] The play is subtitled "A Fable"; in the prologue, the field hand even suggests it is a poem:

47. Lloyd Brown, "Dreamers and Slaves: The Ethos of Revolution in Derek Walcott and LeRoi Jones," *Caribbean Quarterly*, XVII (September–December, 1971), 37.

"Lastly, that, to distort my position. To divert you . . . in your hour of need. Before the thing goes on. Before you get your lousy chance." The figure blurs as the first act begins, and the end of the second act blurs to produce the figure of the prologue in dream fashion. Walker answers Grace's accusation that at the end of their marriage he had "align[ed] [him]self with the worst kind of racists and second-rate hack political thinkers" with the retort "I've never aligned myself with anything or anyone I hadn't thought up first."[48]

The old field slave is a deceptive figure, as he warns: "I am much older than I look . . . or maybe much younger. Whatever I am or seem . . . (*significant pause*) to you, let that rest. But figure, still, that you might not be right. Figure, still, that you might be lying . . . to save yourself" (44). Initially, he evokes the rebellious "field nigger," as opposed to the "house nigger," in Malcolm X's famous distinction. However, as at the end of the prologue he slips into the language of "blues people moaning in their sleep, singing, man, oh, nigger, nigger, you still here, as hard as nails, and takin' no shit from nobody," he suggests a more ambiguous image, for he acknowledges that he has been as deceitful as those he addresses and as enslaved to his own projections, as full of "a stupid longing not to know . . . which is automatically fulfilled. Automatically triumphs" (45, 43–44). Moreover, the revolutionary leader he becomes in the body of the play, self-admittedly is still in many ways a slave to the world he has rejected.

> Walker.   The point is that you had your chance, darling, now these other
>   folks have theirs. (*Quietly*) Now they have theirs.
> Easley.   God, what an ugly idea.
> Walker.   I know. I know.
>
>   (73–74)

Walker is not denigrating the revolution by this comment, but he is acknowledging that a better world may not result, for creating it will "be up to individuals on that side just as it was supposed to be up to individuals on this side" (74). He also understands that in order to create the moral vacuum necessary for wholesale bloodshed, he has had to destroy humane impulses in himself.

> In spite of the fact that I have killed for all times any creative impulse I will
> ever have by the depravity of my murderous philosophies . . . despite the
> fact that I am being killed in my head each day and by now have no soul or
> heart or warmth, even in my killer fingers . . . despite the fact that all my

48. LeRoi Jones, *The Slave,* in *Dutchman and the Slave,* 45, 71, hereinafter referred to parenthetically by page number in the text.

officers are ignorant motherfuckers who have never read any book in their lives, despite the fact that I would rather argue politics, or literature, or boxing, or anything with you, dear Easley, with you . . . (*Head slumps, weeping*) despite all these things . . . I want those girls, very very much. And I will take them out of here with me.

(66–67)

Significantly, his definition of these impulses arises from the culture he has chosen to reject, and as in *The Toilet*, their expression, to Walker, seems possible only in white society. The only love that Walker consciously admits is his love for his children. In the course of the play, however, in spite of mutual abuse, he also spontaneously shows feeling for Grace, their mother.

"Clay, in *Dutchman*, Ray in *The Toilet*, Walker in *The Slave* are all victims," Jones wrote in "the revolutionary theatre."[49] Their victimization is expressed, in part, by the dichotomy, or rupture, between emotion and the forms available for its expression, which, in all three plays, perverts the main character into self-destructive cynicism. Both the slave at the opening of *The Slave* and Walker provide portraits fraught with existential inauthenticity, and those portraits are stripped bare: Walker leads the revolution, but he does not therefore embody what the revolution could or ought to be. *The Slave* is the pivotal play in Jones's corpus and the first of his theater of cruelty plays because it is primarily about becoming—becoming free.

As Richard Lederer suggests in his article "The Language of LeRoi Jones' 'The Slave,'" the play is bound by language and by roles.[50] Walker embodies the Tower of Babel as he recites William Butler Yeats and mimics Irish, "nigger," Indian, Japanese, and gangster accents. He suggests that he has played Othello to Easley's Iago and is accused by Grace of playing "a second rate Bigger Thomas." Walker protests: "I swear to you, Grace, I did come into the world pointed in the right direction. Oh, shit, I learned so many words for what I've wanted to say. They all come down on me at once. But almost none of them are mine" (53).

Mangled communication becomes the verbal reflection of the play's violence, and the child's cry at the end suggests the basic expression to which Walker is reduced and from which new language must come. As Walker assumes voices and Easley grants him titles (when Easley

49. Jones, "the revolutionary theatre," in *Home*, 211.
50. Richard Lederer, "The Language of LeRoi Jones' 'The Slave,'" *Studies in Black Literature*, IV (Spring, 1973), 14–16.

remarks, "So now we get a taste of Vessels, the hoodlum," Walker responds: "Uh, yeah. Another title, boss man"), Walker achieves something of the stature of Ellison's character Rinehart in *Invisible Man* (65). Like Rinehart, Walker is capable of masking his true identity by playing many roles. Moreover, his protean facility suggests traces of the trickster devil of black religious tradition, who has come to plague "ole massa," now damned. But the effect of Walker's *tour de force* is primarily tragic: his voices come from the Western cultural tradition, often from the stereotypes that culture has used to portray the oppressed: "(*He starts dancing around and whooping like an 'Indian'*) More! Bwana, me want more fire water!" (56). Although he mocks the powerlessness of Easley and Grace and all they represent, Walker's impersonations also suggest impotence.

The accusations that both Easley and Grace level at him, and of which Walker himself in a different form admits the truth, suggest the pervasiveness of performance in his actions. At one point Grace remarks: "There are so many bulbs and screams shooting off inside you, Walker. . . . I don't even think you know who you are any more" (61). Easley observes, "You know he just likes to hear himself talk . . . so he can find out what he's supposed to have on his mind" (63). Walker himself says, "I've never aligned myself with anything or anyone I hadn't thought up first" (71).

His performance recalls the poems in *Preface to a Twenty Volume Suicide Note* in which the poet combs Western culture for images adequate to his despair; however, in *The Slave* the performance is a retrospective for the benefit of Easley and Grace. Walker has tried the masks before and found them wanting. However, his debate with Easley and Grace is real; during it, one senses, he reencounters and finally sheds his white intellectual legacy. The poetry he recites for Grace is Yeats—appropriately, the second part of "News for the Delphic Oracle." He accuses those who once were his friends of having "moved too far away from the actual meanings of life . . . into some lifeless cocoon of pretended intellectual and emotional achievement, to really be able to see the world again" (76). He reminds Easley that although "the Western ofay thought . . . that his rule somehow brought more love and beauty into the world . . . that was not ever the point" (73). And he admits that he has turned from idealism to pragmatism.

In *Dutchman*, Jones externalized the debate between the black man and white culture through the figure of Lulu. In *The Slave* the figure of white culture is split into Easley and Grace. Easley represents the world of ideas, the intellectual legacy of the West—ideas that, as the field hand in the prologue comments: "are still in the world. They need judging. I mean, they don't come in that singular or wild, that whatever they are, just because they're beautiful and brilliant, just because they strike us full in the center of the heart. . . . My God! . . . My God, just because and even this, believe me, even if, that is, just because they're *right* . . . doesn't mean anything. The very rightness stinks a lotta times. The very rightness" (44).

Easley accuses Walker of bad art, inconsistent principles, and irrationality. Walker's retorts must be seen in the light of the field hand's comment. He does not deny Easley's accusation; rather, he remarks on Easley's lack of masculinity and his "sick liberal lip service to whatever was the least filth. [His] high aesthetic disapproval of the political" (74). Walker's accusation that Easley is homosexual and impotent suggests the perversity of Easley's ideas, which, although they may be right, have proved ineffectual. Walker states: "The aesthete came long after all the things that really formed me. It was the easiest weight to shed. And I couldn't be merely a journalist . . . a social critic. No social protest . . . *right is in the act. And the act itself has some place in the world . . . it makes some place for itself.* Right?" (75, emphasis added). Thus Easley comes to represent the weakness of constructs about the world that have ceased being rooted in action and experience.

If Easley symbolizes the intellectual and cultural aspects of white society, Grace symbolizes what lies beneath intellectual and cultural constructs—the emotional, experiential aspects of life. Vestiges of affection remain between Grace and Walker. Several times Grace expresses concern for Walker and even is protective of him. When all are shaken by an explosion, Walker automatically rises to see how Grace is, even before Easley does. As well, the argument in which they relive the breakup of their marriage suggests the intensity of the former bond.

> *Walker.*   No, I couldn't understand it. We'd been together a long time, before all that happened. What I said . . . what I thought I had to do . . . I knew you, if any white person in the world could, I knew you would understand. And then you didn't. . . .
> *Grace.*   You stopped telling me everything!
> *Walker.*   I never stopped telling you I love you . . . or that you were my wife!
> *Grace.*   (*Almost broken*) It wasn't enough, Walker. It wasn't enough.
>
> (71)

The union of Walker and Grace represents the bond between white and black America. Walker claims: "I don't hate you at all, Grace. I hated you when I wanted you. I haven't wanted you for a long time. But I do want those children" (65).

The children are symbolic of all that was fruitful in the bond between their parents. When Grace turns on Walker, calling him "a nigger murderer," she demonstrates the validity of what he later contends: that the children are better off among black people (which legally they are) than in a society that will regard their father as "some evil black thing" (54, 68). The same society would regard them as "freakish mulattoes" (68). Moreover, if, when threatened, Grace turns on Walker *as a black man,* she will never entirely accept her children. Furthermore, as they are both girls, the family constitutes the end of a line, not the beginning of a dynasty; and any generations issuing from their children will be part of black society, not white. Nevertheless, there are children, and Grace is their mother. Thus it is symbolically important that she dies as the result of an explosion—as a result of the history Walker has set into motion—rather than, like Easley, by his hand.

While *The Slave's* judgment of white society is harsh, its cruelty is directed most intensely at the figure of Walker Vessels himself. In the course of the play, Vessels admits all that pollutes the purity of his political actions and motives. In the prologue, he suggests, "We need, ahem, a meta-language. We need something not included here" (45). Like Clay's, his insight is deceptive: the metalanguage of which he speaks is action itself, and while the violence Clay represses provides the background in *The Slave,* the protagonist nevertheless chooses a poem-play, a play about a discussion, to express himself. The violence in the background emphasizes primarily the torment of the protagonist and reflects more mangled communication than the uncompromising nature of the act that approaches as the dialogue comes to an end.

The use made of the metaphor of drama in *The Slave* is complex. While in *Dutchman* Lulu runs the show, in *The Slave* Walker does, and his performance is itself a search for and creation of identity. Since in the course of the play, his audience is killed off, none of the masks, a traditional metaphor for the faces blacks show to whites, are of any use, and from what remains, Walker must form his new identity. The slave to whom Walker reverts at the end of the play, therefore, is not the same slave as at the beginning: once his fantasy has been articulated (in the play itself), his ambiguity is lost. The slave's stereotype has been redeemed: by playing Walker, he, like Walker, has discovered who he is.

The play's use of ritual drama is both straightforward and ironic. Easley accuses Walker of writing "a flashy doggerel for inducing all those unfortunate troops of yours to spill their blood in your behalf. But I guess that's something! Ritual drama, we used to call it at the university. The poetry of ritual drama" (56). Grace suggests that Walker's threats to kill them are "metaphors" and "ritual drama," and Easley dies with the words *ritual drama* on his lips. The use made of ritual drama elaborates on the ironies in *Dutchman* about the relationship of word and act. Grace and Easley suggest that a ritual drama is a substitute for action; Easley's death mocks their misunderstanding visually and verbally. Walker tells Easley that the only thing the latter is permitted to say on dying is, "I only regret that I have but one life to lose for my country"; thus he turns Easley into a caricature of both an American patriot and a Christ figure (81). As Easley and Grace ought to have remembered, in the archetypal ritual drama, the Mass, word and act are united in the words of consecration; in fact, words are actions since transformation (transubstantiation) occurs through speech.

The Slave is redemptive for the slave; the ritual drama that Easley scorns and of which he is victim is the ritual through which Walker is redeemed. Walker's ritual is the converse of the ritual Lulu reenacts, for in her encounter with Clay she neither changes nor grows, while Walker, in his meeting with Grace and Easley, experiences a process of becoming.

The biographical implications of *The Slave* are inescapable. Like Walker, Jones was married to a white woman, Hettie Cohen Jones, and had two daughters by her. Shortly after the production of *The Slave* the two parted. There is, however, no evidence that Jones's personal affairs are directly reflected in the portraits in *The Slave*. The degree to which the play involves autobiography is less important than the intensity of the spiritual and physical violence with which the play exorcises the ties that bind the American family. If *Dutchman* is about the death of a black man, *The Slave* concerns his painful, phoenixlike rebirth.

The year 1964 marked a turning point for black theater and for American theater as a whole, as well as for Baraka's career as a dramatist.

Langston Hughes's comment about the corpses of stage Negroes reaching around the globe cites *Dutchman* as continuing the tradition. But in a later piece, Hughes notes: "It was not until 1965 when LeRoi Jones came along with *The Toilet* and *The Slave* that a leading Negro character on stage took a gun and shot a whiteman down. At last the theatrical tables had turned."[51]

While Hughes recorded the historical effect of Baraka's work, the playwright himself redefined his sense of the theater in "the revolutionary theatre," which he wrote in 1964. He defines the theater he seeks to create in Artaud's terms: "The Revolutionary Theatre should force change; it should be change. . . . White men will cower before this theatre because it hates them. Because they themselves have been trained to hate. The Revolutionary Theatre must hate them for hating."[52]

He sees the task of the theater as giving reality to dreams, as serving as food for the hungry and "propaganda for the beauty of the Human Mind." The function of revolutionary theater is religious—a summoning of the world spirit. Its purpose is to move people to an understanding "of what the world is, and what it ought to be." It condemns the decadence of white theater and the white world, and seeks to eradicate the distinction between "theater" and "life." Its ultimate aim is "THE DESTRUCTION OF AMERICA. The heroes will be Crazy Horse, Denmark Vesey, Patrice Lumumba, and not history, not memory, not sad sentimental groping for a warmth in our despair; these will be new men, new heroes, and their enemies most of you who are reading this."[53] This conception of revolutionary theater extends beyond a simple notion of "consciousness raising," to which it is often reduced. The function of this drama is not merely education but exorcism; its basis is spiritual as well as political. And Baraka's writing moved quickly in the direction of his manifesto.

This development begins with plays that assault the possibility of further dialogue with either internalized or external white America. In *Experimental Death Unit #1*, *A Black Mass*, and *Police*, for example, images of whites are grotesque, and intercourse with these images meets with retribution. In the same manner that the Negro must ultimately

51. Langston Hughes, "The Negro and American Entertainment," in *The American Negro Reference Book*, 847; Langston Hughes and Milton Meltzer, *Black Entertainment: A Pictorial History of the Negro in American Entertainment* (Englewood Cliffs, N.J., 1967), 217.
52. Jones, "the revolutionary theatre," in *Home*, 210–11.
53. Ibid., 211–12, 213, 215.

be understood as a construction of white consciousness, in Baraka's theater-of-becoming plays, the white must be understood as, and is therefore portrayed as, a projection of black consciousness, as symbolizing its death wish or its urge toward evil. Contact produces degradation; those who survive the contact become heroic in the classical sense of having survived the valley of death.

Images of the Negro in these plays, either as stereotype or as black bourgeoisie, are redeemed, as in *Jello*, or unmasked as embodying self-betrayal, as in *Great Goodness of Life: A Coon Show*. Baraka's mythology inverts American mythology by having whites assume the roles generally delegated to blacks in America. When portrayed humorously, they become the object of ridicule; when portrayed as threatening, they assume grotesque stature and embody evil. A major difference between the culture that produced the Negro and that which produced the white devil is that the latter does not deny its sexuality by attributing it to the devil's world. A provocative twist in his mythology that Baraka must have enjoyed is that black culture rather attributes perversion and sterility to the culture that has acknowledged that sterility as its own malaise.

In a symposium published in *Black Theatre* magazine, Baraka urged: "What we have to do at this point in our lives . . . is try to say it like a big poster—what we're doing. . . . Move. Or get up. Or shoot." [54] The analogy to poster art is suggestive. Like posters, many of Baraka's 'theater-of-becoming' plays concern the task of identifying evil and portraying the action necessary to overcome it. With few exceptions, the plays, like medieval morality plays, identify the good with the beautiful and the evil with the ugly. Neither good nor evil is portrayed as complex, for the playwright now seeks to induce emotional identification rather than intellectual analysis. Because of this, during the period of his prominence white critics often accused Baraka of sheer demagogy. Rather, he set a particular, important task for himself as artist.

In the symposium mentioned above, a discussion of Ed Bullins' *We Righteous Bombers*, Baraka was the most insistent defender of Bullins as playwright. Participants attacked the play for raising questions about the black revolution rather than defining a clear ideology for it. Baraka responded to these charges: "A play may not always give you an an-

---

54. "A Symposium on 'We Righteous Bombers,'" *Black Theatre*, No. 4 (April, 1970), 25.

swer. Like, here's your answer. . . . And your answer comes out to be black so-and-so-and-so-and-so, some kind of cliche that is meaningless. . . . *We have to cut past our own cliches. I say this and I helped make them*" (emphasis added).[55] This reflection on his work suggests the deliberateness of Baraka's choice of direction.

In the original production of *The Slave*, Walker wore as revolutionary emblem "a red-mouthed grinning field slave . . . [thus taking] one of the most hated symbols of the Afro-American past and radically alter[ing] its meaning."[56] Baraka has chosen the particular task of freeing the oppressed from the stereotypes that live in their imagination and replacing them with a viable and liberating mythology. This task requires the theater of cruelty—but Baraka does not deny the validity of other artistic enterprises, as his defense of Bullins shows.

The plays that follow *The Slave* become increasingly difficult to discuss as they become less dependent on language and more dependent on *mise en scène*. They defy generalizations because, when examined closely, each reveals that it embodies a different experiment in form and focus. *Experimental Death Unit #1*, written in 1964, was Baraka's first play after *The Slave*. In it, the encounter between two white men and a black prostitute results in the death of all three. One man is killed by the other; the murderer and the prostitute are then killed by soldiers of the black revolutionary army. Diane Dippold suggests that Loco and Duff, the two derelicts, are modeled on Samuel Beckett's Vladimir and Estragon. Certainly, something of Beckett's tramps is echoed in their opening speculation on the meaning of life, but the cosmos they discuss resembles that of Baraka's earlier poetry more than Beckett's empty landscape. Loco, the immigrant, despises beauty, those who call themselves artists, and knowledge, except "when it means intelligence." Duff calls intelligence "the open sore," and Loco refers to it as "the open sore in the blizzard." Duff has dulled his consciousness with heroin: "My windows are as icy as the rest of the world."[57] He is portrayed as more corrupt than Loco. When the prostitute approaches them, he says: "Help! Help us, nigger. Help us, slick pussy lady. Let me eat your sanity, gobble your gooky mystiques. . . . I'm in an icebox. . . . We die without this heat." He calls himself a

55. *Ibid.*, 20.
56. Neal, "The Black Arts Movement," 35.
57. Dippold, "A Tramp with Connections," 230; LeRoi Jones, *Experimental Death Unit #1*, in Jones, *Four Black Revolutionary Plays* (New York, 1968), 6, 5.

"ready youth. Made to be used, under and because of you." Duff proclaims: "I differ, unfair lady, only in the sense of my use. I am to be
used in all your vacancies. All those holes in your body I want to fill."

Duff's sexual needs are as perverse and abusive as the insults he
later heaps upon her. When he asks her price, she replies, "I charge
just what you owe," and Loco realizes "we owe everything." When she
grabs at his testicles, Duff calls her a "symbolic nigger from the grave."
Although all sentiments are voiced either in obscure phrases or in
obscenities, it is clear that Loco harbors a simple, powerful need of
the woman's warmth and earthiness. In contrast to Loco, Duff desires
a sadistic encounter with the woman, although at first, angry at her
scornful attitude, he refuses to admit his equally powerful need.
When she and Loco couple in the hallway, Duff pulls him off the
woman and kills him before taking her himself; so degraded is the
final image that the soldiers' entrance is a relief to the audience. Duff
and the woman are startled by them; she reassures him: "It's just a
soulbrother . . . don't worry. I'll cool everything out." When executed,
she falls "terribly surprised, ignorant."[58] In the prostitute are con-
densed both mammy and whore, the stereotypical images of the
black woman in white American culture: Loco perceives her as the
first (possibly because he is younger and an immigrant), and Duff as
the second. Her death is retribution for fulfilling the stereotypes; as
the play visually and verbally illustrates, the prostitute's moral death
long preceded her execution.

Jello, written in 1965, approaches the issue of stereotype differently.
It purports to be the final episode in the Jack Benny program because
it reveals the dynamics upon which the entire program is based: the
stereotypical interplay between "massa" and his devoted Uncle Tom,
Rochester. In Jello, Rochester behaves as black audiences of the show
undoubtedly had always wished he would. He refuses his role, emerges
"with long hair, postuncletom," and proceeds to rob Jack Benny and
the other characters of what they value most: their money and, by
implication, their fantasies of power over him, their identities as
masters.[59]

Jello opens as just another episode in the Jack Benny program. The
white characters are "close to what they are on TV / Radio"; the set-

58. Jones, Experimental Death Unit #1, in Jones, Four Revolutionary Plays, 8, 9, 7,
14, 15.
59. Imamu Amiri Baraka, Jello (Chicago, 1970), 9.

ting is Jack Benny's house, rigged for the taping of a show.[60] A carica-
tured Benny enters, singing a song in which he identifies himself as a
white Christian; when threatened, his language turns vicious, racist,
and obscene. His safe contains a skull bearing a tiara. Yet the play
retains enough of the characteristics of the real Jack Benny show
to maintain the illusion that the characters would behave thus if
Rochester were to unmask himself and emerge as the militant street
dude of *Jello*.

Jello emphasizes both Benny's love of money and his purported love
for and dependence on Rochester. The effect of Rochester's actions is
not only to "end" the show but, more important, to redeem the stereotype by suggesting that the potential for what he does in the play has
always been in him: "And you talking about my shitty li'l life, man I
tol' you you don't know nothin' about my life. . . . Except you might
know a little something about what I think of you . . . ha, ha, now. But I
watch your little white nasty bullshit imitation of life all the time . . .
lookin' at the TV. . . . If I was you, or any of them people look like you,
I'd stick a shot gun in my mouth."[61]

The basic metaphor of *Jello* is that of the script. The play slightly
overlaps air-time; it begins with Benny's song—which, the stage action suggests, is overheard, rather than a part of the "program"—and
ends with Rochester knocking out Don Wilson, who has just finished
his Jello commercial and bid the audience good night. The dialogue
between Benny and Rochester throughout the play gives the sense of
script violation. Benny finally makes this explicit to Mary: "No, Mary,
this is not the script. This is reality. Rochester is some kind of crazy
nigger now. He's changed. He wants everything."[62] Since the show is
still "on the air," the play now becomes the new Jack Benny show. The
white characters frequently attempt to return to the old script, but
because Rochester is in control, all attempts are foiled.

Benny's statement that reality is occurring suggests his awareness
that the script has always been just artifice and masked the real dynamic of the relations among the characters. To produce as thorough
an Uncle Tom as the old Rochester, one must fear him. However,
Rochester mocks conventional suspicions when he approaches Mary

60. *Ibid.*, 9.
61. *Ibid.*, 26. The speech is something of an inversion of Clay's outpouring in
Dutchman.
62. *Ibid.*, 31.

as if to rape her (thus responding to her expectations of what happens when a "nigger goes wild"), only to put his hands up her skirt and remove the bag of money she secrets there. Rochester's attitude toward the money he takes is in marked contrast to Benny's. He is businesslike and portrays none of the concern or perverse, almost sexual, affection that Benny lavishes on his riches. Taking the money does not mean partaking of the corruption white America attaches to it; Rochester simply knows its value.

Thus the script metaphor and the stereotype the old script included work in two directions: on one hand, Rochester's actions destroy the script that has become legend in American popular culture; on the other hand, his actions and words rewrite the script and reverse the roles: in the last show, Rochester acts the part of master. Yet the role does not essentially interest him; when Rochester calls to a woman waiting for him, he suggests that he has a life outside the show, one considerably better than the lives of those he leaves—Mr. Wilson, Mr. Day, Miss Livingston, and Mr. Benny.

Baraka's next play, A Black Mass, written in 1965, is less concerned with old stereotypes than with the creation of new, vivid images of blacks, whites, and the relations between them. Larry Neal calls this play Baraka's most important because it is "informed by a mythology that is wholly the creation of the Afro-American sensibility."[63] Based on "Yacub's History," the Black Muslim myth concerning the origin of the white race, it is the first play to assume the Black Muslim mythology as the imaginative world of a black audience. In the Muslim myth, the white devil enters creation as a carefully bred mutant created by a vengeful black scientist. In Baraka's version, Jacoub is a black artist who creates a white beast, believing he can teach it to serve black mankind.

As William Fischer suggests, Baraka sees Jacoub's sin as one of mistaking both his role as artist and the "true" nature and purpose of art. He overreaches in thinking he can create an original vital form, and depends unduly on rationality in believing that through it he can master life. The creature Jacoub creates transforms all it touches into an image of itself. Together with the woman it transforms, it kills the other characters before moving into the audience. After the two leave, the narrator explains: "And so Brothers and Sisters, these beasts are

63. Neal, "The Black Arts Movement," 36.

still loose in the world. . . . Let us find them and slay them. Let us lock them in their caves. Let us declare the Holy War. The Jihad. Or we cannot deserve to live. Izm-el-Azam."⁶⁴

The verbal content of A Black Mass expresses much of its meaning. The play also utilizes music in a fashion that approaches Artaud's directions for *mise en scène*. William Fischer's description is based on the Jihad recording of the play.

> The opening stage directions include performed music, in particular the music of pianist-percussionist Sun-Ra. . . . Although the opening sounds are appropriately harmonious and tranquil as the Mass proper is being concluded, once the action and dialogue of Jacoub's betrayal begin, the music changes its character to the more familiar tensions and intricacies of contemporary black rhythm and tonalities. The first stage directions conclude by suggesting that "Music can fill the entire room, swelling, making sudden downward swoops, screeching." . . . Its screeching becomes most intense in chorus with the vocal screams of black victims and the white beast, Jones instructing at this point "Sun-Ra music of shattering dimension. . . ." [The music] is part and parcel of the language of the play, infusing the formal English of the speakers with Afro-American sonorities that the unadorned language of the play script could not otherwise convey. . . . Live music now gives predicate motion to stage speech.⁶⁵

By using a separate mythology, A Black Mass becomes perforce a rite for its black audience, inaccessible to outsiders. The title puns on the blasphemous form of the black mass and suggests that what makes this distinct mythology sacred is its inversion of the traditional sacred delineation of good and evil. If whites attend the play, at best it will make vivid to them the dilemma of being black in a culture that identifies black with evil; they will remain outside the community the play creates during performance.

Experimental Death Unit #1 and A Black Mass were written expressly for the Black Arts Repertory Theatre and School, which Baraka established in Harlem in April, 1965. The brevity of the theater and school's history belies its influence on the black theater movement, particularly as a model for the community theater-workshop-schools that sprang up in many black communities.⁶⁶ The organization functioned for a little more than a year, and enraged the press because its plays

64. Fischer, "The Pre-Revolutionary Writings of Imamu Amiri Baraka," 298; LeRoi Jones, A Black Mass, in Jones, Four Black Revolutionary Plays, 39.

65. Fischer, "The Pre-Revolutionary Writings of Imamu Amiri Baraka," 298–99.

66. See Hudson, From LeRoi Jones to Amiri Baraka, 20–25; Dippold, "A Tramp with Connections," 212–15, 235, 239–44, 256–62.

were antiwhite although some of its financial support came from federal monies. Moreover, Baraka barred white audiences from its productions. In addition, highly militant organizations in Harlem were
rumored to be connected with the theater. By all accounts, within the
year artistic and educational activities had decreased and overtly political activities predominated, and by the time the theater was the
object of a police raid in which an arsenal was discovered, Baraka had
broken his ties with the theater and moved to Newark.

There Baraka established a new theater company, the Spirit House
Movers and Players, who performed his next work, *Great Goodness of
Life: A Coon Show*, written in 1966. In this play, Baraka concentrates on
the black bourgeoisie. Its dedication reads, "For my father with love
and respect," and the name of its protagonist, Court Royal, suggests
the name of Baraka's father, Coyt. Black bourgeois respectability blinds
Court Royal; he becomes his son's executioner because he fails to realize that in America, he, too, is a "nigger" and thus a victim. The title
obviously plays on Genet's subtitle for *The Blacks*, "A Clown Show"; like
Genet's work, it concerns a trial and an execution, but its setting and
language evoke the stark world of Franz Kafka and George Orwell,
rather than Genet's world.

As the play begins, a voice calls Court from "an old log cabin—with
morning frost letting up a little"—the traditional stage dwelling of
Uncle Tom. When Court questions the summons, the voice becomes
abusive and informs him that he is charged "with shielding a wanted
criminal. A murderer." Court protests: "Of course I'm not guilty. I work
in the Post Office. . . . I'm a supervisor; you know me. I'm no criminal.
I've worked at the Post Office for thirty-five years."[67] His protestations
satirize the tenuous, deceptive security of the Negro in the civil service, historically one of the few organizations in which blacks were
able to obtain white-collar jobs.

Court demands his attorney, John Breck, but the voice insists that
he use a "legal aid man," a mechanized puppet finally revealed as the
true manifestation of his own lawyer. When Breck urges him to plead
guilty, Court refuses. A nightmare follows, consisting of noises of si-
rens, machine guns, and clanking chains, and finally "low chanting
voices, moaning, with incredible pain and despair," reducing Court to
the stature of the "frightened coon" of the stage tradition. The voice

67. LeRoi Jones, *Great Goodness of Life: A Coon Show*, in Jones, *Four Black Revolutionary Plays*, 45, 46, 47.

informs him that he is in heaven, and hooded figures bring him a "greasy-head nigger lady," inviting him to smell her breath. He refuses. The voice asks him if he is ready for sentencing. He requests a trial: "A simple one, very quick, nothing fancy. . . . I'm very conservative . . . no frills or loud colors, a simple concrete black toilet paper trial." The hooded figures then bring in a body on a stretcher, which, the voice's description suggests, is the body of Malcolm X. The voice asks Court if he knows the man, as images of Malcolm, Martin Luther King, Marcus Garvey, Medgar Evers, and black children killed by police are flashed on the screen behind him. Forced to confront the images, Court first denies the people they represent, then finally breaks down, acknowledging: "Oh, son . . . son . . . dear God, my flesh, forgive me. . . . My sons." [68]

In a conceit reminiscent of *The Blacks*, Court is informed he is to be sentenced to die and that the murderer of the dead man is already dead, and then told he is to be spared since he "can see the clearness of [his] fate, and the rightness of it." He thus is beautiful and "no one beautiful is guilty. So how can you be?" He is free but must first give "the final instruction," which is

> the death of
> the murderer. The murderer is dead and must
> die, with each gift of our God. This gift is the
> cleansing of guilt, and the bestowal of freedom. . . .
> The murderer *is dead*. This is
> his shadow. This one is not real.
> This is the myth of the murderer. His last
> fleeting astral projection. It is the murderer's
> myth that we ask you to instruct. To bind it forever
> . . . with death. [69]

When Court Royal protests that he is not guilty, and thus need not shoot the young man brought before him, he is answered:

> This act was done by you a million
> years ago. This is only the memory of it.
> This is only a rite. You cannot kill a shadow,
> a fleeting bit of light and memory. This is only
> a rite to show that you would be guilty but for
> the cleansing rite. The shadow is killed in place of
> the killer.

68. *Ibid.*, 53, 54, 55, 58.
69. *Ibid.*, 59, 61.

As Court pulls the trigger, the young man cries out "Papa." The voice says, "Case dismissed," and the lights are turned up in full. Court mopes about the stage as though shaking off the experience, and calls offstage: "Hey, Louise, have you seen my bowling bag? I'm going down to the alley for a minute."[70]

Great Goodness of Life (the title parodies those of "darky" plays) employs several kinds of metaphor and image. A metaphor suggested by the title and setting is that of the minstrel and "darky" stage tradition. Its presence suggests that the bourgeoisie unwittingly continue the comic and tragic stage stereotype because they do not realize the falsity of their position "at the Post Office."

The voice, a primary image in the play, is both external (that of American society) and internal, for as Richard Wright suggests in Black Boy and Native Son, white society makes being black a reason for feeling guilty, and makes resenting oppression (the murderer within) a further reason for guilt. The same theme occurs in Dutchman. The defendant's position at this improper trial conducted by an unseen judge represents the condition of all black Americans.

A cluster of metaphors involves the judgment that Court is not guilty because he is beautiful and the execution of the young man. By recognizing that he is "a nigger," Court becomes "beautiful"—that the image is aesthetic links him to another version of the stage Negro: the folk character (Porgy, for example). The beautiful Negro to white America is one who harbors no hatred; he is opposed to the image of Bigger Thomas, for example, who is "ugly." Court kills "the myth of the murderer," the image of the black man willing to kill for freedom. Thus, Court Royal kills his own subconscious impulse, for the young man is called "the last issue," and with his demise all hope for liberation dies: the "shadow" turns out to be Court's son. In playing out his role, the black bourgeois destroys his own children who have moved beyond him in their fight for freedom.

In Great Goodness of Life Baraka employs a combination of verbal precision and visual elegance rare in his drama. By remaining stark and avoiding the visual hyperbole he uses in other plays (A Black Mass and Madheart, for example), he forces members of the audience to draw on their own inner landscapes for experiences to match the horror of the

70. Ibid., 61–62, 63. The ritual execution suggests the ending of The Blacks, in which the shadow (play) execution diverts the audience from the "real" execution off stage.

play. Energies like those in Artaud's drama dominate the nightmare miasmic vision in the center of the play, and the denouement is linguistically articulate and equally cruel. The process of becoming is left to the audience, for at the play's conclusion, the protagonist shakes off his dream, but the audience cannot. In addition, its play on Genet's *The Blacks* serves as a critique of Genet's use of black people as metaphor, and also possibly makes the point that the many black actors who kept themselves alive by working in *The Blacks* during its New York run extended a theatrical tradition that black theater seeks to bury.

Madheart (*A Morality Play*) was written the same year as *Great Goodness of Life*. Its language returns to the dense, violent images of *Experimental Death Unit #1*, and its characters reside in the mythology of *A Black Mass*, which *Madheart* amplifies. The white Devil Lady whom Black Man kills, though his sister and mother worship her, comes from: "blood. Snow. Dark cold cave. Illusion. Promises. Hatred and Death. Snow. Death. Cold. Waves. Night. Dead white. Sunless. Moonless. Forever. Always." [71]

These images clearly connect her to the white beast of the earlier play, and if *A Black Mass* concerns her origin, *Madheart* attempts her exorcism. Devil Lady, a vampire, is "dead and will never die." In two dialogues and a tableau, Black Man confronts and rejects her, then kills her with a wooden stake; however, she remains alive, and Black Man must forcibly eject her from the stage. During the battle, Sister identifies so closely with Devil Lady that when Black Man strikes the latter, Sister falls. The often distasteful behavior of Sister and Mother counterpoints that of the third black woman in the play, Black Woman, whose interaction with Black Man symbolizes liberated consciousness.

Devil Lady is clearly a grotesque, magical version of a figure who has appeared before in Baraka's work: Lulu, in *Dutchman*. Like Lulu, she symbolizes both the role white women have played as pawn and prize in the racial struggle for domination that white society imposes on blacks, and also that society and its culture themselves. Grace, from *The Slave*, is present in Devil Lady as well. In *Madheart* Black Man must deliberately and forcibly reject Devil Lady and deliberately choose Black Woman, who, in turn, embodies and symbolizes both all

71. LeRoi Jones, *Madheart* (A Morality Play), in Jones, *Four Black Revolutionary Plays*, 71.

black women and black culture and society. In *The Slave*, Walker Vessels does not finally divorce himself from his affection for Grace, nor does he turn from her voluntarily—and there is no image in that play of a black woman to whom he can turn. Thus Devil Lady completes the transformation of an image that has a central place in Baraka's writing and completes as well the exorcism that *Dutchman* began.

In doing so, *Madheart* demonstrates an aesthetic Manichaeism more frequent in Baraka's poetry than in his plays. The language and images of Devil Lady and her worshippers are abrasive and violent; those of Black Man and Woman are lyric and harmonious. Although aspects of the play evoke an Artaudian *mise en scène*, the play is overtly didactic in the tradition of the morality play. Black Man, whose ritual the play is, mediates the action for the audience, and thus the play is about a theater of cruelty experience, rather than being the experience itself. The white Devil Lady is so revolting that the understanding of the conflict that necessitates her violent exorcism is extrinsic to the play. In the traditional morality play, a measure of the hero's strength and virtue is the seductive power of the temptation he resists. However, while *Madheart* focuses on the struggle of the black man with the white woman, the force of her seduction is not revealed in the play. Thus, the aesthetic Manichaeism works against the morality play intent. The same difficulty exists with the figures of Mother and Sister: the reasons for their love of the white Devil Lady must be brought to the play rather than discovered in it. If the experience of the play is to become a ritual for the audience, terror cannot be so neatly encapsulated.

That Baraka sought to give his audience a more powerful emotional transformation than *Madheart* could provide is clear, for the work he created just a year later, *Slave Ship*, perfectly embodies the theater of cruelty and becoming toward which he was working. In *Slave Ship*, the emotional journey afforded the audience finally equals that of the character in the play.

Two plays Baraka wrote between *Madheart* and *Slave Ship*, *Home on the Range* and *Arm Yrself or Harm Yrself*, experiment with poster art and with language meant to engender the sense of chaos crucial to a truly Artaudian theater-of-cruelty experience. *Arm Yrself or Harm Yrself: A Message of Self Defense to Black Men* is a simple representation of poster art that warns of the necessity for carrying arms in self-defense.[72] Its

---

72. Imamu Amiri Baraka, *Arm Yrself or Harm Yrself: A Message of Self Defense to Black Men* (Newark, 1967).

opening image is of policemen breaking down a door and shooting those inside. As a woman mourns the death of one of those slaughtered, two brothers discuss and come to blows over the question of whether blacks should arm themselves or trust to "them" for their survival. While they fight with each other, the police approach and begin firing: both are killed.

In *Home on the Range*, Baraka began experimenting with theatrical language close to that conceived of by Artaud. The play is a curious amalgam of Baraka's earlier work as well as an experiment in language, and bears comparison especially with *The Slave*, which it seems at times to parody. In *Home on the Range* a Black Criminal breaks in on a white family. As he approaches the house, he observes a Mother, Father, Son, and Daughter watching television and speaking to one another in gibberish. He knocks at the door and, when the Daughter opens it, forces his way in.

> *Daughter.* Vatoloop? . . . Bastoloop, Baspobo.
> *Criminal.* Back up dollbaby, don't die in the doorway. . . .
> *Father. Seeing* CRIMINAL, *makes nervous step forward.* Lulurch. Crud. Daddoom. Crench . . . Vatloop Lulurch. Crench. Crench. *Shakes with fear, anger.* Vacuvashtung Schwacuschwactung. Yiip!

The Criminal is flabbergasted by their behavior. When laughter on the television sends them into virtual hysteria, he shoots the television set and attempts to threaten them into making sense: "What the hell's going on? Look you . . . I don't have time to look at your bony ass trying to dance. I'm just a working man. And I've come, quite frankly, to commit a crime. . . . This is the reign of terror and I'm Robespierre." Since this comment merely increases their hysteria, he adds: "If you want to talk, talk. For instance, you should have said, this is not the reign of terror, and Robespierre is dead, and was white, anyway."[73]

The situation becomes increasingly bizarre. A concealed loudspeaker announces the voice of God, which repeats "EVERYTHING'S COOL!" until the Criminal shoots the loudspeaker as well. In the next scene, the Criminal leads the family in singing "America the Beautiful" and a "soupy version of The Negro National Anthem 'Lift Every Voice and Sing.'" At the climax of the latter, a crowd of Black People rush in and begin a party, from which the Criminal detaches himself to address the audience: "This is the tone of America. My country 'tis of thee. He *shoots out over the audience.* This is the scene of the Fall. The

73. Imamu Amiri Baraka, *Home on the Range*, in *Drama Review*, XII (Summer, 1968), 107, 108.

demise of the ungodly. He *shoots once. Then quickly twice*. This is the cool takeover in the midst of strong rhythms, and grace. . . . Faggot Frankensteins of my sick dead holy brother. You betta' get outta here. He *shoots again three times*. The World!" [74]

The last scene discloses that only a few have survived the party: the Criminal, the Father, two black men, and a black woman. The others lie strewn about the room while the criminal questions the Father, who is finally talking normally: "I was born in Kansas City in 1920. My father was the vice-president of a fertilizer company. Before that we were phantoms. . . . Evil ghosts without substance." The play closes at dawn, as the Black Woman greets the others: "Good morning, Men. Good morning." [75]

Primarily comic and satiric, *Home on the Range* uses what Artaud calls "humor as destruction," which, according to Artaud, "can serve to reconcile the corrosive nature of laughter to the habits of reason." [76] Most of the black people on the stage, and presumably in the audience, are seduced into believing the idiocy of the family and the acceptance implied by the mock integrated singing and party. Few on stage survive it, as the Criminal's address forewarns. When the Father finally "confesses," he relates a genealogy that links him to the White Beast of the earlier plays, and the remaining characters indicate that they had suspected as much. The play's humor both entices the audience to let down its guard (by laughing) and makes judgment simple (the family is too ridiculous to be attractive—or dangerous). It ends on a serious note, however, reminding the audience to resist the seduction of humor as well as other types of seduction; the family in *Home on the Range* is far from innocuous.

Deflecting rage by portraying whites as humorous, and diminishing their power by making them objects of ridicule, are frequent devices in Afro-American folklore and literature. *Home on the Range* both employs and criticizes these traditional defense mechanisms (its title, of course, alludes to other aspects of the American folk tradition). But its mood and atmosphere have a Kafkaesque quality alien to those black traditions. The play suggests both the danger and the absurdity of "playing along with whites," a necessary aspect of using humor to deal with them.

74. *Ibid.*, 110–11.
75. *Ibid.*, 111.
76. Artaud, *The Theatre and Its Double*, 91.

While *Home on the Range* falls short of the theater-of-cruelty intensity Baraka sought with his linguistic experimentation, *Slave Ship*—
which was first presented by his Spirit House Movers and Players
in 1967 and later in Brooklyn, in November, 1969—embodies the theater of cruelty and becoming completely. *Slave Ship* recreates the
Middle Passage, the journey on the slave ship between Africa and
the New World; its principal metaphor thus is the historical event that
holds both psychic and physical danger—the danger of which Artaud
speaks.

In using this metaphor, Baraka seeks to transform its meaning. The
historical Middle Passage brought the slave from Africa to the hell of
American slavery; in Baraka's play, the journey is from that hell to liberation. The effect produced by language used primarily as incantation and evocation of human anguish; music; and the sound of whips
and chains is augmented by the heavy stench of both incense and
human excrement. During the first part of the pageant, the stage re-
creates the hold of a slave ship. The laughter of white men mingles
with the groans and cries of the slaves in the hold as they call out for
one other, curse their captors, and even kill themselves and their children. In the early part of the play, the gods they invoke are African, as
are the names they call each other. Later, spirituals mingle with cries
for Jesus. Images of African warriors dancing are contrasted with the
image of a shuffling plantation Negro who "yass's" his master and
then informs on Reverend Turner's uprising in return for a pork chop.
The scene is filled with the humming of slaves and "cold hideous
laughter." [77]

Following the betrayal are screams and "gun shots, combination of
slave ship and break up of revolt. Voices of master and slave in combat." The old slave Tom becomes a black preacher who speaks gibberish and phrases about integration while trying to hide the bodies
of burnt children that a woman lays at his feet. A chant backed by
saxophone and drums gathers might, and the slaves rise, dancing,
and kill the preacher; they then turn on the white voice to which he
was speaking. The play then briefly returns to the slave ship and to
the screams of the "killed white voice": "All players fixed in the half
light, at the [moment] of the act. Then lights go down. Black. Lights
come up abruptly, and the people on stage begin to dance. . . . Enter

77. LeRoi Jones, *Slave Ship*, in *Negro Digest*, XVI (April, 1967), 69.

audience; get members of audience to dance. To same music. Rise up. Turns into an actual party. When the party reaches some loose improvisation, etc. audience relaxed, somebody throws the preacher's head into the center of the floor, i.e., after dancing starts for real. Then black."[78]   Clayton Riley's review of *Slave Ship* acknowledged the power of the theatrical experience: "Here the thing is coming, bigger, more intensified than most dreams will allow, will permit or contain."[79] Other black and white reviewers concurred. *Slave Ship* sought, among other things, to translate historical fact into experiential knowledge and succeeded, incarnating the horror that history describes, in an image that delivers its emotional meaning directly.

Slave Ship embodies the quintessential theater-of-cruelty experience, for it creates for its audience not only the experience of the horror of the Middle Passage and black life in America but also an energy that gathers strength in the course of the play to emerge as celebration in the end. Its audience survives as Afro-Americans have survived, by channeling that energy into resistance and revolt.

Langston Hughes's chronicle play *Don't You Want to Be Free?* covers the same historical territory as *Slave Ship*; the differences between the two are a measure not only of the differences between their authors but also of the distance black theater traveled between 1938 and 1967. *Don't You Want to Be Free?* describes the emotional history of black Americans in considerably greater detail than *Slave Ship*. Hughes, however, relies on poetry and traditional black music, that is, on the experience of that emotional history as already shaped by the artists' imagination; and part of that shaping is itself a celebration of survival of that experience. Consequently, although pain is not distanced, horror is. Moreover, the movement of the play as a whole, from outrage to revolt, recapitulates the movement of individual scenes; the voices in the play gradually gather force, and the final plea for unity comes from people whose vitality and strength have been depicted throughout the work. There is no single epiphany.

In *Slave Ship*, so intense and inarticulate is the image of black enslavement portrayed that its horror supercedes all other qualities. No distance is possible, and the only release for emotion requires the audience join in the final dance—a dance that celebrates both a victory and the means used to effect it, for the dancing surrounds the

78. *Ibid.*, 69, 74.
79. Clayton Riley, "Theatre Review," *Liberator*, IX (December, 1969), 19.

severed head of the black preacher. While Hughes's play demands pride in black people as they are and have been, Baraka's work insists that the audience reexperience the actual terror of its history in order to free itself from that history, and to free trapped energy so that liberation, and dancing, are possible. Contrary to *Don't You Want to Be Free?*, only at the end of *Slave Ship* is the suffering, both on stage and in the audience, redeemed. Finally, whereas in Hughes's play blacks and whites join in at the end, it is highly improbable that white members of the audience would feel comfortable dancing at the end of *Slave Ship*. Thus, the play becomes theater of cruelty for whites in another sense: there is no drain for their abscess.[80]

Slave Ship brings to fruition Baraka's poetic and theatrical work in several ways. Its technique grows from his earlier experiments with language, with spectacle, and with creating a *mise en scène* through music, movement, and various uses of the human voice. More important, it makes vivid the cruelty of which he speaks in both his poetry and his other plays: it seeks to recreate for others the experience of his own agonizing Middle Passage and painful rebirth, which find their most eloquent expression in this particular segment of racial and social history.

Following *Slave Ship*, Baraka created a series of rituals in which the context of such works as *A Black Mass* and *The Motion of History* is expressed through movement, music, poetry, chant, and incantation.[81] An extension of the theater of *mise en scène* of which Artaud speaks, these rituals depict chaotic, cruel struggle resolved and made harmonious by a new black order, or they depict beautiful, compelling images in praise and celebration of the liberated black imagination. Their imagery either is drawn from African or Black Muslim mythology, or consists of portraits of the idealized man and woman of the future black world. In his ritual theater, even more than in his earlier work, Baraka addresses a black audience, for the imagination expressed is deliberately particular in meaning attributed and reference; like any religious iconography or service, it is dependent on the communion of the participants.

80. Artaud, *The Theatre and Its Double*, 31.
81. The published rituals written before 1970 include *Bloodrites*, in Woodie King and Ron Milner (eds.), *Black Drama Anthology* (New York, 1971), 25–31; *Black Power Chant*, in *Black Theatre*, No. 4 (April, 1970), 35; *Chant*, in *Black Theatre*, No. 5 (1971), 16–17; and BA-RA-KA, in Rochelle Owens (ed.), *Spontaneous Combustion: Eight New American Plays* (New York, 1972), 175–81.

During this period, Baraka wrote expressly political plays as well. *Police* attacks black members of the police force as traitors to their community; *Junkies Are Full of* (SHHH . . .) wages war on heroin dealers; *The Death of Malcolm* accuses the white establishment of responsibility for Malcolm's death. However, *Slave Ship* marks the end of Baraka's major influence on transforming the stage reality so that black theater might exist on its own terms. This is so, not only because of the rapid growth of black theater and the proliferation of talented black dramatists during the decade of his major work, but also, and perhaps more critically, because of his political shift during the mid-seventies from black nationalism to Marxism-Leninism, which entailed his rejection of cultural nationalism. While he continues to write plays and to see theater as an important didactic tool, his most recent work operates on a rational rather than on an affective level, and insists that the black experience must be examined and understood from the larger perspective of the class struggle in a capitalist society. Three plays have been published from this phase of his work: *The Motion of History*, *S-1*, and *What Was the Relationship of the Lone Ranger to the Means of Production*.[82] *S-1* takes its title from a not yet actual but, according to Baraka, entirely possible federal law allowing suppression of political activity challenging American capitalism and government. The other two titles more clearly suggest their plays' directions.

The best of the three, *The Motion of History*, in effect a long political tract, is an agitprop play of considerable merit. Possibly it was influenced by and is a comment on Hughes's *Don't You Want to Be Free?* [83] *The Motion of History* takes two innocent, or at least mystified, narrator protagonists, one black and the other white, through various scenes in American history. As in Hughes's play, the narrator protagonists both observe and participate in the action. The history they reenact focuses on active revolts in the Afro-American struggle for liberation, and reveals that struggle as masking the larger class struggle, in

82. Imamu Amiri Baraka, *Police*, in *Drama Review*, XII (Summer, 1968), 112–15; *Junkies Are Full of* (SHHH . . .), in King and Milner, *Black Drama Anthology*, 11–23; *The Death of Malcolm*, in Ed Bullins (ed.), *New Plays from the Black Theatre* (New York, 1969), 11–23; *The Motion of History* and *S-1*, both in Baraka, *The Motion of History and Other Plays* (New York, 1978); and *What Was the Relationship of the Lone Ranger to the Means of Production*, in Baraka, *Selected Plays and Prose of Amiri Baraka / LeRoi Jones* (New York, 1979).

83. Werner Sollors, *Amiri Baraka / LeRoi Jones: The Quest for a "Populist Modernism"* (New York, 1978), 247–61.

which those in power use racism to divert whites from how they also are exploited. Through most of the play, the two protagonists maintain an uneasy friendship and alliance, but as the lessons of their history take effect, they decide to part and return to their separate homes to examine the roots of oppression in their own communities. When they reunite in the final scene, a Marxist-Leninist party convention, their friendship stands on the solid basis of comradeship in a mutual struggle.

While *The Motion of History* reveals Baraka's considerable talents as a didactic and political dramatist, neither the form of politics he espouses in it nor the overtly didactic approach of his work has gained much following. This is not to say, however, that *The Motion of History* makes no contribution to black theater. Although it concerns itself with the larger shape of American history rather than the particulars of Afro-American history, it is through the latter that the former is understood. The play's white protagonist, Moriority, in marked contrast to Loco and Duff in *Experimental Death Unit #1*, learns from the black experience, his self-understanding made possible by his ability to see and heed its implications. Moreover, unlike the interracial alliance proposed at the end of Hughes's *Don't You Want to Be Free?*, that in *The Motion of History* extends unselfconsciously throughout the play, with an assurance in part made possible by Baraka's earlier work. In terms of stage reality, the play's class analysis produces an interesting reversal: Afro-American history and the perceptions it engenders become symbolic of the history and perceptions of the majority of Americans, likewise exploited by the capitalist system. The black stage reality functions as primary ground for both black and white characters; acknowledging it as such liberates the white characters as well as the black.

Given the centrality of Baraka's work to the Black Arts Movement, and given that he alone of the dramatists we have considered demanded, by the nature of his work, an exclusively black audience, it is perhaps ironic that he completes the process of making the black experience the primary metaphor in a play for a mixed audience, and that he does so under the influence of Marxist-Leninist ideology. His current position is, however, a logical progression from rather than a break with his earlier cultural nationalism. His insistence in *Blues People* that black music involves attitude, or stance, translates easily into an analysis that perceives certain cultural expressions and forms

as representing the world view of the dominant class defined not only
racially but economically as well. Also, certain Marxist premises have
informed much of the recent writing on racism, and given Baraka's
consistent interest in how culture shapes internal and other personal
conflict as well as social and political conflict, it is not surprising that
he finds the left persuasive.

Having achieved phenomenal success on the mainstream stage,
Baraka abandoned it and the criteria by which he had been so highly
praised. His deliberate, dramatic gesture brought black theater into a
new phase. Like Hughes's gospel plays, Baraka's poster-art theater and
his rituals constitute exact but limited solutions to the problem of
creating a black stage reality. However, his artistic career made possible the final resolution of the problem: as the critic Toni Cade has
commented, after Baraka black theater simply was.[84] Three plays high-
light his accomplishments: *Dutchman*, *The Slave*, and *Slave Ship*. In the
first two, the characters operate as metaphors for each other: Lulu
and Clay encounter each other as stereotypes; Walker reexperiences
his personal and literary ties with the white world in his meeting with
Grace and Easley. In both plays, the setting is white, though in *The
Slave* the changeover is imminent. In *Slave Ship*, however, the white
presence exists only as perceived in historical memory and as internalized voice; the stage reality is entirely the product of the black
imagination.

Black theater's indebtedness to Baraka cannot be overestimated.
Ed Bullins' tribute speaks for a whole generation of recent black playwrights: "I went to see *The Toilet* and *Dutchman*, and when I saw *The Toilet*
the whole world opened up to me. . . . [He] essentially created me
as a playwright and created many other young black playwrights."[85]
The indebtedness extends to the larger American stage as well, for
Dutchman shattered the rules about how the black experience could
be depicted; the work finally strips the black image of its metaphorical quality, investing metaphor in the white figure instead. Thus
the black stage reality exists simply because, as Ed Bullins often
notes after his list of characters, the people in the play are black.

Hughes accomplished this process earlier by embedding his im-

84. Toni Cade, "Black Theatre," in Addison Gayle, Jr. (ed.), *Black Expression:
Essays by and About Black Americans in the Creative Arts* (New York, 1969), 137.
85. Marvin X, "An Interview with Ed Bullins: Black Theatre," *Negro Digest*,
XVIII (April, 1969), 15–16.

ages in Afro-American history and culture, in the ground in which they "belonged." Baraka, however, began his artistic career imaginatively divested of his roots, as a middle-class, northern, black intellectual. His journey "home" could not be accomplished by merely turning to his past, for his grandfather was not a slave but a nightwatchman, as Clay tells Lulu. The black world recreated by Langston Hughes brings the black past into the present. That depicted by Baraka originates both in present black culture and in white, and constitutes a genuinely new black language and a new black imaginative world.

FOUR ❧
"LIKE NIGGERS"
Ed Bullins' Theater of Reality

> All their faces turned into the lights and you work on them black nigger magic, and cleanse them at having seen the ugliness and if the beautiful see themselves, they will love themselves.
>
> —LeRoi Jones

With this epigraph to his first volume of plays, Ed Bullins acknowledged Jones's influence on his work. But while Jones chose the theater of symbol and allegory to show the beautiful themselves, Bullins, early in his dramatic career, chose what he termed a "theatre of reality": "Any theatrical style or method can be used separately or in combination to reach the truth of the play . . . dramatizing the journey of the character through his own psyche to reach his loss of innocence, self-awareness or illumination. To reach what individually is called reality. The method is not the goal in this theatre; the result must elicit the single response of 'Yes!'" [1]

Bullins' dramatic focus has remained consistent throughout more than fifty plays: the loving and relentless exploration of inner forces that constrain black people from realizing their freedom and potential. In directing his attention to this concern, Bullins simply assumes what Baraka chooses to explicate, that racist America has formed and deformed aspects of the black experience and consciousness. The constraints that most interest Bullins reside within his characters and are of their own choosing; even his portrayal of interracial encounters focuses on the behavior of the black character rather than on the perversity of the white.

The penetrating honesty characteristic of Bullins' work indicates his imaginative and literary assurance. In his plays, a black stage reality and a black audience are assumed. The matters he takes up often are intimate, sensitive, and particular to the black experience. As one critic observed, whites in the audience of a Bullins play are "interlopers"; they are generally ignored, not threatened.[2] Nevertheless, white audiences and critics have praised Bullins as wholeheartedly as

---

1. Ed Bullins, "Theatre of Reality," *Negro Digest*, XV (April, 1966), 65.
2. Catherine Hughes, quoted in "Ed Bullins," *Contemporary Authors*, XLIX-LII (1975), 91.

the black audiences for whom he writes; many critics, both black and white, consider him among America's finest playwrights.

Once Bullins arrived in New York in 1967, he established his reputation quickly.[3] He went there at the invitation of Robert Macbeth, the director of the New Lafayette Players, a company of black actors and actresses who had been working together for several years. Impressed by some scripts Bullins had sent him, Macbeth wanted Bullins to write for the company, which had just opened a theater in Harlem. In this ideal situation, Bullins' considerable talent flourished.

In 1968 the New Lafayette Players gave Bullins' work two productions. The first, done at the American Place Theatre because their own theater had burned down, was called *Three Plays by Ed Bullins*. It included *Clara's Ole Man*, *A Son, Come Home* and *The Electronic Nigger*, and earned Bullins the Vernon Rice Drama Desk Award for that year. In December, 1968, the players opened their new theater with a production of Bullins' first full-length work, *In the Wine Time*; it, too, was highly praised.

Also in 1968, Bullins' impact was felt when he edited the influential black theater issue of the *Drama Review*.[4] His selection of plays included what he called "Black Revolutionary Theatre" and "Theatre of Black Experience," the latter realistic portrayals of ordinary black life. The plays and the articles in the issue proposed a definition of black theater as politically radical, situated in the black community, conforming to a black aesthetic, and dedicated to a black audience. This anthology, followed the next year by *New Plays from the Black Theatre*, which he edited and which contained works fitting his definition, made Bullins a powerful arbiter of what constituted the new black theater.

3. The information for the following biography of Bullins is derived from several sources: "Ed Bullins," *Contemporary Authors* (1975), 89–91; "Ed Bullins," *Current Biography* (1977), 90–93; Jervis Anderson, "Profiles," *New Yorker*, June 16,1973, pp. 40–79; Marvin X, "Interview with Ed Bullins," in Ed Bullins (ed.), *New Plays from the Black Theatre* (New York, 1969); Richard Wesley, "An Interview with Playwright Ed Bullins," *Black Creation*, IV (Winter, 1973), 8–10; Clayton Riley, "Bullins: 'It's Not the Play I Wrote,'" New York *Times*, March 19, 1972, Sec. D., pp. 1, 7.

Details about the New Lafayette Theatre are derived primarily from Jessica B. Harris, "The New Lafayette Theater: 'Nothing Lasts Forever,'" *Black Creation*, IV (Summer, 1973), 8–10; Anderson, "Profiles"; and the magazine published by the New Lafayette Theatre, *Black Theatre*, Nos. 1–5. The journal, edited by Bullins, was published erratically from 1968 to 1971.

4. *Drama Review*, XII (Summer, 1968).

Bullins is reticent about his life, although much of his experience emerges in his fiction and plays. He grew up in the slums of north Philadelphia; he once characterized himself as "a street nigger."[5] He quit high school at seventeen and joined the Navy soon after; his tour of duty, from 1952 to 1955, left him time to read, and when he returned to Philadelphia, he finished high school. Apparently, he also resumed his street life; Bullins speaks of his move to Los Angeles in 1958 as a necessary escape from a desperate existence. As a student at City College of Los Angeles, Bullins observed the city's interracial population, whose activities formed a microcosm of the changing race relations and growing black nationalism of the early 1960s. What he saw provided him with material for many stories and plays; in 1961 he began writing poetry and fiction, and in 1965, a year after moving to San Francisco, he turned to drama: "I was reading a lot of plays and I was going to a lot of plays. . . . And I wanted to write a play. . . . And then I got drunk one night and I wrote HOW DO YOU DO. So since I had written one play I had to write another one. Two weeks late [sic], I wrote DIALECT DETERMINISM. . . . We needed another play to fill the bill. So I sat down and wrote CLARA'S OLE MAN."[6]

Bullins became deeply involved in the beginning of black theater in San Francisco. He participated in the Blacks Arts Alliance, Black Arts / West, and Black House, the headquarters of the Black Panther party, in which he served briefly as minister of culture. However, a split occurred between the party's "artistic" and "political" members; the latter insisted that culture served only in so far as it pushed people into the streets, and found the work of the artistic group, Bullins among them, suspect. In 1967 Bullins left Black House, which disbanded shortly thereafter. At loose ends, he wrote to Macbeth and went to New York.

Bullins is an enormously prolific writer, and his work is uneven. At its best, it is brilliant and his talent is frequently acknowledged. In 1971 Bullins received a Black Arts Alliance Award and Obies for two plays, In New England Winter and The Fabulous Miss Marie. In 1975 he won the New York Drama Critics' Circle Award for The Taking of Miss Janie.

In 1972 Bullins incurred a reputation of a different sort when he roundly condemned the Lincoln Center production of his play The Duplex: A Black Love Fable in Four Movements, accusing Jules Irving, the di-

5. "Ed Bullins," Current Biography (1977), 90.
6. Marvin X, "Interview with Ed Bullins," xiii–xiv.

rector of the Repertory Theater of Lincoln Center, of turning it into a minstrel show. In response, Gil Moses, the show's black director, defended his production, as did several critics; others had reservations about The Duplex, not always those of Bullins.[7] Bullins denied the accusation that he created the controversy to cause "a play in the real world," an admitted delight of his.[8] Nevertheless, the situation was probably enjoyable to him. His turning on the establishment that had just given him what many would consider a break caused intense discomfort at Lincoln Center and among New York theater critics.

From 1968 to 1973, there were fifteen productions of Bullins' plays in New York theaters, an astonishing achievement. Five were at the New Lafayette Theatre, on 137th Street and Seventh Avenue, the center of Harlem; others were at an impressive array of theaters throughout the city, including La Mama Experimental Theatre Club, New Federal Theatre of Henry Street Playhouse, American Place Theatre, Chelsea Theatre, Lincoln Center Forum, the Public Theatre, and Perry Street Theatre. After the New Lafayette, La Mama, with four productions, gave Bullins his most frequent support.

The New Lafayette productions are particularly noteworthy because, until its closing in 1972, the theater provided an exciting, influential model for black theater on the principles outlined in Bullins' issue of the Drama Review. Not incidentally, most of its productions were of his own plays. This favoritism aroused accusations of cliquishness, and resulted in, for a time, many encountering the new black theater through Bullins' works. His productions at the American Place Theatre, La Mama, and other houses similarly extended his influence.

Bullins' plays express contemporary black theater's new artistic freedom and maturity. The stage reality Bullins assumes, the themes he chooses, the characters and settings he creates, and the language he uses clearly build on the work of his predecessors and proclaim black theater's new assurance. He pursues his central theme, the inner constraints hampering freedom, in his plays of the Black Revolutionary Theatre, which comment directly on politically revolutionary concerns; in his plays on race relations, which examine those relations

7. Several of these critics are quoted in Anderson, "Profiles," 42. For the first salvo in the debate over The Duplex, see New York Times, March 19, 1972; Riley, "Bullins: 'It's Not the Play I Wrote'"; and Walter Kerr, "Mr. Bullins Is Himself at Fault," New York Times, March 19, 1972, Sec. D, pp. 1, 7.

8. Anderson, "Profiles," 75.

from a social rather than a political perspective; and in his Theatre of Black Experience works, which depict life in black communities about the country.

Certain general aspects of Bullins' technique especially reveal the new imaginative assurance on which the black stage reality is based: his attempt to establish a particular relationship with his audience, his use of street language, and the way that the reappearance of certain characters in different works builds up a sense of a black world beyond the limits of any particular play. Bullins' attitude toward his audience is at least in part influenced by Macbeth. On his productions of In the Wine Time and We Righteous Bombers, Macbeth commented:

> My attitude toward theatre is that there is no audience, and no actors, that the separation is very slim, and that the people who come to "The Room" come to be in the "play," because their being there is part of the play. . . . But in the theatre we're finally going to reach the point where the communication between the people who perform the rituals and the people who sit through them—the communication will be much more direct; it will even be physical, the actors will touch the audience and the audience will then come with the actors into the play.[9]

Audience participation in a Bullins play is sometimes literal, as in It Bees Dat Way, first performed in 1970, a short piece that prescribes that its audience be at least two-thirds white. The audience is admitted into a room with only a streetlamp to suggest a Harlem street corner. The actors, portraying various street types, molest the white members of the audience at will, jostling them, soliciting the men, propositioning the women, and picking pockets. Finally, as the atmosphere becomes abrasive and violent, the whites are slowly dismissed from the room because, as one character admonishes the others: "Des hare people ain't the ones to get . . . they ain't got nothin' . . . just like you and me . . . they just work for them that made dis mess. . . . The ones to shoot is who what made this mess."[10]

Several levels of audience participation occur in this play. While the harassment of the whites may arouse pleasure, anxiety, or concern in black members of the audience, for the whites the experience is unpleasant, even fear provoking. Both blacks and whites are challenged to act, and their responses reveal their basic racial and social atti-

9. Marvin X, "The Black Ritual Theatre: An Interview with Robert Macbeth," Black Theatre, No. 3 (1969), 21.

10. Ed Bullins, It Bees Dat Way, in Bullins, Four Dynamite Plays (New York, 1972), 15.

tudes. It Bees Dat Way slyly and pointedly actualizes the experience whites desired when they flocked to Baraka's plays to, as Mick Jagger says, "get their fair share of abuse." However, ultimately, the play addresses the members of its black audience, for they alone remain after the whites have been ushered out and the final comments are addressed to them.

In In the Wine Time Bullins not only invites audience participation but challenges his audience to identify with and thus at least imaginatively join the activities on stage. In this play, two central characters, Cliff Dawson and his wife, Lou, are passing a summer evening lounging on their front stoop, drinking wine. Early in the play, they quarrel over their boisterousness, resented by their neighbors:

> Cliff. (Raises his voice) Make up yo' mind, broad. Now what is it . . . do we cuss and drink like sailors or cuss like sailors and drink like . . . like . . . what?
> Lou.   Like niggers. (At the last word lights go up on the other stoops, revealing the occupants looking at Cliff and Lou.)[11]

With the exception of the Krumps next door, the entire neighborhood is black; Lou's comment dares both stage and house audience to identify with the couple. Nigger in this context is a black word, the term of insult and endearment spoken by blacks among themselves and thus a mark of the stage reality giving rise to Lou's utterance. If, like the Krumps, whites are present, they are on black turf, and must participate in and accept its sense of reality at their own risk. Furthermore, in a different but equally pointed fashion, black middle-class members of the audience are challenged to identify with their ghetto brethren.

Moreover, Lou's comment is not simply an address to the audience but may be taken as "signifying," implying an invitation to respond. Bullins' plays often create such opportunities for members of a black audience to participate in the event on stage in traditional black ways: commenting on the action among themselves and entering into dialogue with the characters. Participating in a Bullins play, however, is a dangerous action. It Bees Dat Way makes the danger physical and explicit, at least for its white audience. The more important danger lies in the painful illumination that awaits those who dare to enter the world Bullins' play unfolds. Through the fate of one of his charac-

11. Ed Bullins, In the Wine Time, in Bullins, Five Plays by Ed Bullins (New York, 1968), 123, herinafter referred to parenthetically by page number in the text.

ters in his very early play *Clara's Ole Man*, Bullins suggests that any audience of his plays is in danger, particularly if it comes to understand what it witnesses. In *Clara's Ole Man*, Jack, a young intellectual, innocently courts Clara, unaware that her "ole man" is not an absent male but Big Girl, the powerful lesbian dominating the party in Clara's kitchen. The news is as brutal as the beating subsequently administered by local toughs to punish his naïveté and intrusion.

The uncompromising challenge Bullins flings to his audience declares that the question of who owns the stage has been forever settled. In the black landscape established by Langston Hughes, a white audience realizes its presence on alien ground, and finds that ground ultimately hospitable. A black audience of a Hughes play participates in familiar forms of celebration and takes special pleasure in the novelty of finding the familiar in a theatrical setting. Baraka's plays portray the stage takeover; in almost all his plays, the stage reality is either contested or in the process of transformation through exorcism. In a Bullins play, the process is complete; the play opens assuming the black stage reality, and proceeds with the kinds of explorations that such a reality makes possible.

Bullins establishes this world, in part, through language and music. As Lindsay Patterson observes, Bullins has a "wonderful ear for the language of the ghetto," and the effect of his fidelity to that speech is not simply verisimilitude but also the creation of a *mise en scène* that is lively, earthy, volatile, and, because its violence is barely submerged, dangerous.[12] In 1961, in *The Toilet*, Baraka similarly used crude street language, but the effect was different; it was a challenge to his audience and a comment on the world depicted. Unlike Bullins, Baraka did not find the speech lyrical; rather, he used the play's language to extend its unsavory setting. Bullins, however, delights in black street argot and reveals its lyricism while keeping its harshness and profanity intact. His plays disclose that ghetto speech ultimately reflects a brutality the speakers turn first on themselves, and that the speech is equally capable of eloquently expressing his characters' search for love, affection, faith, and security. In Bullins' plays, black street argot comes into its own.

Equally a part of the atmosphere of a Bullins work is black music. In his plays, a radio, a stereo, or a group of live musicians is always

12. Lindsay Patterson, Review of Ed Bullins' *In the Wine Time*, in New York *Times*, December 22, 1968, Sec. 2, p. 7.

playing. Jazz, blues, or rhythm-and-blues provides the background—more accurately, is the ground—for his characters' activities. Some of his later works, for example, *The Fabulous Miss Marie* and "Home Boy," approximate the structure of a jazz piece, allowing characters to step out of the action and speak a solo that expresses their particular handling, understanding, or experience of the play's theme. Several plays, notably *The Duplex*, include blues songs written by the author, sometimes occurring within the action and other times as interlude. Like his use of language, Bullins' use of music to establish setting extends beyond verisimilitude. He suggests what Baraka concluded in *Blues People*: that music is black America's primary language.

Perhaps the most daring mark of Bullins' imaginative and literary assurance and the resulting black stage reality is his extension of the dramatic landscape to include the world outside the individual play. Six of Bullins' plays form the opening of a planned project, the "Twentieth Century Cycle." [13] Its characters, both major and minor, appear in many other of his works as well. By announcing the cycle, Bullins made explicit his attempt to create an extensive, imaginative black world that he and his audience can revisit for further exploration and understanding. His works keep returning to a group of characters who live on or wander between the east and west coasts, and particularly between the cities of Philadelphia and Los Angeles in the late 1950s and the 1960s. Three figures are central to the plays and fiction to date: Cliff Dawson, his half-brother, Steve Benson—the protagonist in Bullins' novel *The Reluctant Rapist*, and often considered the author's persona—and Michael Brown, the central character in the cycle's most recent play, "DADDY!"

The range of setting in Bullins' work constitutes a break with the tendency of both black and white writers portraying black life to locate their characters in places traditionally associated with black Americans. For example, Richardson and Edmonds, both southerners, situated most of their plays in the Deep South. When Hughes specified place in his plays and particularly in his poetry, he usually located his characters in Harlem, which, for him, was both an actual

13. The six plays in the cycle to date are *In the Wine Time*; *In New England Winter*, in Bullins (ed.), *New Plays from the Black Theatre*; *The Duplex: A Black Love Fable in Four Movements* (New York, 1971); *The Fabulous Miss Marie*, in Bullins (ed), *The New Lafayette Theatre Presents* (Garden City, N.Y., 1974); "Home Boy" and "DADDY!," both unpublished.

place and an imaginative landscape that he continually explored and celebrated.

Bullins eschews both the South and Harlem as settings. The reason is partly autobiographical: he writes about places he knows; and he has never lived in the Deep South and until 1967 had never lived in Harlem. The absence of traditional black settings has a larger, paradoxical significance as well. Although Bullins' characters are often situated someplace (Philadelphia, the eastern shore of Maryland, Los Angeles), they seem rooted nowhere. This rootlessness suggests a black attitude, arising from historical experience, that in spite of long tenancy, the land is never really theirs. At the same time, in Bullins' works the black world is simply wherever there are black people, for their characteristic ways of speaking, their music, and their perspectives on the world transform the space they inhabit. Thus Bullins extends the black imaginative domain from coast to coast.

Most of Bullins' characters are wanderers; they locate themselves in familial ties and community relationships rather than in place, and these relationships provide a nexus for identity. For example, Cliff's Philadelphia companions reappear in Los Angeles, in *In New England Winter*; his unknown father surfaces in *The Duplex* (although Cliff is not in that play, and Steve, who might have caught the allusion to their mutual mother, is absent when her name is mentioned). Relationships provide the only real grounding of the characters. Through these relationships, which frequently dissolve or are disrupted, the characters strive valiantly to compensate for their geographic rootlessness. An important effect of this focus on persons and relationship rather than on place is that the concern of the audiences of Bullins' plays is directed to the characters themselves: one wonders where they will appear next and what is happening to them during the plays from which they are absent. More important, the focus makes central to Bullins' plays the as yet fragile but developing sense of community among Afro-Americans that transcends physical proximity and that is ultimately the meaning of black nationalism.

Eugene O'Neill's fragmentary cycle aside, the project in American literature analogous to Bullins' is William Faulkner's fictive South, Yoknapatawpha County, a particular corner of the world in which the southern experience and history are elaborated and made meaningful. Both his similarities to and differences from Faulkner are helpful in understanding Bullins' work. As in Faulkner, although the fictive reality reflects and comments on actual history, its persons, relation-ships, geography, and history are sui generis and elaborations of the artist's vision, not just allegories of personal, regional, or racial his-tory. Just as Faulkner in part created his fictive South to reveal to southerners and the rest of the country the richness and coherence of the region's native culture, Bullins seeks to create a literary landscape through which a significant part of America can come to know itself and be known. With the possible exception of Langston Hughes, no black writer has attempted to create such an extended black landscape.

Literary creations such as Nathaniel Hawthorne's New England, Mark Twain's West, Henry James's New York, and James Fenimore Cooper's frontier have served a particular function in the American imagination. In a country so extensive and so rapidly changing, litera-ture has often provided the only mode of apprehending places, people, history. The Negro has been part of all of these literary creations but, before Bullins, had been seen from a white perspective, as a figure in someone else's landscape. Bullins' plays reveal black America and its midcentury perspective on the country as a whole. In this vein, Bullins commented about his cycle: "All the statements about the black experience have already been made, all the truths have been told. But the artist also re-creates reality in a new atmosphere—gives you a fresh illumination, a fresh view of things . . . he extends your vision." [14]

However, while geography describes the perimeters of Faulkner's territory, "Black" describes the perimeters of Bullins' imaginative world. "The people in this play are Black," frequently ends his drama-tis personae, and his plays define and elaborate that comment. Bul-lins depicts Black as a way of being in the world, as a perspective, as a language, and as a life lived to music: blues, jazz, rhythm-and-blues. Black is also being in bondage, not only to the white man, but to chains forged by those who wear them, and worn because they are familiar, predictable, secure. Bullins entitled an anthology of his plays The Theme Is Blackness; the title appropriately describes the rest of his work as well. [15]

A passage in The Reluctant Rapist illuminates the author's central

14. Anderson, "Profiles," 73.
15. Ed Bullins, The Theme Is Blackness: "The Corner" and Other Plays (New York, 1973).

concerns. In this passage, Steve Benson relates that the first book his mother bought him was Richard Wright's *Black Boy*: "[She] gave me *Black Boy* to enlighten me. My life has held recurrences of that horrible experience ever since. . . . In all my reading until then and most of it since then . . . that was the single character that I felt a definite spiritual kinship with, and I attempted to strangle that apparition's first breath. My hands are still partially encircling its black throat."[16]

In a long, moving passage, Steve explains his fear that Wright's life could have been his; his child's mind protested against what he understood, but he suspected that the character spoke truly. The most painful aspect of Wright's gradual understanding of his childhood centers not on the repressive influence of the white South but rather on the internalized repressiveness of the black community, and of his own family, which sought to stifle his growing awareness of the world. In *Black Boy*, love is expressed brutally lest an even greater brutality strike from the outside, white world.

In Bullins' plays, the white world is remote, the oppression is completely internalized, and the violence is that among brothers and without purpose. His characters enslave themselves to drugs, alcohol, love relationships. They founder in traps of their own making, erected to prevent encounter with perhaps a more terrible trap beyond their control—or even with freedom itself. Bullins' often harsh evaluation of his characters' choices does not diminish his insistence that they can make other choices if they relinquish their illusions and come to know themselves. Although an admirer of the Absurdists, Bullins does not perceive the jagged edge of black existence as reflecting existential necessity.[17] Pandora, a character in *Goin'a Buffalo*, proclaims: "Nothin' bad comes out of me or from my box, baby. Nothin' bad. You can believe that. It's all in what you bring to us."[18] "Us" is all women; in *Goin'a Buffalo* women represent life.

In Bullins' plays, every situation has the potential for order and for

16. Ed Bullins, *The Reluctant Rapist* (New York, 1973), 144–45. This novel, Bullins' first, relates the childhood and young adulthood of Steve, also known as Chuckie and Dandy, depending on his surroundings. The novel is clearly heavily autobiographical, and for that reason certain passages are particularly useful for understanding Bullins' dramatic work.

17. For his admiration of Absurdism, see "Ed Bullins," *Negro Digest*, XV (October, 1966), 80.

18. Ed Bullins, *Goin'a Buffalo*, in Bullins, *Five Plays*, 4, hereinafter referred to parenthetically by page number in the text.

chaos: what his characters bring to it determines what ensues. Bullins' use of several recurring symbols—wine, parties, and especially women—reiterates this point. Drinking wine allows communion or unleashes destruction; parties engender community or end in discord; women give life or are the occasion for despair—the choice remains with his characters. With this insistence, Bullins delivers to his characters and to his audience their freedom.

Plays depicting violent political revolution or the destruction of both whites and blacks who accept American political and social ideology are those most commonly associated with black theater, particularly of the late 1960s. Rightly so, for revolution constituted the central metaphor of the 1960s black theater movement. The metaphor included the imaginative overturning not only of black self-perception but also of the entire social order; it predicted that the imaginative act would be made literal. Bullins created a few of what he called "Black Revolutionary Commercials," and he anthologized revolutionary drama in the black theater issue of the *Drama Review* and in *New Plays from the Black Theatre*. His usual approach to stage revolution, however, differed markedly from that of his fellow artists. For Bullins, plays depicting revolution were objects of concern in themselves, and typically his plays examine the implications of both revolutionary rhetoric and physical violence. Unlike his companions, Bullins sought not to convert blacks to the belief in revolution but to assume and test the revolutionary mentality. In short, from the very outset of his dramatic career, Bullins was the only black playwright of the 1960s to question what was becoming a dramatic and imaginative cliche.

One of Bullins' earliest plays, *Dialect Determinism (or The Rally)*, written in 1965, portrays the confidence man turned political opportunist, the false prophet whose facile and gratifying rhetoric distracts the people from the real leader when he appears to them. The play depicts a composite political rally and church service during which Boss Brother assumes the garb of Hitler, Lenin, Marx, and finally, Jesus. He claims also to be Malcolm X, but Malcolm's spirit rises from the audience to defend itself, and incapacitates half the men present before being forcibly evicted. Finally, Boss Brother tells his audience that their cause requires a martyr, and assenting, they turn on him.

Alternately humorous and terrifying, the play decries the illogic and mystification that were frequently the bases of revolutionary rhetoric. In a concise parody of what could be heard on any street corner of the ghetto in 1965, Boss Brother moves from declaring black people the most honest in the world and thus not needing to fool themselves "by sayin' it's some sort of holy crusade . . . if [they] get [their] chance finally to kick the hell out of somebody for a change" to admitting that blacks are dishonest at times, for to be so is to be human—and blacks are human. And finally he states: "The reason we's don't have to worry 'bout honesty is because dis ain't our society no way and what's ain't yours you don't have to care about no way." The audience accepts each proposition with uncritical enthusiasm, including Boss Brother's plan to take over: "DIALECT DETERMINISM . . . YAWL!" [19]

The presence of the "Visitor" at the rally, at whom Boss Brother winks during a crucial moment, establishes a frame for the theater audience. The visitor is only momentarily drawn into challenging the speaker, and withdraws at the end when the audience turns mob; it is his first time at such a gathering, and his distress at the proceedings contrasts with the enthusiasm of the others. Both the visitor's withdrawal and the doorman's comment to him as he leaves, "Never seen my people in such high spirits," apparently distance the event depicted.[20] However, although the parody of revolutionary rhetoric is obvious and the visitor seems easily to extricate himself from the proceedings, an ambiguous tone in the ending suggests that distance does not imply safety.

Terrifying in a different way is Bullins' later play Death List, written in 1970. While a black man prepares rifle and bullets, he methodically recites the names of the black men and women who signed a New York Times statement in support of Israel; he terms each "Enemy of the Black People." Counterpoint to his appalling recitation is a black woman's pleading with him to give up his concentration on ending the lives of others and on "revolutionary suicide" learned from "the supreme killer of the Universe, the white / beast / devil," and to turn to building the future with her instead. Finally, she challenges him: "Are you not the true enemy of Black People? Think hard now. Are you not the white-created demon that we were all warned about? Is it far more than superstition that you accuse me of to say that you are our

19. Ed Bullins, Dialect Determinism, in Bullins, The Theme Is Blackness, 24, 25, 34.
20. Ibid., 37.

greatest threat to survival now, in these times?"[21] Her plea and challenge remain unacknowledged; the play ends with the cry of his first victim.

Death List questions whether the image of the death-dealing revolutionary is not finally perverse and a self-destructive fantasy of "power, manhood and identity."[22] The woman pleads for an awareness that behind his roll call are sixty black lives—a plea her companion ignores. Whether the audience can ignore it depends partially on the emphasis given her voice in the production.[23] The cold recitation is in itself a chilling experience one cannot imagine an audience easily accepting; so extensive is the list of names that the inclusion of at least some would be protested by most members of the audience.

Bullins' only full-length play treating revolution directly, We Righteous Bombers, was produced and published under the pseudonym "Kingsley Bass, Jr., a twenty-four-year-old black man murdered by Detroit police during the uprising."[24] Both the play and the controversy surrounding it further reveal Bullins' attitude toward dialogues about revolution.

We Righteous Bombers is a thinly disguised version of Albert Camus' The Just Assassins.[25] Camus' play, set in Moscow, 1906, portrays the conflicts of a group of terrorists who assassinate the Grand Duke. The first attempt fails because Yanek, the man entrusted with the mission, sees the duke's children with him in the carriage and does not wish to harm them. Successful the second time, when he finds the duke alone, Yanek is immediately taken into custody and, refusing to bargain for his life, is executed. The play meditates on the meaning of taking another's life for ideological reasons, even in the name of justice; it also explores each character's search for a return to innocence in the face of the gravity of the act.

Certainly Bullins believed that the ethical issues raised by Camus

21. Ed Bullins, Death List, in Bullins, Four Dynamite Plays, 36, 37.

22. Ibid., 28.

23. How strong Bullins intended the woman's voice to be is not clear. However, given his concerns about drama depicting such revolutionary acts, it is likely that he desired her objections stressed.

24. Ed Bullins, We Righteous Bombers, in Bullins (ed.), New Plays from the Black Theatre, "Biographical Information." Bullins still denies he wrote the play, at least "for the record" (Ed Bullins to author, February 24, 1982).

25. Albert Camus, The Just Assassins, in Camus, Caligula and Three Other Plays, trans. Stuart Gilbert (New York, 1958).

were critical to the facile talk of revolution and bloodshed popular with black audiences, and his handling of the original adds questions beyond those of Camus. While Camus establishes a realistic setting and linear time frame in *The Just Assassins*, Bullins creates an open playing space with only a jail cell in the center and a fluid time frame. Lights, sound, and images on screens provide the *mise en scène*. The time of his play is not the past but the future; a news bulletin explains that apartheid and a complete dictatorship have existed in America since black revolutionary activity intensified. Blacks live behind barbed wire in camps governed by black prefects and patrolled by black soldiers.

Although essentially he retains the original text, Bullins reorders its sequence and adds a twist to the plot that reveals his additional intent. In Bullins' play, Murray Jackson (his version of Yanek) discovers that the man he thought was the Grand Prefect (who represents Camus' Grand Duke) is an imposter, and that the chief of police who interrogates him is actually the Grand Prefect. Moreover, he is informed that all the people his cadre has assassinated are actors; thus it has accomplished only useless murder. Furthermore, one of the women terrorists persists in speculating that all the killings have been manipulated by whites since all their targets have been black people and since the orders they have carried out were from an unknown superior.

A further alteration of Camus' plot elaborates and articulates the question of illusion versus reality raised by the woman's doubts. In *The Just Assassins*, a fellow prisoner acts as executioner, his sentence reduced a year for every person he kills. He excuses his treachery by saying he merely follows orders. Bullins retains this character, but in *We Righteous Bombers* the executioner is himself betrayed. The chief of police forces Jackson to consent to replace the inmate executioner in order to save his comrades. Thus the scene closing the play and witnessed by all the characters, apparently Jackson's execution, is actually Jackson executing his predecessor.

We Righteous Bombers challenges every aspect of plays dealing with revolutionary violence. Not only does it, through Camus' text, comprehensively raise the ethical issues that must be confronted if the new society emerging after the revolution is to approach those ideals in whose name it has been won, but, further, it suggests that the black revolution envisioned on American soil most likely will result in even greater repression of blacks than they previously experienced, and in a genocide cruelly manipulated so as to appear self-inflicted. For Bullins, whenever blacks talk of killing other blacks or actually kill them, for any reason, only the oppressor is served. In *The Reluctant Rapist* his hero sadly observes, "The world prepares the black man in a single skill: treachery to his fellows."[26] For Bullins, internecine revolutionary acts fall into that category.

Bullins' play was produced at the New Lafayette Theatre in 1969 amid a storm of controversy, and provoked a heated symposium, reported in *Black Theatre*.[27] The symposium particularly addressed the question of the responsibility of the black artist.[28] Ernie Mkalimoto and Askia Muhammad Touré insisted that the philosophical confusion that the play exhibited was destructive for its audience. Baraka, Larry Neal, and Robert Macbeth responded in various ways that the opposition the play generated was the very mark of its success. Baraka particularly noted its necessary attack on the cliches he had "helped create," and while both Neal and Macbeth had reservations about aspects of the play, they also defended its production.

Bullins, who generally avoids commenting on ideological issues, absented himself from the discussion. In a 1973 interview he observed: "It's very strange that some people will say that I'm a raving radical and others will say that Bullins doesn't stand for anything. I don't write the kind of plays they want me to, because I believe in trying to come at the audience fresh. . . . We are having a discourse, a discussion, a dialogue between black and black—writers and audience."[29]

In Bullins' plays concerning social relationships between blacks and whites, there is a similar challenge of the usual vision and the self-gratifying fantasy. In these plays, blacks often control whites and have access to white women. However, as in *We Righteous Bombers*, their power is simply an illusion, masking the same deadly enslavements.

26. Bullins, *The Reluctant Rapist*, 148.
27. Bullins' use of the Camus text requires some explanation. Since the New Lafayette shunned works by writers who were not black (with the exception of *The Blood Knot*, by Athol Fugard), to present *The Just Assassins* would contravene theater policy. More important, if the ideas in the Camus play were to gain a hearing, their source needed to be suppressed, for their importance could have been dismissed through the likely attack on the work as expressing decadent European philosophies.
28. *Black Theatre*, No. 4 (April, 1970), 16–25.
29. Anderson, "Profiles," 72–73.

Thus, as in his plays about political revolution, Bullins grants certain fantasies, tests them, and asks if anything has really been accomplished by achieving them.

It Bees Dat Way, for example, in forcing an encounter between typical Bullins' street characters and whites in the audience, explores the "liberal" reaction to black life by testing it. The effect is to enlighten both the white and black members of the audience. In its concluding comment to the black members of the audience, the play admonishes them that any pleasure they might have experienced watching the whites being harassed arises from their own misdirected hostility.

An earlier short piece, A Minor Scene, written in 1966, is a cartoon of the sixties. It depicts "black-militant-white-liberal" interaction, this time in a playful mode. In it, Peter Black asks Miss Ann, "Hey you scummy lookin' bourgeois white bitch, take me to dinner?"[30] Taken aback at first, Miss Ann even threatens to call the police, but within minutes she is offering him a choice of cuisine and herself for dessert—in polite language that contrasts ludicrously with his obscene suggestions.

Other pieces examine relationships between blacks and whites more comprehensively. His early one-act play It Has No Choice, written in 1966, concerns the relation between Steve and Grace (a character possibly named after Walker's wife in The Slave). The play bears this inscription from Kafka: "You do not need to leave your room. Remain sitting at your table and listen, simply wait. Do not even wait, be quite still and solitary. The world will freely offer itself to you to be unmasked, it has no choice, it will roll in ecstasy at your feet."[31]

With this passage, we are informed, Steve courted Grace in the beginning of their relationship. Now, on the last day of a two-week vacation, apparently spent in bed, Grace asks him to repeat it because, she says, every time he does, she "get[s] a little more out of it." Ironically, she has most difficulty understanding the phrase "it has no choice." In the course of the play, she confesses to Steve that although her physical relationship with him has made her happier then she has

30. Ed Bullins, A Minor Scene, in Bullins, The Theme Is Blackness, 78.
31. Ed Bullins, It Has No Choice, in Bullins, The Theme Is Blackness, 38. The passage comes at the end of a collection of aphorisms, "Reflections on Sin, Suffering, Hope, and the True Way," in Franz Kafka, Wedding Preparations in the Country and Other Posthumous Prose Writings, trans. Ernst Kaiser and Eithne Wilkins, ed. Max Brod (London, 1954), 53. This translation is not the one Bullins quotes, however; I have not been able to trace it.

been in years, she wishes to end it because she does not love him. Steve replies: "I told you, Grace, not to come to me until you had fully made your free choice . . . remember, when it happens 'it has no choice' . . . no, not at all, baby. It was your choice the moment you decided. And I'm holding you to it!" They begin to fight hysterically; he subdues her and almost strangles her, then releases her and dresses. Looking down at Grace as she struggles back to conscious-ness, he says: "Same time tomorrow, okay? . . . I think I'll enjoy making love to you tomorrow, darling." [32]

At the play's conclusion, it is Grace who has no choice: having placed herself in Steve's power, she must remain his. And he is as bound to her by his self-confessed love and hatred as she is to him by force. "The dream of myself isn't complete without you," he tells her. [33] Thus, his sense of power is finally illusory, and the world unmasks itself neither to Grace, the victim, nor to Steve, the philosopher, but only to the audience. The play's inscription is in every sense ironic.

For Bullins, then, the image of the black man apparently in control of a white woman, while a gratifying fantasy of historical and sym-bolic significance, is bitterly ironic. His first full-length play depicting race relations, The Pig Pen, written in 1970, must be understood in this light. The Pig Pen portrays an interracial party set in Los Angeles' bohemia in 1965, on the night of the assassination of Malcolm X. The announcement of his death brings the party and the play to a close and lends significance to its earlier, random activity.

Although the action on stage is essentially realistic, slight distor-tions of time and space and unlikely dimensions of characterization direct attention to the symbolic significance of what occurs. Ostensi-bly the pig referred to in the title is a "white pig," dressed in a police uniform and blowing a whistle, and occasionally dancing across the stage. But the pig cop, a cliche caricature representing the silent American majority, is something of a decoy. Pig also means loose woman, and perhaps the most striking feature of the hospitality offered by Len and Sharon, the interracial couple who give the party, is that white Sharon spends most of her time in the bedroom accom-modating any guests who desire her. Len does not object; sancti-moniously, he tells the others: "There is no need to envy me . . . my brothers. . . . (Len throws his hands out in a yoga position) I willingly share

32. Bullins, It Has No Choice, in The Theme Is Blackness, 42–43, 53, 55.
33. Ibid., 52.

with my brothers all I have. For what we have to share is really love." [34]
Almost all the guests take a turn with Sharon during the course of the
evening.

As the play opens, Sharon, Len, and Ray Crawford (a character from
In the Wine Time) are having breakfast. Ray had come to visit at three
o'clock in the morning, much to Sharon's annoyance. The play opens
on her nagging, which Len endures but which Ray rebukes. "Don't ever
try that with me," he warns her. [35] His way of responding to Sharon is
in marked contrast to Len's frustrated anger and to the behavior of all
the black men who later appear for the party. Ray alone never approaches Sharon for sexual favors and later leaves the party with Margie, the black girlfriend of Mackman, who is white.

The morning breakfast gradually becomes the party, which brings
together "as motley a group as you can find," as Ray observes. Present
are Ray; Len and Sharon; the three Carroll brothers, who provide the
live music; Margie; Carlos, a friend; Ernie, a black nationalist who
has come uninvited, apparently to see Ray but actually lusting after
Sharon; and, finally, Mackman, who tries to act hip but succeeds only
in being a ready target for almost all the guests. It is Mackman who
first hears of and then announces Malcolm X's death. His grief is
genuine; only Margie and Ray react with similar intense emotion. The
others are too preoccupied, stoned, drunk, or intent on Sharon to
care. Ironically, Margie's sorrow finally turns her away from Mackman,
although earlier in the play she had affronted all the black men
present by announcing, "I pour wine for my man . . . the Mack . . .
that's all." [36]

Bullins' treatment of Mackman is gentle. However, he leaves few
others of his motley group unscathed. Len's self-emasculating relationship to Sharon forms the centerpiece of Bullins' portrait of relationships between blacks and whites. Len enmeshes himself in abstract language and inappropriate generalization, the pitfalls of most
intellectuals. Yet he is not portrayed in a totally negative light. He is
knowledgeable about both African and Afro-American history, literature, and other aspects of culture, and generously shares his learning
with Ray and Ernie. Moreover, Len's insight exposes the shortcomings
of his companions.

34. Ed Bullins, The Pig Pen, in Bullins, Four Dynamite Plays, 99.
35. Ibid., 48.
36. Ibid., 93, 85.

Ray, the poet, Len correctly observes, is "nationalistic emotionally
. . . but seeking this scene out . . . and refusing to become really part
of it." On the other hand, Len observes, Ernie is "nationalistic completely . . . in rhetoric . . . and not in thought or deed." Len needles
him, "[Why] do you lust after my wife?"[37] Finally, the Carroll brothers
and Carlos have no political pretensions, but all of them seek their
turn in Sharon's bed, thus qualifying as residents of Bullins' pigpen.

Margie acts as counterpoint to Sharon. Before the party, as Ray and
Sharon converse and Len is elsewhere, talking on the telephone, Margie wanders in unnoticed; she speaks to Sharon and Ray but is un-
heard, wanders off, and returns hand in hand with Len, dancing—an
action sharply contrasting his earlier acrimonious interaction with
Sharon. Later, when Sharon is absent and Ray and Len absorbed in
Ray's poetry, Margie "takes a large banana from her large grass hand-
bag, peels it slowly and begins to eat as if it is luscious," but the men
do not notice. Thus, in some scenes, Margie represents the sympathetic and passionate black woman who is the appropriate lover for
black men, but whom they often neglect in their preoccupation with
white women. But Margie is tainted by white culture as well: when the
dancing starts, her long hair is described as "flying, in greased imitation of Sharon's," and, of course, she arrives at the party with
Mackman.[38]

Sharon clearly represents a caricature of aspects of white America:
she combines middle-class aspirations with the proclivities and behavior of a bohemian liberal. She berates Len for his inability to provide her with a maid and a good car, although by marrying him she
has chosen a life-style that clearly precludes such luxuries. Furthermore, Len's comments suggest that he sees Sharon as representing
something beyond herself. When John Carroll, her first bed partner,
approaches her, Sharon protests, "But it's kind of early," to which Len
replies, "Yes, it is early, Sharon . . . but some other people have different time senses."[39] Through this parody of "why can't they go slow,"
Len invokes history as context for the ensuing action.

Both the interracial and fraternal conviviality implied by the party,
the play's central metaphor, are easily disrupted. Almost every conversation and encounter during the party ends in hostility, and this hos-

37. Ibid., 99.
38. Ibid., 58, 79.
39. Ibid., 89.

tility intrudes from the very beginning through the abrasive nagging between Sharon and Len. While the party in The Pig Pen represents the tenuous fellowship in those corners of American society where blacks and whites interact with apparent ease, the goings-on at the party suggest an underlying, deadly mutual exploitation. And the rapaciousness is not confined to interracial relationships. In The Pig Pen, several characters, especially Ray, invoke Malcolm X as symbol of the truth about the black condition. His death at the hands of black assassins reflects and amplifies the activity on stage. Bullins has no illusions about the politics of a pigpen; he knows of what he speaks. In The Reluctant Rapist, Steve describes feeding real pigs during his summer vacation.

> The pigs were always ready to feed. No matter how [he] filled their troughs to brimming, when he returned the next day all had been swilled up and nothing remained but the stained, weathered boards of the troughs. When he turned the buckets up and splashed the food into the troughs, the pigs made oinking sounds which he had never gotten used to. He watched the fat beasts feeding, pushing each other aside, and remembered the story he had read of a man who had lain helpless in a pig-pen and been eaten alive.[40]

Bullins' metaphorical pigpen does not seem so horrifying, and compared to the interaction in Dutchman, for example, that at the party is mild. But there is danger in his depiction, lying in the fact that all the characters are off guard, deluded into thinking that they are safe, and that they have something, though what is not clear. The presence of the policeman and the sound of his whistle, as well as the death of Malcolm X announced at the play's end, remind the audience of the wider political context for the party, of which its underlying viciousness is only a shadow.

The black man's desire for the white woman is a central image in Bullins' plays that explore American race relations, particularly in The Taking of Miss Janie, the sequel to The Pig Pen. This play is Bullins' retrospective comment on the turbulent decade that encompassed the civil rights movement, the rise of black militancy and nationalism, and the flowering of black theater. Like The Pig Pen, The Taking of Miss Janie uses the medium of the party and an interracial group of characters to explore American race relations. The play begins and ends with the rape of Janie, a blond California college student, by Monty, a black

---

40. Bullins, The Reluctant Rapist, 29.

poet and her friend of thirteen years. Between the opening scene, in which Janie remonstrates with Monty over what has just occurred, and the end of the play, prelude to the rape to follow, the entire decade is reviewed.

The setting is Monty's party, which is attended by Len and Sharon (from *The Pig Pen*); Rick, a strident black nationalist who appears in *The Reluctant Rapist* and is a version of Ernie, but who scorns whites completely; Lonnie, Janie's white boyfriend, an unsympathetic variation on Mackman; two black women, Peggy and Flossie, both of whom are far more racially and politically aware and bitter than Margie; and Mort Silberstein. Flashback and monologues interrupt the party, reviewing the characters' pasts and foretelling their futures.

Len and Sharon are still courting as the play opens. In Sharon's monologue, she reports that it was not easy to survive the past decade, but now Len has settled into financial stability by becoming a capitalist, and that they are the proud parents of a rather spoiled son who looks just like his father. Len's arrogance, aparent in his rhetoric, and pride in himself as a teacher remain unchanged. He comments on the play itself: "Ah . . . many things are spoken of here. And the writer of this integrated social epic hints at only some surface manifestations of the times, for he did not know the impact of these accidental associations. He did not know that through me he would discover the kernel of political truth of the era, the seminal social vision of the sweep of so much history. . . . But remember, more political and cultural phenomena came out of southern California in the mid-century than Richard Nixon and Walt Disney."[41]

The kernel of political truth of which Len speaks Peggy utters succinctly: "We all failed. Failed ourselves in that serious time known as the sixties. And by failing ourselves we failed in the test of the times. We had so much going for us . . . so much potential. . . . And we blew it. . . . We just turned out lookin' like a bunch of punks and freaks and fuck-offs." This bitter accusation is leveled at the audience as well as the characters on stage, and spoken by the character least prone to self-delusion and least judgmental of others. Peggy's comment sums up the play's underlying tone and message. The play's delivery of that message, brilliantly comic and even sardonic, shows that Bullins, like Peggy, is finally not judgmental: all who lived through the decade, in-

41. Ed Bullins, *The Taking of Miss Janie*, in Ted Hoffman (ed.), *Famous American Plays of the* 1970s (New York, 1981), 222.

cluding the playwright, bear responsibility for "blowing it," but need not be blamed for their failure since blame is unproductive. The play mourns what occurred, yet while vindicating no one, is not vindictive. All the characters' failings and follies are scathingly revealed, but their humanity is never denied. Lonnie, for example, the least likable of all the characters and one who overrates himself, a third-rate jazz musician and thus parasitic on black culture yet ultimately condescending to "spades," opens his monologue admitting, "It wasn't the times that betrayed us. It was ourselves." [42] He is not fairly treated by Janie, who discards him because he will never go anywhere, and when he comments wistfully that he would have liked to be consulted about her three abortions, he seems deserving of some measure of sympathy.

The other white male in the play, Mort Silberstein, is a brilliant, if somewhat vicious, comic creation, representing various groups of whites who have been connected to and had influence on the black community: the intellectual Jewish community; the left, particularly the Communist party; the beats; and, finally, the hippie communities of the sixties. Mort attends as the party's drug supplier. He begs Monty for money to attend a freedom rally that Monty himself would not consider attending, and denounces Sharon for marrying a black man, while confessing that he himself lives with a German woman, who is acceptable because she is a Marxist. Besides, he says, he would never marry her. He also attacks Monty, first, for talking like a black militant while sleeping with a white woman and, second, for loving not white women but rather "my father . . . and his father's father," as well as Karl Marx, Sigmund Freud, Albert Einstein, and Jesus. [43] Hysterically countering Mort's accusations, Monty replies that he takes his inspiration from Mao Tse-tung, Franz Fanon, and voodoo, and vanquishes Mort in an epic battle that brings the party to a close and precedes the rape that brackets the play.

Peggy and Flossie are the most sympathetic characters in the play. Peggy, for a while Monty's wife, while bitter over his manipulation of her and his infidelity with Flossie, her best friend, still acknowledges that for a time they really loved each other in an intense, special way. She also admits that even though she left Monty, married a white man, and finally became a "liberated lesbian," she still misses his

42. Ibid., 230, 219.
43. Ibid., 233.

love. Bitter in its details, her story, which reveals her emotional
strength, is tempered by biting humor and clear-sighted analysis of
both Monty's failings and her own gullibility. Flossie, streetwise and
independent, also sees Monty clearly and remains unperturbed. It is
to Flossie, finally, that Janie reveals she is capable of some insight,
and it is Flossie who takes her aside to share some wisdom that is
never disclosed. It is Peggy who finally unmasks the insufferable Rick,
not so much for his rhetoric as for his condescension to her as a lesbian, and it is Peggy who speaks the final truth.

Monty meets "Miss Janie" (his nickname for her, whose implications she does not understand) in a creative-writing class, in which
she approaches him. From the beginning of their friendship, Monty
plans to take her, but for more than a decade respects her insistence
that their relationship remain platonic. Arrogant about his ability to
get what he wants, particularly from women, Monty is also capable of
friendship, love, and generosity—aspects of his character to which
Peggy, Flossie, and Janie attest. He is intelligent and perceptive of
others' weaknesses, but apparently confused and directionless in his
own life. His only consistent ambition during the thirteen years cov-
ered by the play is to continue his friendship and obsession with Miss
Janie, and she similarly relies on him. Although during the play he
constantly denigrates her and their relationship, he acknowledges at
the end, just before the rape, that on some level their relationship has
been authentic.

Oddly and yet appropriately, Janie is the least clearly delineated
character in the play—appropriately, not only because she represents
a type and state of mind, but also because, desired so intensely by
Monty, she cannot possibly be seen clearly by him. Blond, brown-
eyed (rather than blue-eyed, as is the devil Rick accuses her of being),
promiscuous, confused, and spoiled by her rich parents, Janie insists
on a kind of naïveté and idealism that, except at two moments in the
play, suggests deliberately cultivated stupidity. The first moment follows Flossie's remark that Monty, her friend and lover of many years,
never regards her as he does Janie. To this comment Janie replies,
"Maybe he's got what he wants from you . . . and he wants what he
thinks he can get from me." The second moment, the last in the play,
sums up the underlying tragedy the play suggests. Janie and Monty
recollect a friend who committed suicide, and as Monty moves to-

ward her, Janie recalls, "She just put the noose over her head and felt her spirit dance away." [44]

In these two comments, the two dimensions of Janie's character are revealed. The first suggests that underlying her hope for an ideal black-white relationship with Monty is the knowledge that she is maintaining it fraudulently—that, whatever else it involves, its shape is that of a seduction and she is the seducer. The second underscores the side of Janie that truly seeks a human and humane relation, one that their sexual encounter will destroy. Given who she is and what she represents, unlike Flossie, she cannot be both Monty's lover and his friend. Her manipulative exploitation of Monty and her idealism cannot be disengaged from each other, much as the idealism and humanity not only of the period depicted but also of society in all ages cannot be separated from any vicious and deliberate destructiveness that also exists.

In *The Taking of Miss Janie*, people fail because they conceal from themselves and one another both their goodness and strengths and their failings, with various kinds of rhetoric, cliches, ideals, indulgences. "Don't blame anybody," Peggy says, which is not to say, in Bullins' terms, that people were not responsible for what they did, but to say that blame prevents seeing what actually occurred and moving past it. If the entire period of the sixties was no more than a stalk and a tease, and if underneath all the rhetoric and high ideals of freedom and identity what Monty wanted was still only Miss Janie, at the end he got her. Presumably, he will have to move on from there. The play's central metaphor is not optimistic in this regard. The play ends with the prelude to the rape that has already occurred, and the present participle in the title suggests that a single taking will not satiate Monty's desire.

Not all Bullins' race-relation plays focus on sex. In *The Electronic Nigger*, written in 1968, one of the plays in Bullins' first collection, he directs his attention to blacks who lose themselves not to white women but to white culture. In this play his vehicle is farce. *The Electronic Nigger* takes place in a college classroom on the first night of a creative-writing course. The class is taught by Mr. Jones, a young black writer described as extremely self-conscious and as speaking in an accent "as unlike the popular conception of how a negro speaks as is pos-

44. *Ibid.*, 227, 234.

sible." His adversary is a student, A. T. Booker Carpentier, "a large dark man in his late thirties [who] speaks in blustering orations, many times mispronouncing words. His tone is stentorian, and his voice has an absurdly ridiculous affected accent."[45] The two portray the gamut of miseducation and cultural assimilation.

As soon as Carpentier enters the classroom, he dominates. In the most complex language he can summon, he continually draws attention to himself, his achievements, and his ideal for art, sociodrama. Carpentier is a "Sociological Data Research Analysis Technician Expert," which, translated, means "wiretapper"; bugging prisons is his specialty. His concept of art "is to scientifically eavesdrop . . . with electronic listening devices and get the actual evidence for any realistic fictionalizing one wishes to achieve. . . . Combined with the social psychologists' case study, and the daily experiences of some habitant of a socio-economically depressed area, is the genius of the intellectual and artistic craftsman."[46]

His sheer bombast finally defeats Jones, who is appalled by Carpentier's professional treachery, particularly because he is black.

> Mr. Jones.   What does all the large words in creation serve you, my Black brother, if you are a complete whitewashed man?
> Mr. Carpentier.   Sir, I am not black nor your brother. . . . There is a school of thought that is diametrically opposed to you and your black chauvinism. . . . You preach bigotry, black Nationalism and fascism. The idea . . . black brother . . . [is] intellectual barbarism![47]

This outbreak finishes Jones. As Carpentier discourses to a rapt audience on adolescent necrophilia, observed by bugging corpses in his family's funeral home, Jones announces his early retirement from teaching and dismisses the class. Few notice, for they have succumbed to Carpentier, whose rhetoric finally evolves into a gibberish of abstract nouns.

The Electronic Nigger constitutes a sly, outrageous replay of the historic debate between W. E. B. Du Bois and Booker T. Washington. Jones, light skinned and "proper-speaking," recalls Du Bois, and Carpentier is named after Washington, although he has frenchified his tradesman's surname ("A. T. Carpentier is the name . . . notice the silent T"). And to those who think of the founder of Tuskegee Institute

45. Ed Bullins, *The Electronic Nigger*, in Bullins, *Five Plays*, 216.
46. *Ibid.*, 239, 241.
47. *Ibid.*, 239–40.

as a Tom, Carpentier's profession provides an analogue to the white-appointed black leader's role as "official spokesman for the black community." Ironically, it is a white student, Sue Gold, who calls Carpentier "Tom," and a black student, Bill, immediately remarks, "That's for me to do, not you, lady!" Later Sue and Bill leave together.[48] It is also the white students who crowd around Carpentier at the end of the play as he discourses on crows, birds frequently associated with black people.

While Carpentier has immersed himself in sociological language to gain power, Jones seeks his authority in literature. He attempts to assert himself to the class by pleading, "I have read Faulkner in his entirety . . . I cut my teeth on Hemingway . . . *Leaves of Grass* is my bible." Jones is doubly ineffectual. In the sense that he represents the traditional arts and humanities in their encounter with the contemporary sociotechnical, pseudoscientific objectification of the world, Jones is appropriately speechless before Carpentier's onslaught. As representative of the young black intellectual, Jones reveals that type's patent inability to deal with the clearly recognizable type evoked by Carpentier: the older, blustering black community leader, frequently a teacher or preacher, whose love of learning consists more in his relish for a complex vocabulary than in the sense that vocabulary embodies, and who, like the prototypical folk preacher, finds in language a source of power. The play drew on the raging debate about the nature of black art and the role of the black artist carried on outside the classroom-theater in the 1960s in radically different language and form, Baraka's, for example:

> Poems are bullshit unless they are
> teeth or trees or lemons piled
> on a step. . . .
>   Fuck poems
> and they are useful. . . .[49]

The play raised other artistic issues as well. The kind of art Carpentier advocates, "community eavesdropping," ironically reflects the realism of playwrights of the black experience, Bullins included. Like them, Carpentier finds the "great themes" at "AA meetings, pris-

48. *Ibid.*, 222, 240. The interchange between Sue and Bill and their subsequent alliance provide a concise synopsis of the long, complex relationship between Jews and blacks, particularly in intellectual circles.
49. *Ibid.*, 243; Baraka, "Black Art," in *Black Magic*, 116.

ons"—wherever he plants his bugs—and ludicrously intones them: "Loneliness! Estrangement! Alienation!"[50] The play delights in depicting the abuse both of the artist's subject and of language, his tool. Thus, in an oblique fashion, *The Electronic Nigger* raises issues that are central to Bullins' serious plays: the danger and even betrayal involved in seeing, understanding, and portraying the truth embedded in ordinary reality, the various failures in human communication, and the confusion of being black in white America.

Bullins' plays about revolution and those depicting the interaction between blacks and whites differ in several crucial ways from those by Baraka treating similar themes. For example, where Baraka dares his audience to consider the imaginative possibility of violent revolution, Bullins assumes and tests this scenario, challenging the taking of human life so that the quality of other human life may be improved. Bullins neither advocates nor deplores violent revolution; he simply mistrusts whether, as imagined, it transcends the violence seething on any ghetto street corner. Moreover, while Baraka depicts blacks as enslaved by white culture and an imposed white consciousness, and focuses on the act of liberation, Bullins depicts his characters as time and again freely choosing white values, often symbolized by white women, over black. In interracial matters as in others, Bullins focuses on the misuse of the freedom his characters possess, rather than on the bondage over which they have little control.

The serious plays included in Bullins' first anthology of his own work, *Five Plays by Ed Bullins*, exemplify his delicate explorations of the vicissitudes of ordinary black life. *A Son, Come Home, Clara's Ole Man*, and the two full-length works, *In the Wine Time* and *Goin'a Buffalo*, are rich, subtle depictions of people who struggle for their freedom but bind themselves to old places and sustain old wounds rather than finally transform their lives.

A Son, Come Home, a brief, delicate sketch performed on a bare stage, relates the history of a black family through an encounter between mother and son. Mother and son are shadowed by a boy and girl, both in black, who enact some of their memories and extend, comment on, or complete their broken dialogue. The story is simple. After an absence of nine years, Michael has come to visit his mother,

50. Bullins, *The Electronic Nigger*, 230.

who has become a religious fanatic and lives in a tyrannical church-run home. Their conversation, desultory and at cross-purposes, evokes painful memories in both. Finally, the mother retreats into her religious environment, and the son returns to his life.

The mood of A Son, Come Home is almost unbearably sad. Each potentially joyous moment in their encounter turns out to be sorrowful or is juxtaposed to an expression of fear, disappointment, or difficulty. The dominant theme of the play is the family bond: the mother repeatedly admonishes Michael to contact his aunt Sophie, rebuking him for losing touch with her and telling him they are so alike. Michael's memories not expressed to his mother reveal that his aunt threw him out of her house after a week's visit and later refused a simple request for help when he was in trouble.

Some memories are joyful. His mother recalls carrying him: "Happy that I was having a baby of my own . . . I worked as long as I could and bought you everything you might need." But recollections of Michael's father mitigate the joy of the memory. He offered no assistance and when, years after Michael's birth, they encountered him on a trolley and he oozed his paternity, the mother remarked: "You never gave him no name . . . his name is Brown . . . Brown. The same as mine. . . . You never gave him nothin' . . . and you're dead . . . go away and get buried." [51]

Through Michael's questions the audience learns that his mother loved and lived with a man named Will for ten years—a man who never married her because, she finally admits to Michael, he had family elsewhere. Michael claims, "Will was like a father to me . . . the only one I've really known." [52] His mother then reminds him that he drove Will out of the house as soon as he was big enough. The rhythm of each exchange is the same: the hope, joy, or excitement experienced by one is denied, refuted, or negated by the response or memories of the other. Twice Michael eagerly proposes an evening out with his mother, and twice she denies him, saying that she never eats out anymore. Religion has become both a solace for her painful memories and a prison protecting her from further encountering the world. Neither mother nor son has become any freer or closer to the other through the visit; neither seems to have gained any satisfaction.

51. Ed Bullins, A Son, Come Home, in Bullins, Five Plays, 196, 205.
52. Ibid., 207.

Michael's rejection of the idea of home at the play's beginning is balanced by the mother's withdrawal from Michael at the close of the visit, their mutual rejections protecting them from each other.

The shadow figures emphasize and make vivid Michael's sense of displacement in time. The crucial, painful displacement actually involves the bond between mother and son, which time necessarily disrupts and which, one senses, also has been deadened and denied because of its earlier intensity, which neither mother nor son could accommodate and of which the audience is only allowed glimpses. A *Son, Come Home* is important because, although Bullins frequently portrays the black family, only in this play does he treat the relationship between mother and son. So delicate and tender is his approach, so unaccommodated, that one suspects it is a theme from which he fled and to which he will have to return.

In A *Son, Come Home*, the black family consists only of mother and son. Michael's natural father gave him nothing; Michael rejected Will because he felt Will displaced him in his mother's affections. But the outline of the nuclear family is there, each break in the image expressed as pain and loss. *Clara's Ole Man* depicts the family as well and provides a grotesque, bitter comment on the structure often used to describe black family organization: matriarchy. For *Clara's Ole Man* recites a litany of failures in nurturing.

Again, the story is simple. In a kitchen in south Philadelphia, an afternoon of wine drinking reveals to Jack, Clara's suitor, that Big Girl is Clara's "ole man." The play opens with a grotesque family portrait: Big Girl, twenty pounds overweight and of indeterminate age, seated at the kitchen table drinking wine; Clara, eighteen and pretty, at the stove cleaning up the bacon she has just burnt; Baby Girl, Big Girl's demented teenage sister, playing on the floor with a homemade toy. Big Girl controls the action throughout. Several times, feeling uncomfortable, Jack attempts to leave, but each time Big Girl detains him, using Clara as bait for her own cat-and-mouse game, whose object is to oust Jack from her domain forever. However, before he goes, he must be her audience: "When I was a little runt of a kid my mother found out she couldn't keep me or Baby Girl any longer cause she had T.B. so I got shipped out somewheres and Baby Girl got shipped out somewheres else. People that Baby Girl went to exposed her to the disease. She was lucky. I ended up with some fuckin' Christians."

While Big Girl's mother failed her because of illness, Clara's parents, a "Christian mammy and a pot-gutted pappy," as Big Girl calls them, seem to have failed her for unknown reasons.[53]

Baby Girl's fantasies reflect a similar preoccupation with nurture: "The cat! The cat! It's got some kittens! The cat got some kittens!" Big Girl tells Jack: "She's been making that story up for two months now about how some cat crawls up under the steps and has kittens. She can't fool me none. She just wants a cat but I ain't gonna get none" (261–62). Baby Girl reflects the world around her in other ways as well. She imitates Clara's hairdo and make-up, and much to Clara's discomfort, she curses like her sister. Whenever displeased, Baby Girl throws back her head, drums her feet on the floor, and screams: "NO! NO! SHIT! DAMN! SHIT! NO!" (254). Big Girl explains to Jack that she taught Baby Girl to curse deliberately.

> It was to give her her freedom, ya know? . . . Ya see workin' in the hospital with all the nuts and fruits and crazies and weirdos I get ideas 'bout things. I saw how when they get these kids in who have cracked . . . they all mostly cuss . . . and some of them really get into it and let out all of that filthy shit that's been stored up all them years. But when the docs start shockin' them and puttin' them on insulin they quiets down, that's when the docs think they're gettin' better but they ain't. They're just learn'n like before to hold it in.
>
> (256–57)

Impressed, Jack immediately translates her insight into psychological jargon and compliments her: "You have an intuitive grasp of very abstract concepts" (257). But her understanding avails little, for the society she creates with all her cursing and drinking is as repressive as the hospital she describes. Clara has not been drinking with the others because "Big Girl doesn't allow me to start drinking too early," and whenever Clara fails to obey her immediately, Big Girl screams: "DO LIKE I SAY! DO LIKE BIG WANTS YOU TO!" (257, 256).

Respect for Big Girl's dominance extends beyond her household. The drinking party is interrupted by three local youths who appear in her back door, trying to escape the cops. Big Girl invites them to join the party and relishes the accounts of their exploits—an earlier gun battle and the mugging of a drunk, whose vodka they offer to those assembled. In spite of their bravado in the outside world, the three

53. Ed Bullins, *Clara's Ole Man*, in Bullins, *Five Plays*, 259, hereinafter cited parenthetically by page number in the text. Bullins first published the play in the black theater issue of *Drama Review*.

boys hesitate to anger Big Girl. When they begin quarreling over how to split the goods from the mugging, Big Girl warns them: "Okay, cool it! There's only one person gets out of hand 'round here, ya understand?" Stoogie replies: "Okay, B. G. Let it slide" (273). However, in her name they become bold, as when Jack speaks of his marine service.

> *Stoogie.*   What kind of boat were you on, man?
> *Jack.*   A ship.
> *Big Girl.*   A boat!
> *Jack.*   No, a ship.
> *Stoogie.*   (*Rising, Bama and Hoss surrounding Jack*) Yeah, man, dat's what she said . . . a boat!
> *Clara.*   STOP IT!!
>
> (276)

This incident foreshadows the scene to follow, in which Stoogie, Bama, and Hoss are the instruments of Big Girl's triumph. She tells them as she and Clara leave: "Before you go, escort my friend out, will ya?" Clara implores: "Please, B. G., please. Not that. It's not his fault! Please! . . . (*With a nod from Stoogie, Bama and Hoss take Jack's arms and wrestle him into the yard. The sound of Jack's beating is heard*)" (281–82).

The meaning of Bullins' subtitle for *Clara's Ole Man*, "A Play of Lost Innocence," extends beyond what happens to Jack. Almost every line protests some violation, some bitter knowledge acquired. The opening lines of the play divide the world into those who know and those who don't, the experienced and the innocent.

> *Clara.*   I wonder how I was dumb enough to burn the bacon?
> *Big Girl.*   Just comes natural with you, honey, all looks and no brains . . . now with me and my looks, anybody in South Philly can tell I'm a person what naturally takes care of business . . . hee, hee . . . ain't that right, Clara?
>
> (252)

Both the sexual innuendo and the boast of practical talents establish the contrast between Big Girl and Clara. Big Girl credits herself with Clara's entire education. She claims that when she found Clara, the girl had never had a drink and knew nothing of personal hygiene. Moreover, she had been abandoned seven-months pregnant and had failed as a whore because "our sweet little thing here was sooo modest and sedate" (261). Clara feels corrupted: "Sometimes . . . sometimes . . . I just want to die for bein' here," she cries, as Big Girl exposes her life's story to Jack (260). Neither Jack nor the audience is prepared, at this point, to understand her shame, for they have the sense that she continues a "lost innocent," who has not been corrupted and will never become hardened to her bitter life. This play on words is concretized by the figure of Baby Girl, physically mature but mentally a child, made to resemble Clara.

Big Girl envies her sister's stunted consciousness: "She was lucky. I ended up with some fuckin' Christians. . . . A dozen years in hell . . . always preachin' bout some heaven over yonder and building a bigger hell here den any devil might have imagination for" (259). So bitter is the life described in Clara's Ole Man that, in response, all its characters have refused to mature. Clara's first encounter with heterosexuality proved so destructive that she had to retreat for more mothering to the big-breasted woman who also acts as father and as lover. Her similarity to Baby Girl, permanently arrested in childhood, intensifies this sense of Clara. As her name implies, Big Girl has not fully matured either. She has managed to deal with the world, but at a high cost, as she tells Jack defiantly: "Well, let me tell you what you see. You see a fat bitch who's twenty pounds overweight and looks ten years older than she is. You want to know how I got this way and been this way most of my life and would be worse off if I didn't let off steam some drinkin' this rotgut and speakin' my mind?" (258–59). The speech is prologue to her life's story.

Yet the environment Big Girl has provided is not without nurturing power. She manages to feed and house an ailing alcoholic aunt and to keep her supplied with gin, as well as to care for Baby Girl and Clara. Furthermore, the whole neighborhood comes to her when in trouble, as the abrupt entrance of Stoogie, Bama, and Hoss indicates. And most important, Jack's presence in the house, no matter how brief, suggests that under Big Girl's nurturing, Clara has gathered enough strength to desire contact with a man again—a man different from those of her previous attempt, an innocent like her. She tells Big Girl: "I only wanted to talk, B. G. I only wanted to talk to somebody. I don't have anybody to talk to. . . . (Crying) I don't have anyone" (281).

Clara needs to go beyond "mother" to return to the outside world and particularly to men. As Big Girl is not only mother but also lover, she cannot, as a mother must, let Clara go; thus Jack must pay the price of daring to invite Clara out into the world beyond Big Girl's walls. Lance Jeffers correctly suggests that Big Girl operates as a prin-

ciple of potential order in the world of Clara's Ole Man.[54] Big Girl has
the capacity for nurture, but so stunted has been her development
that she must make of her home a prison, and of her love, perversity.
Big Girl's household consists of women who do not "know" men—
women who are therefore innocent in a special sense, distancing
themselves from a world too cruel to be admitted. The innocence,
which in Baby Girl is idiocy, defies Jack's "ordinary" innocence and
ordinary expectations.

Clara's Ole Man is quite sympathetic and, for its time, courageous in
its treatment of Big Girl and Clara's lesbianism and in its investigation
into matriarchy, for which Big Girl is a symbol. The play adopts the
tolerance of the insiders in the community—the three toughs; Miss
Famie, the aunt's drinking companion; C. C., Baby Girl's drunken baby-
sitter—but, in a subtle, complex fashion, also shares Jack's outrage.
Like Jack, the play desires something different. Just as Big Girl's household excludes Jack, the lesbian world excludes men completely. In
Bullins' plays, women represent life; the lesbian life is life denied to
men and to the future—life turned in on itself. Moreover, the lesbian
family suggests an accentuated image of the family created when
a woman is abandoned with her children. If, like Michael's father in
A Son, Come Home, a man fails in his initial responsibility to acknowledge and care for his child, he may be locked out of the relationship
later; if the woman succeeds in being both mother and father, the
man may become superfluous. This fear of having no place underlies
Jack's horror, which is so intense that he vomits when he discovers the
true nature of Clara's living situation. Just as she seems within reach,
just as, finally drunk, he relaxes enough to ask her for herself, Jack
discovers he cannot ever have the woman he wants.

The audience is in a position similar to Jack's in several ways. It is
not among the insiders; like Jack, it must gradually discover the nature of Clara's relationship to Big Girl. Until the revelation, the audience, like Jack, has gradually come to feel that the world depicted is
within its understanding and become comfortable with its bizarre or
simply alien characters. Moments before the final revelation, Jack confesses that he grew up in this neighborhood, although he escaped
and has been away. Similarly, the audience just begins to feel a shared

54. Lance Jeffers, "Bullins, Baraka and Elder: the Dawn of Grandeur in Black
Theatre," College Language Association Journal, XVI (September, 1972), 35.

origin with the characters when the world of the play turns violently on Jack, shutting him out, and the audience with him. In this very experience of being punished for the physical and emotional trespass, they can understand a crucial aspect of the world of *Clara's Ole Man*. Jack's presence, and, by extension, that of the audience, forces all the characters to perceive themselves anew; Jack's beating is a reflection of their subsequent painful reassertion of themselves. The audience must respect Big Girl and her world at the end of the play; the members of this world ask for no pity, and none is possible.

Similarly, in Bullins' first full-length play, *Goin'a Buffalo*, the presence of an outsider forces the characters to reveal themselves, and strips them of certain illusions. But Art, the outsider in this play, is not innocent; when the characters open to him, they become his victims.

Each member of the community of pimps, whores, and hustlers depicted in *Goin'a Buffalo* has individual illusions, and together they share a single dream: "goin'a Buffalo" to start anew.

> *Curt.*   It's a good little hustlin' town, I hear. . . .
> *Pandora.*   With me workin' on the side and with Curt dealin' we'd be on our feet in no time.
>
> (31–32)

However, their dream does not come to pass in the way they imagined it. The dream itself is problematic. Their plan, the same hustle but with a clean record, suggests the characters can imagine no real change or moral rebirth. Moreover, Los Angeles—the city Bullins refers to as "the last shore" in *The Reluctant Rapist*—has been kind to none of the characters, and their desire to go east suggests that even the hustlers' version of the American Dream has crumbled.[55]

Principally, however, the characters fail to escape their environment because they depend on the very instruments of their imprisonment—crime, drugs, prostitution, their illusions—for their release. Thus they become vulnerable to Art, an unscrupulous realist and a better hustler than any of them. They ought to suspicious of him, but caught in their personal needs and fantasies, they fail to heed the many danger signals. The trap that closes in on them at the end of the play is even more vicious than the one they sought to escape.

The events of *Goin'a Buffalo* are as follows. Curt and his wife, Pandora; Mamma-Too-Tight and her pimp, Shaky; and Curt's friend Rich,

55. Bullins, *The Reluctant Rapist*, 53.

are accumulating money to escape Los Angeles. At Curt's invitation, Art, whom Curt met in prison and who saved his life there during a riot, joins them. Although the others are initially wary of Art, he gradually wins over the women and fends off Rich's continued distrust.

Later in the evening, they adjourn to the club where Pandora dances, so that she and Mamma can go to work. A brawl develops at the club because Pandora's boss, Deeny, refuses to pay her, and during the fight Curt severely injures him. When the police arrive, most of the main characters flee. They are forced to abandon Shaky, who is too hurt to move. A known peddler carrying a large amount of heroin, Shaky is arrested.

As the scene opens three days later, Curt has been gathering money to leave town before Deeny either dies or returns to consciousness and presses charges. He and Rich plan to sell the rest of Shaky's heroin, use the money to free him on bail, and then, with Art and the women, leave for Buffalo. Curt and Rich exit to make the sale, bringing Pandora as driver; they leave Art to care for Mamma and prevent her from taking a fix. As the scene ends, Art makes a phone call then comforts Mamma with drugs and sex.

The final scene is brief. Pandora returns distraught: the police, who were waiting for them, have arrested Curt and Rich with the drugs in their possession. Pandora wants Art to use the money they have saved to free the men on bail, but Art, forcing her to pack, intends to bring her and Mamma-Too-Tight to Buffalo. Art's treachery is possible only because the characters refuse to admit the truth about themselves and their world, while Art does not.

Bullins uses lighting to concretize this crucial theme of personal and communal illusion. In Act 1, set in Curt and Pandora's apartment, both decor and lighting establish the "illusion of a world afire, with this pocket of atmosphere an oasis" (4). The seeming safety of the oasis blinds them not only to the danger embodied in Art but also to the implications of the frequent outbursts of violence that mark their own interactions. Within the opening minutes, for example, Curt is testy with Rich while beating him at chess, and almost strikes Pandora because she grumbles about serving them beer. Shortly after, a flippant remark by Art about his ability to handle a gun brings the atmosphere to the breaking point again. This rhythm of violence governs the entire play.

In Act 2, lighting is used to accentuate the nightclub setting, making it garish and sensuous like the women who work there. The stage directions insist "reality is questionable here" (48). In this act, Bullins intermittently freezes the background activity in the club, frequently at the point of violence, and spotlights interchanges between his principal characters. Finally, the menace that has remained in the background erupts, and during the fight one feels that Curt, Art, and Pandora finally express the violence they barely held in check in the previous act.

Act 3 returns to the apartment, which, in the first scene of the act, appears "sterile, unlived in and motel-like," lit only by the harsh California sun (82). The stark lighting suggests the characters' feelings of vulnerability. Curt feels vulnerable because he fears Deeny may die; Mamma, because she is suffering from heroin withdrawal and misses Shaky; Rich, because he is increasingly suspicious of Art. The illusion of safety created by the lighting in Act 1 has been disrupted, but the harsh glare in this scene is no more revealing. The audience cannot hear Art's treacherous phone call, and he comforts Mamma with sex and drugs in the dark. By the time Pandora returns in the final scene, Art has recreated the original lighting, visually restored the opening illusion. The effect is simply to reaffirm and reveal its real function— that of a bitter trap—a revelation experienced only by the audience since Art already knows it, the other men are all in jail, Mamma is high on drugs, and Pandora is too stunned to understand.

A related motif in *Goin'a Buffalo* is the game of chess. Only Curt and Rich play, and Curt always wins. One senses that they have been playing for years and that through the game Curt dominates his lifelong buddy. In chess, a good player can see every move coming. Weak players do not think far enough ahead, and they allow themselves to become distracted. In the first scene, Curt and Rich have forgotten whose turn it is, and they ask Art if he has noticed. "I ain't in it," he demurs (16). But he watches the game, and although he claims not to have played in a long time, he is obviously good. Rich asks Art to comment on a game he has just lost. Art reaches over and picks up the black king.

> Art.   Most kings need a queen to be most powerful but others do the best
> they can. (*He places the king upon another square*) That's what I'd do, Rich.
> Curt.   (*Perceiving*) Yeah. I see . . . I see.
>
>   (91)

Rich is slow to understand.

Curt. (*Matter-of-fact*) A stalemate. . . .
Art.   When you play the game you look for any break you can make.
Curt. We should play some time, Art.
Art.   I'm looking forward to it, Curt. But you name the time.

(92)

The game Curt is unaware of playing precludes the one offered, and, a comparative amateur, he has, by this time, already lost it. In the larger game, Art is not satisfied with a stalemate—he wins with two queens.

Not only is Art a better player, but he does not share the fantasies with which the others delude and protect themselves. The most dangerous fantasy is Curt's. He tells Art: "You're like me in a lot of ways. Man, we're a new breed, ya know. Renegades. Rebels. There's no rules for us . . . we make them as we break them." Art remarks, "Sounds kinda romantic, Curt." Curt responds: "And why shouldn't it? Man, this ain't a world we built so why should we try to fit in it? We have to make it over the best way we can . . . and we are the ones to do it. We are, man, we are!" (68–69).

Curt's romanticism is one from which Bullins is not completely immune. It also comments ironically on Theater of Black Experience that would seek to endow street life and street people with mythical proportions. *Goin' a Buffalo* explores the deadly nature of that world and finds little redeeming in it. For if there is a rule in the world of the renegade, as Curt admits, it is that all rules can be broken, and particularly vulnerable are those affecting human bonds of trust and affection. Thus, for example, Curt's rebel attitude challenges his own commitment to Art as his "little brother," an implication Curt misses —but that Art does not.

Moreover, Curt's romanticism protects him from self-knowledge. Since he generally makes his money by his wits rather than by force (by forgery rather than by armed robbery), Curt believes that he can easily extricate himself from any crime by making restitution. Thus he believes himself freer than Rich, for example, who is still on probation for an unnamed offense and is a heroin addict.

More important, Curt's dreams, as well as the legal nature of his relationship to Pandora, protect both of them from admitting that Curt functions as her pimp. That Pandora provides the steady income and that both resent it is disclosed in the opening scene; and the relationship of Mamma and Shaky, who enter in the second scene, counterpoints their relationship and clarifies its economic dimension. In the midst of a chicken dinner, Pandora reveals to all that the chicken is Curt's extravagant gesture—they have been eating beans all week. Curt is about to turn on her when Mamma interrupts and relieves the tension: "Girl, you don't have ta tell me a thing . . . these here men think that money can be just picked up off'a them pavements out there like chewin' gum paper . . . until they got ta get out there for themselves. . . . I know that Curt is a big strong man . . . he's always lettin' Pan know. (*Strong dialect*) . . . So he don't need no help from us frail-ass women but maybe ole fuzzy wuzzy face [Art] here needs some help. (*Her audience is in better humor once more*) You wants Mamma-Too-Tight to feeds him some food, baby boy?" (20–21).

She follows her humorous remarks with a playful yet poignant account and partial reenactment of her first hours out of jail with Shaky. "Umm . . . chile . . . I nearly thought I was on that honeymoon I never had," she tells Pandora. But just as soon as "things got really gettin' romantic . . . this mathafukker says . . . 'I want you to bring in a yard tonight, baby,'" to which Mamma responds, "How do you want them, daddy . . . in fives or tens?" (22–23). Pandora's empathetic laughter reveals an understanding that arises from experience. Moreover, when Mamma questions why Shaky never visited her in jail, Curt defends him for acting as a good pimp should, incidentally revealing that he has performed the same function for Pandora: "Pan ain't been snatched since before we were married. . . . A self-respectin' man won't let his ole lady stay in jail." Mamma remarks, "Aww . . . Curt, you try and make it sound so smooth," and Pandora says, "He can really make it do that, girl" (25). Finally, by Act 3, Curt has replaced Shaky on the streets through his attempt to sell Shaky's heroin to raise bail money—thus giving lie to his earlier assurance that he could restrict himself to "lesser" crimes.

As long as Curt does not admit he is a pimp, Pandora can maintain her illusion. She tells Art: "Well, I ain't no whore . . . I'm just makin' this money so Curt and me can get on our feet. One day we gonna own some property and maybe some businesses when we get straight and out of this town" (60). Thus she protects herself from her bitter profession and distinguishes herself from Mamma-Too-Tight, a self-admitted whore, who uses heroin to help her endure her work. When Art expresses pity for Mamma, Pandora lashes out: "Don't sing no sad songs for that woman, you understand? She's not askin' for your pity.

She's a real woman in some ways and she won't let you take it away from her by your pity. She'd spit on your pity" (60).

Pandora's impassioned defense of Mamma-Too-Tight speaks even more eloquently of her own condition. In a fantasy sequence, Curt recalls to Art the first time he met Pandora. He knew instantly that he wanted her, and simply took her. Although she is only eighteen in the reenactment, "her face has that expression that prisoners sometimes have when they are shifted without prior explanation from an old cell to an unfamiliar cell, equally as old" (66). In *Goin'a Buffalo*, the women are the least free, and Bullins' treatment of them perceptive and sympathetic. However, his portraits are traditional, and the play's perspective is male.

Bullins approaches his investigation of women through the motif of Pandora's box. The actual box introduced in Act I, Scene 3, contains marijuana—and, in a sense, all their dreams. Pandora brings it out so that they can smoke before going to the club. As the dope begins to take effect, Art smiles and asks, "So that's what's in Pandora's box?" (42). Mamma remarks, "Most people think that a girl's box is in other places," and she and Pandora agree, with a wisdom born of the prostitute's experience, that the bad attributed to that box, as well as to the mythical one, is only in what men bring to it (43).

Pandora's box also contains a gun, and Curt says: "Right now this is the most important thing. There's always something new in there. (*Handing gun to Art*) Feel it, brother" (44). Art compares its gleaming to that of Pandora's eyes, and she tells him, "Nothin' bad comes out of me or from my box, baby." Curt and Art continue:

Curt.   It's all yours now, Art, as much yours as mine. Can you handle it, brother?

Art.   (*Looking at Pandora and taking a new reefer*) If that's my job, brother.

(44)

The symbolism is suggestive in several ways. Art's initial refusal to smoke reveals that he does not share the others' illusions, and when he does smoke, at Pandora's insistence, the dream he adopts is not the shared fantasy of Buffalo but that of Pandora and her box. Pandora's interchange with Mamma ironically foreshadows her own fate. What Art will bring her is his own version of the same bondage. In a later scene, Art asks her, "And what if I wanted you, Pandora?" She replies: "You don't have enough to give me, Art. What could you give me that would make things better for me?" Art answers: "I'm not a giver, Pan. I'm a taker" (61–62).

Pandora is vulnerable to Art because Curt has given her over to him, implicitly with the gun and later explicitly. Just before the fight in the club, Curt tells her that if he is ever arrested, she should live with Art until his release. Afraid, Pandora protests, "But I'm your woman, remember?" (72). Curt believes that his attitude expresses his immense trust in Art, but as the symbolism of the gun points out, his trusting Pandora to Art is more complex. What Pandora senses is that Curt actually is offering her to Art as an expression of his latent sexual desire for Art—for which Pandora is medium.

Pandora's reversal of the Pandora's box myth—"nothin' bad comes out of me or from my box, baby. . . . It's all in what you bring to us"— implies that women reflect and express the world men have created. Obviously, Pandora's box—both literal and figurative—is emblematic of the play's relationships between males and females. The box is a treasured object in which both she and Curt store their dreams and in which Curt's masculinity feels secure. At the same time, because Pandora is a prostitute, her box is for sale, an instrument of utility—like the gun, to be "handled"—and to the men who buy it, simply a means to an end. Prostituting the woman one loves involves exploiting what one values most in other contexts. Moreover, prostitution forces the woman to deny and distance herself from her body in order to endure unwelcome, often revolting intimacy. Finally, the man's separating the woman he loves from the whore he has created is but a pale reflection of the woman's radical self-alienation.

The pimp makes a mark of his masculinity what, in another context, might be considered emasculating—that the woman supports the man. Curt's ambivalence about using Pandora as a source of income, and the contrast established between their relationship and Mamma's more typical one with Shaky, suggest a painful truth embedded in this aspect of *Goin' a Buffalo*. The world of pimp and prostitute makes a virtue of a particular fact of black existence—that because of her marketability, the black woman has often had to be the breadwinner. The ironies of this situation reverberate in an interchange between Art and Pandora.

Art.   Curt and Shaky are really into something.
Pandora.   Yeah! Because they're men!
Art.   Is that what bein' a man is, bein' lucky?

Pandora.   No. It's from gettin' what you want.
Art.   And how do you get what you want, Pan?
Pandora.   You go after it.
Art.   And after you have it?
Pandora.   Then maybe it's yours and you can do whatever you want with it.
Art.   And what if I wanted you, Pandora?

(60–61)

Pandora's ironic and unconscious self-objectification, and her defense of both Curt and Shaky (classing them together although she resents Art's insinuation that they are alike), eloquently express the confusion implicit in her relationship with Curt.

If the similarities between Curt's relation to Pandora and Shaky's to Mamma suggest the perversity of love relationships in *Goin'a Buffalo,* the differences, particularly Curt and Pandora's loyalty to and respect for each other, suggest the presence of real love—however abused. Pandora and Mamma, and Curt and Rich, show genuine affection for each other as well. But love requires a world in which trust is possible, and Curt's affection for Art symbolizes the danger of loving in the world depicted in *Goin'a Buffalo.* What is endearing about Curt is that he is a lover, genuinely attached not only to Pandora but to Rich and Art as well; but given his world, Curt is therefore a fool.

Goin'a Buffalo also strikes a related and favorite Bullins theme: that of treachery inside the black community—a treachery that leaves it open to destruction from outside. In prison, Art saved Curt from a white man in a fight that developed from strife between Muslim and non-Muslim black prisoners. The prison violence mirrors the constant undercurrent of violence in the outside world, which marks all interactions in *Goin'a Buffalo.* Art manipulates that violence to his own ends; for example, both Pandora and Mamma are accustomed to physical brutality from Curt and Shaky and thus vulnerable to Art's apparent gentleness.

Bullins directs that Deeny, the bouncer in the club, and one of the customers may be cast as white, thus adding interracial tension; but the play does not require it. Its focus is on the intense, vital black men and women who misuse, repress, and abuse their strength and creativity, and thus live in constant danger from themselves and one another. However, the white world is present in *Goin'a Buffalo,* in a fashion possibly unique in the corpus of the black theater. Mamma-Too-Tight is white. Likable from the moment she appears, Mamma seems completely accepted and a part of the black world of the play. Her pres-

ence certainly suggests that the social and personal ills depicted in
Goin'a Buffalo are not unique to black people; in fact, Mamma is far
more deeply enmeshed in street life than Pandora, for she is openly
a prostitute, and an addict as well—a complication Pandora has
avoided. Mamma is on the streets to stay, while Curt and Pandora
hope to leave.

Some references are made to Mamma's color, and aspects of her
portrait suggest stereotyping. Mamma's original name is "Queenie
Bell Mack. . . . No self-respectin' whore in the world can go 'round
with a name like that unless she's in Mississippi" (29). The others ride
her for calling Art "boy"—"How fuckin' big do boys grow where you
come from?"—and Curt complains that she never uses the back door
(20). Her name may be intended to contrast Pandora's ample box—
evoking epithets often used in black literature to refer to white women.
Finally, Mamma provides the only source of humor in the play, thus
suggesting a reversal of the stereotypical role of the black comic in
white drama. In Bullins' use of Mamma-Too-Tight, the process of de-
metaphorizing the black characters and metaphorizing the white, for
which Hughes and Baraka prepared the ground, is perfectly realized.

Mamma's color also reminds the audience that the world depicted
is black, in the same way that the presence of the Krumps, the white
family in In the Wine Time, insists on the black reality of that play.
Mamma fits in because she has learned to "talk like a spade." Pandora
reminds her, "When you brought your funky ass from Mississippi . . .
we couldn't even understand you . . . we taught you to speak, if
anything!" (69). Her reminder is eloquent. If her black friends gave
Mamma language, it was to voice a pain that was in her already and
that she could not express in Biloxi, Mississippi. The language provided her is not only the spoken black dialect but also the cool jazz
that forms a constant background to the action in Goin'a Buffalo.

In Goin'a Buffalo Bullins accentuates all that is perverse about the
hustling street world. In contrast to Mamma-Too-Tight, his black characters do dream, but the only one who "gets what he wants" and thus,
in Pandora's terms, is really a man, is also practically devoid of humanity. The world of the renegade is not one of infinite possibility, as
Curt wants to believe. Because it recognizes no rules, in it no community, no love, no trust, and thus no real future is possible.

To demystify characters like Art is not to say the black community
lacks heroes, for in contrast to the worlds portrayed in the plays of

Richardson, Edmonds, Hughes, and Baraka, the worlds depicted in
Goin'a Buffalo, A Son, Come Home, and *Clara's Ole Man* need not be perceived as "the black community," nor are they intended to bear such
comprehensive symbolic weight. Rather, they describe segments of
that community, and to the extent that those segments express universal aspects of the black experience and of the human experience,
they have significance beyond themselves. All works not deliberately
allegorical or abstract function in this fashion, but for black drama to
arrive at the point where it could freely be eloquent through the particular, the assurance of a black stage reality was required.

Like *A Son, Come Home* and *Clara's Ole Man, In the Wine Time,* the first
play in the "Twentieth Century Cycle," takes place in a poor black
neighborhood in Philadelphia. The themes of this play are similar to
those in *Goin'a Buffalo.* But while in *Goin'a Buffalo* dreams are the dangerous self-deceptions of trapped people, in *In the Wine Time* the
dreams, which belong to a sixteen-year-old adolescent, Ray Crawford,
are legitimately romantic and full of possibilities. The relationship between Cliff Dawson and his wife, Lou, although difficult, is loving;
their affection for Ray, Lou's orphaned nephew, is nurturing. Moreover,
whereas *Goin'a Buffalo* focuses on people who block themselves from
the future, *In the Wine Time* depicts the selfless and heroic action by
which Cliff makes Ray's future away from the ghetto possible. Cliff pur-
chases Ray's future at a high price: he kills Red, the figure symbolically
blocking Ray's path to manhood, and is arrested.[56] Thus, while *Goin'a
Buffalo* exposes various flights from genuine love and manhood, *In the
Wine Time* meditates on the real meaning of these qualities, and displays, through Cliff's sacrifice, the strength and dignity of the ordinary
individual. Through this meditation Bullins conducts his search for
heroes in the black community.

In the Wine Time opens with a long prologue, spoken by Ray, which
establishes the most gentle variation of the play's central themes and
provides the undercurrent harmonious melody for the apparently random and often discordant action that follows. As in *The Pig Pen,* the
play's direction is vague—aimless like the summer evening of wine

56. It actually seems as through Ray kills Red and Cliff takes the blame.
However, the killing occurs offstage, and the real culprit is left ambiguous. In
In New England Winter, in Bullins (ed.), *New Plays from the Black Theatre,* 138–40,
Cliff seems to admit the killing—although, of course, it is possible he is still
protecting Ray.

and drinking it depicts—until the concluding moments give shape and meaning to what precedes them.

"She passed the corner every evening during my last wine time" (103). So begins Ray's opening account of his semimystical love affair with a beautiful woman whom he saw daily but only spoke to once (103). During their last encounter, the woman addressed him: " 'I love you, little boy,' she said. I nodded trying to comprehend. '. . . I have to go away but I wanted to tell you this before I left' " (105). Ray wanted to go with her, but she refused him, saying: "No, not now, but you can come find me when you're ready. . . . Out in the world, little boy, out in the world . . . all you have to do is leave this place and come to me, I'll be waiting" (105). Ray watched her disappear into the evening and then "turned back to meet autumn and Cliff and Lou in our last wine time, meeting the years which had to hurry so I could begin the search that I have not yet completed" (105).

The prologue, originally a short story, is a favorite of the author; he also uses it in *The Duplex*, the third play in the cycle, by having Steve read it to Thelma.[57] In it two voices mingle: the voice of the confused, naïve, but eager adolescent is tempered by that of the more mature and weary poet and seeker. The prologue's mythical equation of the meaning of life with the equally evasive beloved woman counterpoints the crude and even violent reality depicted in the play proper. The prologue also sets the action into a larger framework, thus relieving the claustrophobic atmosphere of the narrow ghetto street: "Summer and Cliff and Lou and me together—all poured from the same brew, all hating each other and loving, and consuming and never forgiving—but not letting go of the circle until the earth swung again into winter bringing me closer to manhood and the freedom to do all the things that I had done for the past three summers" (104).

The wine-time world offers Ray myriad images, models of manhood, each commenting on the others. He reflects all of them, tests some of them, and beyond them, through his encounter with the mystical woman on "The Avenue," retains his private portrait of the woman he seeks, and the man he wants to be. The models vary in value, and the drunken advice Cliff offers him in Act 3, which he almost immediately thereafter puts into practice, finally dominates the play.

57. The short story "In the Wine Time" is in Ed Bullins, *The Hungered One: Early Writings* (New York, 1971), 63–66.

> *Cliff.*   Ray . . . just learn this one thing in life. . . . When the time comes . . .
> be a man . . . however you've lived up till then . . . throw it out of your
> mind. . . . Just do what you have to do as a man.
> *Ray.*   (*Not sober*) Sure, Cliff . . . sure.
>
>   (171)

Until that moment arises, and even giving rise to it, is the wine
time. Cliff, Lou, Ray, and their companions are wine drinkers—and
thus different from the others in the neighborhood, the Garrison family next door, for example, who drink "pure'dee cooked corn whiskey."
Most of Bullins' ghetto characters are wine drinkers (in *Clara's Ole Man,
In New England Winter, The Duplex*) until they move up the social ladder
to scotch drinkers, as in *The Fabulous Miss Marie.* Wine affords long
nights of good times (for wine comes in gallons and is cheap), and
symbolically, it recalls sacrament and a sense of community. Lou says
of wine, "Ain't good for none of us . . . but it sho' do relaxes me" (131).
Wine elicits from both Lou and Cliff their sense of the divine. Under
its influence, Lou appeals to Ray to "listen to what I say . . . and not to
the devil" as embodied in Cliff, and she deplores her failure to be a
good example to Ray, whom she rescued from a foster home when he
was twelve (131). As she lectures Ray, Cliff intones a prayer that
renders her sermon almost incomprehensible: "Lord? You old shyster.
You pour white heat on these niggers, these Derby Street Donkeys, in
the daytime and roast and fry them while they shovel shit for nex' to
nothin', and steam them at night . . . they believe in You and Your lies.
Stupid donkeys!" (130–31).

Cliff's sacrilege shocks Lou.

> *Lou.*   You better get some of the fear of the Lord in you, Cliff.
> *Cliff.*   (*Disgust*) Every night. Every goddamn night when you start in feelin'
> your juice.
> *Lou.*   'Cause I know better, that's why.
> *Cliff.*   Is that why when I get you in bed every night you holla: (*Whining
> falsetto*) "Yes, Lord. Yes, Lord. Ohhh . . . Jesus . . . one more time."
>
>   (131–32)

With this revelation, the religious discussion ends, much to Ray's delight, and all three return peaceably to drinking.

Wine also evokes the sacred as it engenders a sense of community.
Act 1 of *In the Wine Time* focuses on Cliff, Lou, and Ray, with interrup-
tions from neighbors and brief scenes on "The Avenue," which contrast with and comment upon the principal action. Act 2 concentrates
on the relationship between Ray and Cliff, but during that act friends

begin to join them, until by Act 3 a whole community of their friends has gathered to drink wine and pass the time. Although moments of violence are as frequent as in *Goin'a Buffalo*, the motion of the play is not toward the point at which violence erupts but rather toward the resolution of discord, the reestablishing of a kind of peace. The most bitter moment between Cliff and Lou typifies the difference.

Ray has just announced his intention to join the Navy, as Cliff had done at his age, and Lou and Cliff quarrel over whether to give their consent, necessary because Ray is underage. Cliff says: "Yeah, you can go, Ray. I'll sign the papers myself. You're goin' to the navy and see how real men live" (135). When Lou objects, Cliff insists: "I'll sign anything I want fo' him. I'm his guardian."

> Lou.   (*Ridicule*) Guardian? How? With what? You ain't never had a job in your life over six months. What you raise him with . . . the few lousy bucks you don't drink up from your government check? You somebody's guardian . . . I . . . (*Cliff slaps her violently*)
>
> Cliff.   (*Low, menacing*) You talk too much, Lou.
>
> (135)

As in *Goin'a Buffalo*, the woman's legitimate attack on her husband's failure as a provider goads him into violence. In *Goin'a Buffalo*, Curt maintains dominance over Pandora and denies his own humiliation by physical brutality. The physical fight in *In the Wine Time* ends quite differently.

> Cliff. Damn it! . . . He's got to get out of here . . . don't you, Ray? . . . Off'a Derby Street and away from here so he can grow up to be his own man.
>
> Lou. (*Crying*) Like you?
>
> Cliff. No, not like me . . . not tied down to a half-grown, scared, childish bitch!
>
> Lou. You don't have to be.
>
> Cliff. But I love you.
>
> (135–36)

Cliff is truly remorseful for striking her, but the argument continues, becoming even more painful and cutting closer to the bone. Lou is three months pregnant, and Cliff admits he does not want the child (who, the prologue reveals, they will name Baby Man) because he cannot support it. They express their conflict simultaneously.

> Lou.   You ain't no man. My daddy he worked twenty years with his hands . . . his poor hands are hard and rough with corns and callouses. He was a man . . . he
>
> Cliff.   I'm going to get me part of that world or stare your God in the eye and scream *why*. I am not a beast . . . an animal to be used for the plows of the world.

worked and brought us up to take pride in ourselves and to fear God. What did I marry? I thought you was a man, Cliff. I thought because you was loud and was always fightin' and drinkin' and was so big and strong that you was a man . . . but you ain't nothin' but a low-down and less than nothin'!

But if I am then I'll act like one, I'll be one and turn this fucken world of dreams and lies and fairy tales into a jungle or a desert. And I don't give much of happy fuck which. There's a world out there, woman. Just beyond that lamppost . . . just across "The Avenue" and it'll be mine and Ray's.

(139)

Their duet eloquently depicts the range of problems confronting the black man, and evokes their historical context. Lou praises her father's diligent responsibility and respectability, but for Cliff, his father-in-law's dogged labor recalls a slave past continued beyond legal emancipation. Thus, while Lou works in a laundry for a dollar an hour, Cliff attends business school on the GI plan, hoping education will bring him mobility. Rather than work in the manner of his father-in-law, Cliff tells Lou he will ship out again or leave to allow Lou and the baby to collect relief, a plan that also has historical resonance. Their dialogue painfully acknowledges that none of the options, including that represented by Lou's father, satisfy the sense of manhood Cliff seeks and hopes to impart to Ray. Cliff's conflict with Lou and with himself cannot be easily resolved, but it at least allows Cliff and Lou, in contrast to the men and women in *Goin' a Buffalo*, to freely and honestly express their pain and anger.

A scene from "The Avenue," juxtaposed to Cliff's admission "But I love you," further illuminates the humanity underlying even the most painful aspects of Cliff and Lou's relationship. The counterpointing scenes all involve two couples: Red and Bunny Gillette; and Bama (from *Clara's Ole Man*, but a few years older) and Doris. Bunny is Ray's girlfriend, although she is flirting with Red; Doris is Lou's best friend. In the scene following Cliff's slap, Red strikes Bunny for a remark he considers offensive. Bama restrains him, and Doris pulls her knife. As in *Goin' a Buffalo*, on "The Avenue" the gratuitous violence of man toward woman is considered a prerogative of male dominance, and the scene ends with violence held at bay rather than resolved through confronting what lies behind it. Red simply reenacts a ritual now completely divorced from the pain that engendered it.

If, in his groping, Cliff aspires to true manhood, Red represents his opposite. He continually acts the bully, displays a spurious bravado, and in foul-mouthed company manages to outdo all the others, frequently by words and gestures violating even his companions' minimal sense of decorum. Red's final insult, which causes the fight during which he is killed, shocks even his companions. He urinates into an empty wine bottle and offers it to the drunken Ray as a toast to his new love. Red's action blasphemes Ray's dreams and all the world *In the Wine Time* honors. He himself represents all that is destructive in that world, for there is no humanity in him, no honor, no loyalty. While Cliff offers Ray wine and with it dreams of leaving the ghetto, of seeing the world, Red proffers him filth and disillusionment. The ensuing battle between Ray and Red is to the death and is conducted out of sight, in an alley between the Dawsons' house and a neighbor's—a space even more confined than the street depicted, the inner sanctum of the ghetto.

Red embodies all Ray must overcome to build a promising future, and to survive their fight he requires Cliff's help. A long, intimate conversation between Cliff and Ray occurs during Act 2; it reveals the strong bond between the two and establishes Cliff's role as mentor in Ray's quest for manhood. The scene opens, ironically, with a comment from "The Avenue." Bunny says to Red, "I like you a lot . . . really I do . . . but what will Ray say?" (141). Bunny's concern is self-aggrandizing, for as the audience learns in this act, Ray has turned his attention elsewhere, to his dream woman. He had been sexually faithful to Bunny because, he admits to Cliff in response to teasing, "me and her's in love" (147). But immediately after his declaration for Bunny, Ray tells Cliff of his new romance—a romance depicted as threatening to the entire world in which "me and her's in love." A pantomime on "The Avenue" accompanies Ray's confession to Cliff, expressing the danger: "The girl appears and stands under soft light. . . . The couples are fixed in tableau but Red and Bama pull away from Bunny Gillette and Doris and dance about the girl in a seduction dance, until the two girls break their positions and dance against the attraction of the girl, in a symbolic castration of the boys" (150). Ray's aspirations extend beyond what Bunny and her companions can imagine—or tolerate.

Counterpointing Ray's confession about his girl, Cliff reveals his own secret. Earlier, Cliff acknowledged Lou's accusations of sexual infidelity; however, his secret concerns not his disloyalty but his wife: "You better not breathe a word of this to your aunt . . . you hear? (*Pause*) Well, Lou Ellen is different because . . . well, because she's got character. . . . And your aunt's got principle and conviction and you have to be awfully special for that. . . . For someone to have all them qualities in these times is close to bein' insane. She's either got to be hopelessly ignorant or have the faith of an angel . . . and she's neither. . . . I don't deserve her, I know" (152).

Thus the play offers two ideal images of woman as crucial aspects of the male quest—the one, Ray's woman on "The Avenue," whose promise matches that of his own unrealized manhood, and the other, flesh-and-blood Lou, who has not only character but also what Cliff praises as a pure Hottentot behind. Against them all other women in the play are measured and found lacking. Bunny is alternately fickle and demanding; Doris is dangerous with her ready knife; Tiny, who appears in Act 3 and who, it is suggested, has slept with Cliff, is bitchy and petty; Beatrice, who flits across the stage in Act 2, is a snob. Similarly, against the relationships the two ideal women share with their men, all other relationships in the play are measured. Pointedly, the most degraded family relationships depicted in In the Wine Time are those displayed by the white Krump family.

Although Cliff's conversation with Ray covers the range of male sexual bravado and fantasy, particularly concerning Cliff's experiences in the Navy, at its core is the revelation that each is secure in his relation to an appropriate anima, and thus his quest begins from a firm basis. As the resolution of sexual identity is central to any definition of manhood, in Goin' a Buffalo, In the Wine Time, and many other plays as well, Bullins seeks to define authenticity in relationships between males and females, and condemns all other modes of sexual interaction as created to compensate for failures in manhood. His examination of the black community always returns to this point.

Approaching In the Wine Time through the theme of the meditation on manhood results in a reading some may regard as too gentle and optimistic. Certainly, much of the play reflects the same quality of imprisonment, suffocation, and self-delusion so oppressively present in Clara's Ole Man and Goin' a Buffalo, and thus the play certainly may be interpreted more pessimistically. For example, pursuing the motif of bondage in the play reveals that most of the principal characters are trapped in some fashion, and that there is little reason to believe— except for the vision of a beyond in the prologue—that Ray will escape Cliff's fate. The Navy functions as symbol of Cliff's experience of freedom, but Act 1 reveals that he spent half of his naval career in the brig—from which he obtained an early release only because Lou married him. All the characters are alcoholics, and one addiction easily leads to others, as Ray's woman warns him. The very act by which Cliff expresses his manhood, killing Red to protect Ray, results in his incarceration—and forces a failure of manhood in another respect, for he must leave his pregnant wife without support. His last words to Lou implore her to sign the papers for Ray, to give him his freedom—paradoxically, by yoking him to the military—thus further depriving her of help and support. Finally, in spite of all his dreams, Cliff has resigned himself to "sit[ting] back and rais[ing] tar babies," a fate he sees as a dismal trap (156).

Lance Jeffers aptly describes Cliff as embodying a fusion of suicide and manhood.[58] This kind of duality is frequent in Bullins' work: order and disorder, vitality and destruction, often originate from the same source. One is reminded of Pandora's box and her insistence that "it is all in what you bring to us," of Big Girl's capacity for nurture and for brutality, of the wine time's ability to build community and to create dissension. In the Wine Time, and more generally Bullins' work, contains its own critique of the world depicted, and imposes no external standards. Lou constantly admonishes the others for their crude language, although she herself finds it the only language appropriate to express certain emotions. Cliff stays with Lou because he loves her, and his staying simultaneously expresses his love and his unwillingness to be free. The nastiness of other relationships between males and females in In the Wine Time—not only Bunny's alliance with Red and Doris' with Bama, but also those that one glimpses in the Krump family—attests to the strength of the Dawson marriage, and insofar as it resembles the relationships around it, the audience understands its defects. That the characters choose to remain in the state that makes them unhappy is central in every Bullins play. Pandora and Mamma hate prostitution, but both continue to practice it. Clara fears Big Girl, but she is not yet strong enough to leave her. Through illuminating its characters' choices, each play establishes clear priorities and unmistakable, rigorous values. It is through his insistence on the potential for good and for evil residing in any person or circumstance that Bullins affirms the possibility for liberation as residing within, and thus available to everyone.

58. Jeffers, "Bullins, Baraka and Elder," 37.

The other plays in the "Twentieth Century Cycle," *In New England Winter*, *The Duplex*, *The Fabulous Miss Marie*, and the more recent, unpublished "Home Boy" and "DADDY!," introduce new characters and new surroundings, but Bullins' chief concerns remain the same. Some of his characters imprison themselves in self-hatred (as in *In New England Winter*), others in relationships (in *The Duplex*) or in places (in "Home Boy"). Each play investigates the meaning of manhood, particularly as developed and experienced through heterosexual relationships. Thus many of his plays also examine the ways men and women habitually abuse each other—thereby taking up the quintessential themes of the form for which Bullins frequently composes lyrics, the blues.

What distinguishes Bullins' quest from others with similar concerns is that he seeks a definition arising from the imaginative and social context in which his characters live, through which they understand themselves. The question "What does it mean to be a black man?" for Bullins means "What does it mean to be a man?" By Black he does not mean black-as-opposed-to-white, like Baraka. He does not, even unconsciously, depict modes of behavior that counter various insidious stereotypes—the pitfall of Richardson, Edmonds, and even, on occasion, Hughes. Rather, Bullins means by his question one of the world's riddles, and in some degree he succeeds in formulating answers in black terms.

For example, in *In the Wine Time* Cliff offers a definition of manhood very much like Hamlet's "the readiness is all." Given the dangerous, uncertain tenor of ghetto existence and poverty subsistence, given also the historical period depicted (the 1950s), which marked the first decisive stirrings of a new, more universally militant approach to the demand for civil rights, Cliff's definition clearly evolves from his milieu. Other definitions, arising from other circumstances and suitable in other contexts, may set out conditions inappropriate to who and where Bullins' characters are, and thus only make their failure inevitable.

Moreover, Bullins generates values out of the experience of his characters, rather than imposing them from outside. In comparison, Richardson and Edmonds employ value systems that clearly reflect a bourgeois morality arising from a completely different world from the one they depict, particularly in the folk plays. Hughes often appeals to the sense of social justice defined by the ideals of American democracy, even while exposing its most painful inadequacies. In the sixties and early seventies, Baraka espoused a system deliberately set up in opposition to those that evolved from the Judeo-Christian tradition. His appeal to African deities and Black Muslim mythology generated the metaphors through which he expressed this value system.

Bullins' focus is the experiential knowledge of good and evil that he believes is present in everyone except those whose understanding is distorted through drugs, violence, and all they represent. He is neither philosopher nor moralist, but he is absolutely certain, ultimately, that the human quest has a purpose. The structure of that quest, the metaphors through which it is revealed and explored, evolves from the people whose quest it is, from the specifics of their experience. To Bullins, the double vision of which Du Bois speaks in *The Souls of Black Folk*, continually present in Richardson and Edmonds, and only occasionally and specifically transcended or transformed in Hughes and Baraka, is no longer an issue. The world Bullins depicts pursues self-understanding on its own terms, in its own language, and by its own standards. The creation of this kind of imaginative reality requires assurance that the audience will understand the language, be able to share the perspective, remain open to the characters, and allow their truth to manifest itself. To speak in this way is to perceive the question of white versus black audience in a new fashion. The white audience attends a Bullins' play as outsider; middle-class blacks may feel differently excluded. However, since the pursuit of meaning is conducted on its own terms, the question of audience is, in a sense, irrelevant. The members of the audience will achieve varying degrees of insight depending on who they are.

For the metaphor to disclose its meaning, it must be examined in context—this rule is axiomatic to interpretation. In Bullins' plays, black figures stand securely in black ground; they no longer symbolize the "Other," and are, therefore, capable of achieving self-understanding. Bullins' work exemplifies black drama's maturity. In doing so it also reveals something of what it means to say a literature has matured, and something of the truth in the paradox that it is only when the particular is most perfectly realized that the universal is most eloquently expressed.

AFTERWORD ൦

Between 1917, the year Willis Richardson's *The Chip Woman's Fortune* was performed in New York, and 1975, when Bullins won acclaim for *The Taking of Miss Janie*, black dramatists gradually constructed the black theater. Richardson, Edmonds, Hughes, Baraka, and Bullins were the most prolific of these playwrights, and each had significant impact on that theater's development. Many dramatists contributed to the process; my attending to five in detail is not meant to obscure the contribution of others. Theodore Ward, Owen Dodson, Lorraine Hansberry, and James Baldwin, for example, are conspicuous by their absence. Ward's militancy and Dodson's language in particular suggested directions to other black playwrights; Hansberry's *Raisin in the Sun* and Baldwin's *Blues for Mr. Charlie*, both extremely successful, demanded a respect from white audiences that precluded condescension, and in this sense foreshadowed the fully established black stage reality. Examining the five in detail provides a context for approaching the work of the others, I would argue, for all are engaged in the same project.

I concentrated on a few writers who had a sizable body of work because doing so allowed me to dissect the necessary, complex, and difficult process of transforming artistic conventions, and of establishing in the context of formal art a fully controlled and assured imaginative landscape. Alternatively, one might think of the process as one of creating a national literature. The problems that confronted Afro-American writers then may be seen as similar to those confronting, for example, novelists in neocolonial countries. In a more obvious sense, these writers had to adapt to a completely different cultural milieu and audience, and to European forms and languages, which were themselves constant reminders of the colonial heritage. A more subtle variation of the same problem emerges when observing how women writers have wrestled with forms and language developed by male writers and validated by a male critical establishment.

I defined the transformation that occurred as one of a change in stage reality, which includes the implicit and explicit assumptions made both in the play and by its audience. In brief, where the black stage reality prevails, there is a community of assumptions shared by the work and at least its black audience. A white audience may share some of these assumptions, but it is impelled to acknowledge, respect, and accept the "Otherness" of what it does not share. It cannot take the black figure as mask for its own experience; rather, it is invited to encounter the "Other" and, insofar as any particular human experience has meaning beyond itself, to be enriched by that meaning.

Each stage in the development of this stage reality both mirrored and influenced the social and political environment in which it occurred. While this is true of any artistic endeavor, the connection between art and its social and political context possesses a wonderful literalness in the theater. Plays are written to be performed, and the play in performance is a public act. Actors perform real actions when they act; this accounts at least in part for the caution of early playwrights like Richardson and Edmonds as well as for the audacity of the playwrights of the Black Arts Movement. The presence of what I call a national literature, to continue the political analogy, does not, of course, signal a resolution to social and political problems. In a pluralist society, however, it does have a particular significance. I would suggest, for example, that Jessie Jackson's 1982 presidential campaign was as much an expression of the imaginative landscape black artists had created as it was of the change in the American political climate. The rhetoric and accents of Jackson's campaign were unmistakably those of black America, although his "rainbow coalition" addressed the political hopes of a wider group of Americans.

Two recent, immensely popular plays exemplify the black theater's freedom and assurance. Ntozake Shange's *for colored girls who have considered suicide / when the rainbow is enuf* speaks eloquently about the lives of black women and their relations with black men. Without mitigating or minimizing how racism has deformed those relationships, the play addresses their pain, and thus implies as well their potential for joy. In so doing, *for colored girls who have considered suicide* made some of its black audiences uneasy. When the play opened in 1976, criticisms ranged from the accusation that it was "washing dirty laundry in public" to the claim that it introduced to the black community a militant, inappropriate feminism borrowed from whites. Yet much of the play's dramatic power lies in its full treatment of the experience of black women as clearly distinct from that of other women, while it also reveals the pain shared by all. Because its images, situations, and language are unmistakably black, the black experience is the lens through which human experience must be perceived and understood.

In a different way, but with equal freedom and assurance, Charles Fuller's Pulitzer Prize–winning A *Soldier's Play* also treats painful tensions within the black community. Set at a southern military base during World War II, A *Soldier's Play* concerns a black officer's investigation of the apparent lynching of Waters, another black officer. His investigation reveals that the murderer is a black private taking revenge for Waters' cruel treatment of a fellow black private. The play thus explores not only white racism but, in the character of Waters, internalized racism at its most brutal, and it does so with infinite sympathy and compassion. Fuller seeks, not to exonerate or to explain, but rather to explore and to understand this internalized racism in all its complexity. No character is demeaned by his portrait, and none, black or white, is judged.

Shange's and Fuller's work represent as well the range of form contemporary black theater assumes. For *colored girls who have considered suicide* is a series of poetic monologues; A *Soldier's Play*, though not naturalistic, uses relatively conventional plot and characterization to unravel its story as well as to comprehend its ultimate subject. The black theater also expresses its freedom and confidence through its command of the theater's formal possibilities.

Other factors have contributed to the vitality of the new black theater. Perhaps the most important is that in New York and other major United States metropolitan areas, there exist black theaters where dramatists can have workshops and full productions of their plays, and find encouragement and criticism from informed black theater professionals and audiences. For *colored girls who have considered suicide*, for example, was developed as a theater piece at Woodie King, Jr.'s New Federal Theatre at the Henry Street Settlement Playhouse before being moved to Broadway by Joseph Papp. A *Soldier's Play* and other works by Charles Fuller were produced by New York's Negro Ensemble Company. In New York, many off- and off-off-Broadway houses now mount black productions, knowing there is an audience for them. More than a few black plays and plays with black casts have achieved success on the "Great White Way" as well.

Of course a full account of the factors contributing to the new black theater requires much more than an analysis of the work of five play-

wrights. It must consider the history of black America and race relations throughout the period of black theater's development, and it
must consider other black and white artistic endeavors. Artistic assurance is greatly affected by the artists' relation to their audience, to
the various traditions they draw on as a resource, and to the social
and political context in which they create. The new black theater is a
product of changes in those factors; but it is also itself a significant
cause.

BIBLIOGRAPHY ✑

PRIMARY SOURCES

Archival Collections

Hatch-Billops Collection. In the possession of James V. Hatch.
    Richardson, Willis. "The Amateur Prostitute." Typescript.
    ———. "The Broken Banjo." (Three-act version.) Typescript.
    ———. "The Flight of the Natives." (Three-act version.) Typescript.
    ———. "The Peacock's Feathers." Typescript.
    ———. "A Pillar of the Church." Typescript.
    ———. "The Visiting Lady." Typescript.

Hatch-Billops Oral Black History Collection, City College of New York.
    Interview with Randolph Edmonds. August 21, 1973.
    Interview with Willis Richardson. March 5, 1972.

Langston Hughes Papers, James Weldon Johnson Collection, Beinecke
Library, Yale University.
    Edmonds, Randolph. "Report of the European Tour: Florida A&M
        Playmakers."
    Hughes, Langston. "Angelo Herndon Jones." Typescript.
    ———. "The Ballot and Me." Typescript.
    ———. "The Barrier." Typescript.
    ———. "Black Nativity." Drafts and typescript, program note.
    ———. "Cock o'de World." Drafts.
    ———. "Colonel Tom's Cabin." Typescript.
    ———. "De Organizer." Typescript.
    ———. "Don't You Want to Be Free?" Drafts and typescripts. 1938,
        1944, 1946, 1949, 1952, 1963.
    ———. "Emperor of Haiti," also called "Drums of Haiti" and
        "Troubled Island." Drafts and typescripts.
    ———. "Esther." Typescript.
    ———. "For This We Fight." Typescript.
    ———. "Front Porch." Drafts and typescripts.
    ———. "Gospel Glory." Drafts and typescript.

————. Interview. Chicago *Defender*, March 25, 1954.

————. "Jericho-Jim Crow." Typescript.

————. "Joy to My Soul." Drafts and typescript, production note.

————. Lyrics for "Just Around the Corner," by Abby Mann and Bernard Drew. Typescript.

————. "Little Ham" (play). Drafts and typescript.

————. "Little Ham" (65-episode radio program). Typescript.

————. "Mulatto," originally "Cross." Drafts and typescript.

————. "Mule Bone." Typescript.

————. "Port Town." Typescript.

————. "The Prodigal Son." Drafts.

————. "St. James: Sixty Years Young." Typescript.

————. "Simple Takes a Wife." Typescript.

————. "Simply Heavenly." Drafts and typescripts.

————. "Soul Gone Home" (opera). Typescript.

————. Lyrics for *Street Scene*, by Elmer Rice. Typescript.

————. "The Sun Do Move." Drafts and typescript.

————. "Tambourines to Glory." Drafts and typescript.

Hughes, Langston, and Arna Bontemps. "When the Jack Hollers." Drafts and typescript.

Hughes, Langston, and Ella Winter. "Blood in the Fields." Drafts.

Books, Periodicals, and Articles

Allen, Donald, ed. *The New American Poetry*, 1945–1960. New York, 1960.

Artaud, Antonin. *The Theatre and Its Double*. New York, 1958.

Baraka, Imamu Amiri. See Jones, LeRoi.

Black Theatre, Nos. 1–5 (1968–1971).

Bontemps, Arna. "New Poets, Then and Now." *Phylon*, XI (1950), 355–60.

————. *The Old South*. New York, 1973.

Bontemps, Arna, and Langston Hughes, eds. *The Book of Negro Folklore*. New York, 1958.

Brooks, Gwendolyn. "Poets Who Are Negroes." *Phylon*, XI (1950), 312.

Brown, Sterling. "Folk Expression." *Phylon*, XI (1950), 318–27.

————. *Southern Road*. 1932; rpr. Boston, 1974.

Bullins, Ed. *The Duplex: A Black Love Fable in Four Movements*. New York, 1971.

————. *Five Plays by Ed Bullins*. New York, 1968.

————. *Four Dynamite Plays*. New York, 1972.

————. *How Do You Do?* San Francisco, 1967.

————. *The Hungered One: Early Writings*. New York, 1971.

————, ed. *The New Lafayette Theatre Presents*. Garden City, N.Y., 1974.

————, ed. *New Plays from the Black Theatre*. New York, 1969.

————. "The Polished Protest: Aesthetics and the Black Writer." *Contact*, IV (July, 1963), 67–68.

————. *The Reluctant Rapist*. New York, 1973.

————. "The So-called Western Avant-garde Drama." *Liberator*, VII (December, 1967), 16–17.

————. *The Taking of Miss Janie*. In *Famous American Plays of the 1970s*, edited by Ted Hoffman. New York, 1981.

————. "Theatre of Reality." *Negro Digest*, XV (April, 1966), 60–66.

————. *The Theme Is Blackness: "The Corner" and Other Plays*. New York, 1973.

Burke, Kenneth. "The Negro's Pattern of Life." In his *The Philosophy of Literary Form*. Berkeley, 1973.

Camus, Albert. *Caligula and Three Other Plays*. Translated by Stuart Gilbert. New York, 1958.

Chandler, G. Lewis. "A Major Problem of Negro Authors in Their March Toward Belles-Lettres." *Phylon*, XI (1950), 383–86.

Cleaver, Eldridge. *Soul on Ice*. New York, 1968.

Drama Review, XII (Summer, 1968).

Du Bois, W. E. B. "Criteria of Negro Art." *Crisis*, XXXII (October, 1926), 290–97.

————. "Krigwa Little Theatre Movement." *Crisis*, XXXII (July, 1926), 134–36.

————. *The Souls of Black Folk*. 1903; rpr. Greenwich, Conn., 1961.

Edmonds, Randolph. "Black Drama in the American Theatre: 1700–1970." In *American Theatre: A Sum of Its Parts*. New York, 1971.

————. *Earth and Stars*. In *Black Drama in America: An Anthology*, edited by Darwin Turner. Greenwich, Conn., 1971.

————. "Education in Self-Contempt." *Crisis*, XLV (August, 1938), 262–63, 266, 278.

————. *The Land of Cotton and Other Plays*. Washington, D.C., 1942.

————. "The Negro Little Theatre Movement." *Negro History Bulletin*, XII (January, 1949), 82–86, 92–94.

————. "The Negro Playwright in the American Theatre." SADSA *Encore* (Spring, 1950), 8–13.

————. *Shades and Shadows*. Boston, 1930.

————. *Six Plays for a Negro Theatre*. Boston, 1934.

————. "Some Reflections on the Negro in American Drama." *Opportunity*, VIII (October, 1930), 92, 105.

————. "What Good Are College Dramatics." *Crisis*, LVI (August, 1934), 232–34.

Ellison, Ralph. *Invisible Man*. New York, 1952.

————. *Shadow and Act*. New York, 1964.

Floating Bear. 1961–*ca.* 1962; rpr. La Jolla, Calif., 1973.

Ford, Nick Aaron. "A Blueprint for Negro Authors." *Phylon*, XI (1950), 374–77.

Gayle, Addison, Jr., ed. *Black Expression: Essays by and About Black Americans in the Creative Arts*. New York, 1969.

Genet, Jean. *The Blacks: A Clown Show*. New York, 1960.

Gloster, Hugh M. "Race and the Negro Writer." *Phylon*, XI (1950), 369–71.

Green, Paul. *In Abraham's Bosom*. In *Five Plays of the South*. New York, 1963.

————. *Lonesome Road: Six Plays for the Negro Theatre*. New York, 1926.

Gregory, Montgomery. "For a Negro Theatre." *New Republic*, November 16, 1921, p. 350.

Harrison, Paul Carter. *The Drama of Nommo*. New York, 1972.

Hatch, James V., ed. *Black Theatre, U.S.A.: Forty-five Plays by Black Americans, 1847–1974*. New York, 1974.

Henderson, Stephen. *Understanding the New Black Poetry*. New York, 1973.

Hughes, Langston. *The Big Sea*. New York, 1940.

————. *The Best of Simple*. New York, 1961.

————. *Don't You Want to Be Free?* In *Black Theatre, U.S.A.*, edited by James V. Hatch. New York, 1974.

————. *Emperor of Haiti*. In *Black Drama in America: An Anthology*, edited by Darwin Turner. Greenwich, Conn., 1971.

————. *Fine Clothes to the Jew*. New York, 1927.

————. *Five Plays by Langston Hughes*. Edited by Webster Smalley. Bloomington, 1963.

————. *The Gold Piece: A Play That Might Be True*. In *Brownies' Book*, II (July, 1921), 190–94.

————. *Good Morning, Revolution: Uncollected Social Protest Writings by Langston Hughes*. Edited by Faith Berry. Westport, N.Y., 1973.

————. *I Wonder as I Wander*. New York, 1956.

————. *Little Ham*. In *Five Plays by Langston Hughes*, edited by Webster Smalley. Bloomington, 1963.

————. *Mother and Child*. SADSA *Encore* (1950), 31–35.

————. *Mulatto*. In *Five Plays by Langston Hughes*, edited by Webster Smalley. Bloomington, 1963.

————. "The Negro and American Entertainment." In *The American Negro Reference Book*, edited by John T. Davis. Englewood Cliffs, N.J., 1966.

————. "The Negro Artist and the Racial Mountain." Rpr. in *The Black Aesthetic*, edited by Addison Gayle, Jr. Garden City, N.Y., 1972.

————. *The Negro Mother and Other Dramatic Recitations*. 1931; rpr. Freeport, N.Y., 1971.

————. *The Prodigal Son*. In *Players*, XLIII (October-November, 1967), 16–21.

————. *Scottsboro Limited: Four Poems and a Play*. New York, 1932.

————. *Selected Poems of Langston Hughes*. New York, 1970.

————. *Simple Speaks His Mind*. New York, 1950.

————. *Simple Stakes a Claim*. New York, 1957.

————. *Simple's Uncle Sam*. New York, 1965.

————. *Simple Takes a Wife*. New York, 1953.

————. *Simply Heavenly*. In *Five Plays by Langston Hughes*, edited by Webster Smalley. Bloomington, 1963.

————. *Soul Gone Home* (play). In *Five Plays by Langston Hughes*, edited by Webster Smalley. Bloomington, 1963.

————. *The Sun Do Move*. New York, 1942.

————. *Tambourines to Glory*. In *Five Plays by Langston Hughes*, edited by Webster Smalley. Bloomington, 1963.

————. "That Boy LeRoi." In *Anthology of the American Negro in the Theatre*, edited by Lindsay Patterson. New York, 1967, 205–206.

————. *The Ways of White Folks*. New York, 1971.

————. *The Weary Blues*. New York, 1926.

Hughes, Langston, and the Editors. "Some Practical Observations: A Colloquy." *Phylon*, XI (1950), 307–11.

Hughes, Langston, and Milton Meltzer. *Black Entertainment: A Pictorial History of the Negro in American Entertainment*. Englewood Cliffs, N.J., 1967.

Hughes, Langston, and William Grant Still. *Troubled Island*. New York, 1949.

Hughes, Langston, and Zora Neale Hurston. *Mule Bone*, Act 3. *Drama Critique*, VII (Spring, 1964), 103–107.

Jackson, Blyden. "An Essay in Criticism." *Phylon* XI, (1950), 338–43.

Jarrett, Thomas D. "Toward Unfettered Creativity: A Note on the Negro Novelist's Coming of Age." *Phylon*, XI (1950), 313–17.

Johnson, Charles, ed. *Ebony and Topaz: A Collectanea*. New York, 1927.

Johnson, James Weldon. *Along This Way*. New York, 1933.

———. *Black Manhattan*. 1930; rpr. New York, 1968.

———. "The Dilemma of the Negro Author." *American Mercury*, XV (December, 1928), 477–81.

———. *God's Trombones: Seven Negro Sermons in Verse*. 1927; rpr. New York, 1969.

Jones, LeRoi [Baraka, Imamu Amiri]. *Arm Yrself or Harm Yrself: A Message of Self Defense to Black Men*. Newark, 1967.

———. *The Baptism and The Toilet*. New York, 1966.

———. [Baraka, Imamu Amiri]. BA-RA-KA. In *Spontaneous Combustion: Eight New American Plays*, edited by Rochelle Owens. New York, 1972.

———. [Baraka, Imamu Amiri]. *Black Magic: Poetry, 1961–1967*. New York, 1969.

———. [Baraka, Imamu Amiri]. *Black Music*. New York, 1967.

———. [Baraka, Imamu Amiri]. *Black Power Chant*. In *Black Theatre*, No. 4 (April, 1970), 35.

———. [Baraka, Imamu Amiri]. *A Black Value System*. Newark, 1970.

———. [Baraka, Imamu Amiri]. *Bloodrites*. In *Black Drama Anthology*, edited by Woodie King and Ron Milner. New York, 1971.

———. *Blues People: Negro Music in White America*. New York, 1963.

———. [Baraka, Imamu Amiri]. *Chant*. In *Black Theatre*, No. 5 (1971), 16–17.

———. *The Dead Lecturer*. New York, 1964.

———. *The Death of Malcolm X*. In *New Plays from the Black Theatre*, edited by Ed Bullins. New York, 1969.

———. *Dutchman and The Slave*. New York, 1964.

———. *Four Black Revolutionary Plays*. New York, 1968.

———. *Home: Social Essays*. New York, 1966.

———. [Baraka, Imamu Amiri]. *Jello*. Chicago, 1970.

———. [Baraka, Imamu Amiri]. *The Motion of History and Other Plays*. New York, 1978.

———. *Preface to a Twenty Volume Suicide Note*. New York, 1961.

————. *Selected Plays and Prose of Amiri Baraka / LeRoi Jones*. New York, 1979.

————. [Baraka, Imamu Amiri]. *Slave Ship*. In *Negro Digest*, XVI (April, 1967), 62–74.

————. *The System of Dante's Hell*. New York, 1966.

————. *Tales*. New York, 1967.

Jones, LeRoi [Baraka, Imamu Amiri], and Larry Neal, eds. *Black Fire: An Anthology of Afro-American Writing*. New York, 1968.

Kafka, Franz. *Wedding Preparations in the Country and Other Posthumous Prose Writings*. Translated by Ernst Kaiser and Eithne Wilkins. Edited by Max Brod. London, 1954.

King, Woodie, and Ron Milner. *Black Drama Anthology*. New York, 1971.

Lee, Ulysses. "Criticism at Mid-Century." *Phylon*, XI (1950), 328–37.

Lewis, Theophilus. "Main Problems of the Negro Theatre." *Messenger*, IX (July, 1927), 229–43.

————. "The Paul Green Menace Increases." *Messenger*, X (January, 1928), 18.

————. "Same Old Blues." *Messenger*, VII (January, 1925), 14–15.

Locke, Alain. "Broadway and the Negro Drama." *Theatre Arts*, XXV (1941), 145–50.

————. "The Negro and the American Theatre." 1927; rpr. in *Drama Critique*, VII (Spring, 1964), 12–122.

————, ed. *The New Negro*. 1925; rpr. New York, 1969.

————. "Self-Criticism: The Third Dimension in Culture." *Phylon*, XI (1950), 391–94.

————. "Steps Toward the Negro Theatre." *Crisis*, XXV (December, 1922), 66–68.

————, and Montgomery Gregory, eds. *Plays of Negro Life: A Source-Book of Native American Drama*. New York, 1927.

Malcolm X. *The Autobiography of Malcolm X*. New York, 1966.

————. *Malcolm X Speaks*. New York, 1966.

McKay, Claude. *Harlem: Negro Metropolis*. New York, 1940.

————. *A Long Way From Home*. 1937; rpr. New York, 1970.

"The Negro in Art: How Shall He Be Portrayed: A Symposium." *Crisis*, XXXI (March, 1926), 219–20, and (April, 1926), 278–80; XXXII (May, 1926), 35–36, (June, 1926), 71–73, (August, 1926), 193–94, and (September, 1926), 238–39; XXXIII (November, 1926), 28–29.

Neal, Larry. "The Black Arts Movement." *Drama Review*, XII (Summer, 1968), 29–39.

Nicholas, Charles H., Jr. "The Forties: A Decade of Growth." *Phylon*, XI (1950), 377–80.

Nichols, Charles, ed. *Arna Bontemps / Langston Hughes: Letters, 1925–1967*. New York, 1980.

Parone, Edward, ed. *New Theatre in America*. New York, 1965.

Patterson, Lindsay, ed. *Anthology of the American Negro in the Theatre: A Critical Approach*. New York, 1967.

Rampersad, Arnold. *The Life of Langston Hughes, Volume 1, 1902–1941: I, Too, Sing America*. New York, 1986.

Reddick, L. D. "No Kafka in the South." *Phylon*, XI (1950), 380–83.

Redding, J. Saunders. "The Negro Writer—Shadow and Substance." *Phylon*, XI (1950), 371–73.

Reid, Ira De A. "The Literature of the Negro: A Social Scientist's Appraisal." *Phylon*, XI (1950), 388–90.

Richardson, Willis. *The Broken Banjo*. In *Plays of Negro Life*, edited by Alain Locke and Montgomery Gregory. New York, 1927.

———. *The Chip Woman's Fortune*. In *Black Drama in America: An Anthology*, edited by Darwin T. Turner. Greenwich, Conn., 1971.

———. *Compromise*. In *The New Negro*, edited by Alain Locke. 1925; rpr. New York, 1969.

———. *The Deacon's Awakening*. In *Crisis*, XXI (November, 1920), 10–15.

———. *The Flight of the Natives*. In *Plays of Negro Life*, edited by Alain Locke and Montgomery Gregory. New York, 1927.

———. "The Hope of a Negro Drama." *Crisis*, XIX (November, 1919), 338–39.

———. *The Idle Head*. In *Black Theatre, U.S.A.*, edited by James V. Hatch. New York, 1974.

———. *The King's Dilemma and Other Plays for Children: Episodes of Hope and Dream*. New York, 1956.

———. *Mortgaged*. In *Readings from Negro Authors*, edited by Othelia Cromwell, Lorenzo Dow Turner, and Eva B. Dykes. New York, 1931.

———, ed. *Plays and Pageants from the Life of the Negro*. Washington, D.C., 1930.

———. "Propaganda in the Theatre." *Messenger*, VI (November, 1924), 353–54.

Richardson, Willis, and May Miller, eds. *Negro History in Thirteen Plays*. Washington, D.C., 1935.

Riley, Clayton, ed. *A Black Quartet*. New York, 1970.

Schuyler, George S. "Carl Van Vechten." *Phylon*, XI (1950), 362–68.

Smith, William Gardner. "The Negro Writer: Pitfalls and Compensations." *Phylon*, XI (1950), 297–303.

"A Symposium on 'We Righteous Bombers.'" *Black Theatre*, No. 4 (April, 1970), 16–25.

"The Task of the Negro Writer as Artist: A Symposium." *Negro Digest*, XIV (April, 1965), 54–79.

Thompson, Era Bell. "Negro Publications and the Writer." *Phylon*, XI (1950), 304–306.

Tillman, N. P. "The Threshold of Maturity." *Phylon*, XI (1950), 387–88.

Toomer, Jean. *Cane*. 1923; rpr. New York, 1969.

Torrence, Ridgely. *Granny Maumee, The Rider of Dreams, Simon the Cyrenian: Plays for A Negro Theatre*. New York, 1917.

Van Vechten, Carl. Review in *Literary Digest*, May 9, 1914, p. 1114.

Walker, Margaret. "New Poets." *Phylon*, XI (1950), 345–54.

Wright, Richard. *Black Boy: A Record of Childhood and Youth*. New York, *ca.* 1945.

———. "How Bigger Was Born." *Saturday Review*, June 1, 1940, pp. 4–5, 17–20.

———. *Native Son*. New York, 1940.

———. *White Man, Listen!* Garden City, N.Y., 1964.

SECONDARY SOURCES

Abrahams, Roger D. *Deep Down in the Jungle . . . : Negro Narrative Folklore from the Streets of Philadelphia*. 1st rev. ed. Chicago, 1970.

———. "The Negro Stereotype: Negro Folklore and the Riots." In *The Urban Experience and Folk Tradition*, edited by Americo Paredes and Ellen J. Stekert. Austin, 1971.

———. *Positively Black*. Englewood Cliffs, N.J., 1970.

Abramson, Doris. "It'll Be Me: The Voice of Langston Hughes." In *Black and White in American Culture*, edited by Jules Chametzky and Sidney Kaplan. New York, 1969.

———. *Negro Playwrights in the American Theatre, 1925–1959*. New York, 1969.

Adam, George. "Militant Black Drama." *American Imago*, XXVIII (1971), 107–28.

Anderson, Jervis. "Profiles." *New Yorker*, June 16, 1973, pp. 40–79.

Aptheker, Herbert, ed. *A Documentary History of the Negro People in the United States*. Vol. III. Secaucus, N.J., 1974.

Archer, Leonard C. "Negro Life as a Folk Basis in Contemporary American Drama." M.A. thesis, University of Toronto, 1939.

Bailey, Peter. "The Electronic Nigger." *Ebony*, XXIII (September, 1968), 96–101.

Barksdale, Richard, and Kenneth Kinnamon, eds. *Black Writers in America*. New York, 1972.

Beck, Robert [Iceberg Slim]. *Pimp: The Story of My Life*. Los Angeles, 1969.

Bell, Bernard W. *The Folk Roots of Contemporary Afro-American Poetry*. Detroit, 1974.

Benston, Kimberly W. *Baraka: The Renegade and the Mask*. New York, 1976.

Bernstein, Samuel J. *The Strands Entwined: A New Direction in American Drama*. Boston, 1980.

Berry, Faith. *Langston Hughes: Before and Beyond Harlem*. Westport, Conn., 1983.

Blassingame, John. *The Slave Community*. New York, 1972.

Bluestein, Gene. *The Voice of the Folk: Folklore and American Literary Theory*. N.p., 1972.

Bond, Frederick W. *The Negro and the Drama*. 1940; rpr. Washington, D.C., 1969.

Bontemps, Arna, ed. *The Harlem Renaissance Remembered*. New York, 1972.

Boskin, Joseph. "Sambo: The National Jester in the Popular Culture." In *The Great Fear: Race in the Mind of America*, edited by Gary Nash and Richard Weiss. New York, 1970.

Brawley, Benjamin. *The Negro Genius: A New Appraisal of the Achievement of the American Negro in Literature and the Fine Arts*. New York, 1937.

Brown, Lloyd. *Amiri Baraka*. New York, 1981.

——. "Black Entitles: Names as Symbols in Afro-American Literature." *Studies in Black Literature*, I (Spring, 1970), 16–44.

——. "Comic-Strip Heroes: LeRoi Jones and the Myth of American Innocence." *Journal of Popular Culture*, III (Fall, 1969), 191–204.

——. "Dreamers and Slaves: The Ethos of Revolution in Derek Walcott and LeRoi Jones." *Caribbean Quarterly*, XVII (September-December, 1971), 36–44.

Brown, Sterling. "Negro Characters as Seen by White Authors." *Journal of Negro Education*, II (April, 1933), 179–201.

——. "Negro in the American Theatre." In *Oxford Companion to the Theatre*. 2nd ed. London, 1957.

————. *Negro Poetry and Drama*. 1937; rpr. New York, 1969.

Butcher, Margaret Just. *The Negro in American Culture*. 2nd ed. New York, 1972.

Chametzky, Jules, and Sidney Kaplan, eds. *Black and White in American Culture: An Anthology from "The Massachusetts Review."* New York, 1969.

Clark, John Pepper. *The Example of Shakespeare*. London, 1970.

Cohen, Ruby. *Dialogue in American Drama*. Bloomington, 1971.

Costello, Donald. "LeRoi Jones: Black Man as Victim." *Commonweal*, June 28, 1968, pp. 436–40.

Dace, Laetitia. A *Bibliography of LeRoi Jones*. London, 1971.

Davis, Arthur P. *From the Dark Tower: Afro-American Writers, 1900–1960*. Washington, D.C., 1974.

————. "The Harlem of Langston Hughes." *Phylon*, XIII (1952), 276–83.

Dennison, George. "The Demagogy of LeRoi Jones." *Commentary*, XXXIX (February, 1965), 67–70.

Dickinson, Donald C. A *Bio-Bibliography of Langston Hughes*. 2nd ed. Hamden, Conn., 1972.

Dippold, Diane. "A Tramp with Connections." Ph.D. dissertation, University of Maryland, 1971.

Dollard, John. *Caste and Class in a Southern Town*. 3rd ed. Garden City, N.Y., 1957.

"Ed Bullins." *Contemporary Authors*, XLIX-LII (1975).

"Ed Bullins." *Current Biography*. 1977 ed.

"Ed Bullins." *Negro Digest*, XV (October, 1966), 23, 78–82.

Elkins, Stanley. *Slavery*. Chicago, 1959.

Emanuel, James. *Langston Hughes*. New York, 1967.

Essien, Ignatius McDonald. "Social Criticism in Three Plays by Langston Hughes." M.A. thesis, Memphis State University, 1971.

Evans, Don. "The Theatre of Confrontation: Ed Bullins, Up Against the Wall." *Black World*, XXIII (April, 1974), 14–18.

Fabre, Michael. *The Unfinished Quest of Richard Wright*. Translated by Isabel Barzun. New York, 1973.

Fanon, Franz. *Black Skin, White Masks*. New York, 1968.

————. *Wretched of the Earth*. New York, 1968.

Fischer, William C. "The Pre-Revolutionary Writings of Imamu Amiri Baraka." *Massachusetts Review*, XIV (Spring, 1973), 259–305.

Flanagan, Hallie. *Arena: The History of the Federal Theatre*. 1940; rpr. New York, 1965.

Frazier, Franklin. *The Black Bourgeoisie.* New York, 1957.

Friedman, Lawrence J. *The White Savage: Racial Fantasies in the Post Bellum South.* Englewood Cliffs, N.J., 1970.

Gibson, Donald, ed. *Five Black Writers: Essays on Wright, Ellison, Baldwin, Hughes and LeRoi Jones.* New York, 1970.

Glicksberg, Charles. "The Negro Cult of the Primitive." *Antioch Review,* IV (1944), 47–55.

Goldman, Michael. *The Actor's Freedom: Toward a Theory of Drama.* New York, 1975.

Goldstein, Malcolm. *The Political Stage: American Drama and Theatre of the Great Depression.* New York, 1974.

Gottlieb, Saul. "They Think You're an Airplane and You're Really a Bird." *Evergreen Review,* XI (December, 1967), 51–53, 96–97.

Guernsey, Otis L., ed. *The Best Plays of 1964–1965.* New York, 1965.

Harris, Jessica B. "The New Lafayette Theatre: 'Nothing Lasts Forever.'" *Black Creation,* IV (Summer, 1973), 8–10.

Hatch, James V. *Black Image and the American Stage: A Bibliography of Plays and Musicals, 1770–1970.* New York, 1970.

Hay, Samuel A. " 'What Shape Shapes Shapelessness?': Structural Elements in Ed Bullins' Plays." *Black World,* XXIII (April, 1974), 20–26.

Hemenway, Robert E. *Zora Neale Hurston: A Literary Biography.* Urbana, 1977.

Herskovits, Melville. *The Myth of the Negro Past.* New York, 1941.

Himelstein, Morgan. *Drama Was a Weapon: The Left-Wing Theatre in New York, 1929–1941.* New Brunswick, N.J., 1963.

Hudson, Theodore. *From LeRoi Jones to Amiri Baraka: The Literary Works.* Durham, N.C., 1973.

Huggins, Nathan. *Harlem Renaissance.* New York, 1971.

Isaacs, Edith. *The Negro in the American Theatre.* New York, 1947.

Jackson, Blyden. *Black Poetry in America: Two Essays in Historical Interpretation.* Baton Rouge, 1974.

————. "The Negro's Image of the Universe as Reflected in His Fiction." *College Language Association Journal,* IV (September, 1960), 22–31.

Jeffers, Lance. "Bullins, Baraka and Elder: The Dawn of Grandeur in Black Theatre." *College Language Association Journal,* XVI (September, 1972), 32–48.

Johnson, Charles S. *et al. The Collapse of Cotton Tenancy.* Chapel Hill, 1935.

Johnson, Helen Armstead. "Playwrights, Audiences and Critics." *Negro Digest*, XIX (April, 1970), 17–24.

Johnson, Lemuel A. *The Devil, the Gargoyle, and the Buffoon: The Negro as Metaphor in Western Literature.* New York, 1971.

Jordon, Winthrop D. *White over Black: American Attitudes Toward the Negro, 1550–1812.* Baltimore, 1969.

Keil, Charles. *Urban Blues.* Chicago, 1966.

Kent, George. *Blackness and the Adventure of Western Culture.* Chicago, 1972.

Kerr, Walter. "Mr. Bullins Is Himself at Fault." New York *Times*, March 19, 1972, Sec. D., pp. 1, 7.

Keyassar-Franke, H. "Strategies in Black Drama." Ph.D. dissertation, University of Iowa, 1974.

Koch, Frederick, ed. *American Folk Plays.* New York, 1939.

Kochman, Thomas, ed. *Rappin' and Stylin' Out: Communication in Urban Black America.* Urbana, 1972.

Krutch, Joseph Wood. *The American Drama Since 1918.* New York, 1957.

Kuhlke, William. "They Too Sing America: The New Negro as Portrayed by Negro Playwrights." M.A. thesis, University of Kansas, 1959.

Lawson, Edward. "Theatre in a Suitcase." *Opportunity*, XVI (December, 1938), 360–61.

Lederer, Richard. "The Language of LeRoi Jones' 'The Slave.'" *Studies in Black Literature*, IV (Spring, 1973), 14–16.

Logan, Rayford. *Howard University: The First Hundred Years, 1867–1960.* New York, 1969.

Logan, Rayford *et al.*, eds. *The New Negro Thirty Years Afterwards.* Washington, D.C., 1955.

Lynch, Hollis, R., ed. *The Black Urban Condition: A Documentary History, 1866–1971.* New York, 1973.

McDermott, Douglas, "Agit-prop: Production Practice in the Worker's Theatre, 1932–1942." *Theatre Survey*, VII (November, 1966), 115–24.

McGhee, Nancy. "The Folk Sermon: A Facet of the Black Literary Heritage." *College Language Association Journal*, XIII (September, 1969), 55–61.

McLeod, Norman. "The Poetry and Argument of Langston Hughes." *Crisis*, XLV (November, 1938), 358–59.

Marvin X. "The Black Ritual Theatre: An Interview with Robert Macbeth." *Black Theatre*, No. 3 (1969), 20–24.

————. "An Interview with Ed Bullins: Black Theatre." *Negro Digest*, XVIII (April, 1969), 9–16.

————. "An Interview with LeRoi Jones." *Black Theatre*, No. 1 (1968), 16–23.

Mason, Clifford. "Clifford Mason Talks with Robert Macbeth and Ed Bullins: 'The Electronic Nigger Meets the Gold Dust Twins.'" *Black Theatre*, No. 1 (1968), 24–29.

Matthews, Brander. "The Rise and Fall of Negro Minstrelsy." *Scribners*, LVII (June, 1915), 754–59.

Mays, Benjamin. *The Negro's God as Reflected in His Literature*. 1938; rpr. New York, 1968.

Meier, August and Elliott Rudwick. *From Plantation to Ghetto*. 3rd ed. New York, 1976.

Meltzer, Milton. *Langston Hughes: A Biography*. New York, 1968.

Mitchell, Henry H. *Black Preaching*. Philadelphia, 1970.

Mitchell, Loften. *Black Drama*. New York, 1967.

————. "Death of a Decade: Black Drama in the Sixties." *Crisis*, LXXVII (March, 1970), 87–92.

————. "The Negro Theatre and the Harlem Community." *Freedomways*, III (Summer, 1963), 384–94.

————. *Voices of the Black Theatre*. Clifton, N.J., 1975.

Neal, Larry. "Cultural Nationalism and Black Theatre." *Black Theatre*, No. 1 (1968), 8–10.

Nelson, Hugh. "LeRoi Jones' *Dutchman*: A Brief Ride on a Doomed Ship." *Educational Theatre Journal*, XX (March, 1968), 53–59.

O'Daniel, Therman B., ed. *Langston Hughes, Black Genius: A Critical Evaluation*. New York, 1971.

Ostendorf, Bernard. *Black Literature in White America*. Totowa, N.J., 1982.

Pawley, Thomas. "The Black Theatre Audience." *Players*, XLVI (August-September, 1971), 257–61.

Peavy, Charles D. "Myth, Magic and Manhood in LeRoi Jones' *Madheart*." *Studies in Black Literature*, I (Summer, 1970), 12–20.

Peterson, Bernard, Jr. "Willis Richardson: Pioneer Playwright." *Black World*, XXIV (April, 1975), 40–48, 86–88.

Quinn, Arthur Hobson. *A History of the American Drama: From the Civil War to the Present Day*. 2 vols. New York, 1927.

Reardon, William, and Thomas Pawley, eds. *The Black Teacher and the Dramatic Arts: A Dialogue, Bibliography and Anthology*. Westport, Conn., 1970.

Reed, Daphne S. "LeRoi Jones: High Priest of the Black Arts Movement." *Educational Theatre Journal*, XXII (March, 1970), 53–59.

Review of *Simply Heavenly*. New York *Daily News*, August 8, 1957.

Rice, Julian. "LeRoi Jones' *Dutchman*: A Reading." *Contemporary Literature*, XII (Winter, 1971), 49–59.

Riley, Clayton. "Bullins: 'It's Not the Play I Wrote.'" New York *Times*, March 19, 1972, Sec. D, pp. 1, 7.

―――. "Ed Bullins." *Liberator*, VIII (May, 1968), 20–21.

―――. "Theater Review." *Liberator*, IX (December, 1969), 19–20.

Rodman, Sheldon. *Haiti: The Black Republic*. New York, 1954.

Rollins, Charlemae. *Black Troubadour: Langston Hughes*. Chicago, 1970.

Rosenberg, Bruce A. *The Art of the American Folk Preacher*. New York, 1970.

Rourke, Constance. *American Humour: A Study of the National Character*. New York, 1931.

―――. *The Roots of American Culture and Other Essays*. Edited by Van Wyck Brooks. New York, 1942.

Sandle, Floyd. "A History of the Development of the Educational Theatre in the Negro Colleges and Universities, 1911–1959." Ph.D. dissertation, Louisiana State University, 1959.

Sartre, Jean-Paul. *Portrait of the Anti-Semite*. Translated by Erik de Mauny. London, 1948.

Silver, Reuben. "A History of the Karamu Theatre of Karamu House, 1915–1960." Ph.D. dissertation, Ohio State University, 1961.

Smitherman, Geneva. "Ed Bullins / Stage One: Everybody Wants to Know Why I Sing the Blues." *Black World*, XXIII (April, 1974), 4–13.

Sollors, Werner. *Amiri Baraka / LeRoi Jones: The Quest for a "Populist Modernism."* New York, 1978.

Spencer, T. J., and Clarence Rivers. "Langston Hughes: His Style and Optimism." *Drama Critique*, VIII (Spring, 1964), 99–102.

Sper, Felix. *From Native Roots: A Panorama of Our Regional Drama*. Caldwell, Idaho, 1948.

Tener, Robert. "Role Playing as a Dutchman." *Studies in Black Literature*, III (Autumn, 1972), 17–22.

Tindall, George Brown. *The Emerging of the New South, 1913–1945*. Baton Rouge, 1967. Vol. X of *A History of the South*. Edited by Wendell Holmes Stephenson and E. Merton Coulter.

Tobin, Terence. "Karamu Theatre, 1915–1964: Its Distinguished Past and Present Achievements." *Drama Critique*, VIII (Spring, 1964), 87–91.

Turner, Darwin. "The Negro Dramatist's Image of the Universe, 1920–1960." *College Language Association Journal*, V (December, 1961), 106–20.

———. "Negro Playwrights and the Urban Negro." *College Language Association Journal*, XII (September, 1968), 19–25.

Vincent, Theodore, G., ed. *Voices of a Black Nation: Political Journalism in the Harlem Renaissance*. San Francisco, 1973.

Wade, John Donald. "Southern Humour." In *Culture in the South*, edited by W. T. Couch. Chapel Hill, 1935.

Wagner, Jean. *Black Poets of the United States: From Paul Laurence Dunbar to Langston Hughes*. Translated by Kenneth Douglas. Urbana, 1973.

Watkins, Charles. "Simple: The Alter-Ego of Langston Hughes." *Black Scholar*, II (June, 1971), 18–26.

Weales, Gerald. *The Jumping-Off Place: American Drama in the 1960's*. Toronto, 1969.

Weisgram, Diane. "LeRoi Jones' *Dutchman*: Inter-racial Ritual of Sexual Violence." *American Imago*, XXIX (1972), 215–32.

Wepman, Dennis, Ronald Newman, and Murray Binderman. *The Life: The Lore and Folk Poetry of the Black Hustler*. N.p., 1976.

Wesley, Richard. "An Interview with Playwright Ed Bullins." *Black Creation*, IV (Winter, 1973), 8–10.

Whitman, Wilson. *Bread and Circuses: A Study of the Federal Theatre*. 1937; rpr. Freeport, N.Y., 1972.

Witherington, Paul. "Exorcism and Baptism in LeRoi Jones' *The Toilet*." *Modern Drama*, XV (September, 1972), 159–63.

Wittke, Carl. *Tambo and Bones*. Durham, N.C., 1930.

Young, Charles M. "Is Rape a Symbol of Race Relations?" *New York Times*, May 18, 1975, Sec. D, p. 5.

Young, James O. *Black Writers of the Thirties*. Baton Rouge, 1973.

INDEX 〜